Language and Translation in Postcolonial Literatures

I0584612

This outstanding collection gathers together a stellar group of contributors offering innovative perspectives on the issues of language and translation in postcolonial literatures. In a world where bi- and multilingualism have become quite normal, this volume identifies a gap in the critical apparatus in postcolonial studies in order to read cultural texts emerging out of multilingual contexts. The role of translation and an awareness of the multilingual spaces in which many postcolonial texts are written are fundamental issues with which postcolonial studies needs to engage in a far more concerted fashion. The essays in this book by contributors from Australia, New Zealand, Zimbabwe, Cyprus, Malaysia, Quebec, Ireland, Scotland, France, the US, and Italy outline a pragmatics of language and translation of value to scholars with an interest in the changing forms of literature and culture in our times. The essay topics include: multilingual textual politics; the benefits of multilingual education in postcolonial countries; the language of gender and sexuality in postcolonial literatures; translational cities; postcolonial calligraphy; globalization and the new digital ecology. This volume looks at translation as a basic feature of contemporary global culture, and argues for a translational model to keep postcolonial studies alive in the age of globalization and the internet.

Simona Bertacco is an Assistant Professor of Humanities at the University of Louisville, USA, and was previously a 'ricercatrice' at the University of Milan, Italy. Her research focuses on issues in postcolonialism, women's and gender studies and translation studies. Her publications include: 'Skepticism and the Idea of an Other: Reflections on Cavell and Postcolonialism', in *Stanley Cavell and Literary Studies* (2011); *Death and Its Rites in Contemporary Art & Culture* (*Altre Modernità* #4 2010) co-edited with N. Vallorani; 'Postcolonialism', in *The Oxford Companion of Philosophy and Literature* (2009).

ROUTLEDGE RESEARCH IN POSTCOLONIAL LITERATURES

Edited in collaboration with the Centre for Colonial and Postcolonial Studies, University of Kent at Canterbury, this series presents a wide range of research into postcolonial literatures by specialists in the field. Volumes will concentrate on writers and writing originating in previously (or presently) colonized areas, and will include material from non-anglophone as well as anglophone colonies and literatures. Series editors: Donna Landry and Caroline Rooney.

Language and Translation in Postcolonial Literatures

Multilingual Contexts, Translational Texts

Edited by Simona Bertacco

Routledge
Taylor & Francis Group
NEW YORK AND LONDON

First published 2014 by Routledge

2 Park Square, Milton Park, Abingdon, Oxfordshire OX14 4RN
711 Third Avenue, New York, NY 10017

Routledge is an imprint of the Taylor & Francis Group, an informa business

First issued in paperback 2018

Library of Congress Cataloging-in-Publication Data

Language and translation in postcolonial literatures : multilingual contexts, translational texts /
    edited by Simona Bertacco.
        pages cm. — (Routledge research in postcolonial literatures ; 49)
    1. Literature–Translations–History and criticism.   2. Translating and interpreting–Social aspects.
3. Literature and globalization.   4. Multilingualism and literature.   5. Postcolonialism in
literature.   I. Bertacco, Simona, 1971– editor of compilation.
    PN241.L295 2013
    418'.04–dc23
    2013028650

ISBN13: 978-0-415-65604-7 (hbk)
ISBN13: 978-1-138-54794-0 (pbk)

Typeset in Baskerville
by IBT Global.

In memory of Barbara Godard (1942–2010)

Contents

Part III
Contexts of Translation

PART IV
Colonial Past, Digital Future

Figures

Acknowledgments

I wish to thank all the colleagues and friends who have helped in the production of this book, from the beginning of this project at the University of Milan, in Italy, to its completion at the University of Louisville, in the United States. In particular, I would like to thank all the contributors for their unwavering support and their patience during the long gestation of this project. Grateful thanks to Emily Ross, Liz Levine, and Nancy Chen at Routledge for their help and editorial advice.

For permission to reproduce portions from their works, the editor and publisher are grateful to: Derek Walcott for excerpts from *Ti-Jean and His Brothers* (Farrar, Strauss and Giroux, 1972) and *Moon-Child* (Farrar, Strauss and Giroux, 2012); Dionne Brand for excerpts from *No Language Is Neutral* (Coach House Press, 1990); Jenan Selchuk for reproducing the English translation of his poem 'The Date Palm' from *91st Meridian, Excerpta Cypriana*, ed. S. Stephanides, International Writing Program, University of Iowa, 6.3 (2009); Katerina Attalidou (as heir to her mother Niki Marangou's rights) for quoting the English translation of Niki Marangou's poem 'Street Map of Nicosia' from *Cadences: A Journal of Literature and the Arts in Cyprus* (2008) 4: 99; Deborah Walker-Morrison and Neil Morrison for reproducing two images from the DVD contained in the volume *Cultural Crossings: Negotiating Identities in Francophone and Anglophone Pacific Literatures* (Peter Lang, 2010).

Introduction
The Fact of Translation in Postcolonial Literatures

Simona Bertacco

The role of the translation/translators as a visible/invisible fact.
—Antoni Muntadas, *On Translation* (Venice Biennale 2005)

On Translation

Each child, Ngugi writes in *Moving the Centre*, should master at least three languages. And each country should foster the teaching of translation and interpreting in its schools (Ngugi 1993: 39), so that instead of a universal language, we would have a universe of different languages. And a universe of translators. A world brimming with languages and translators is exactly what one finds at the center of the work by Catalan artist Antoni Muntadas, *On Translation*—a multimedia and transnational art project consisting of installations, lectures, websites, public projects and interventions, everyday objects, videotapes, publications—that the artist has been exhibiting since 1995.

I saw Muntadas's *On Translation* for the first time at the 51st Venice Biennale in 2005 and was struck by the way in which the various installments of the project reveal the pervasiveness and materiality of translation in our contemporary and 'networked' societies. Yet, in the educational systems of the 'Old World'—Europe as well as the United States—monolingualism is still taken to be the norm. Muntadas's projects make us question the monolingual myth of national cultural identities (Edwards 2004: 5), and realize that, literally, we would not be able to live in this world without translation.

The works included by the artist in the general project are extremely diverse, both in the media used (installations, photographs, videos, websites, lectures, pieces of furniture, objects, etc.) and in the declension of the notion of translation each 'installment' conveys. So, for example, the adapter dominates one of the series—and each traveler can easily see why—*il telefonino* (Italian for mobile phone) is the key image for triptychs of photographs of Italians speaking on a mobile phone (a huge 'cultural' phenomenon in Italy since the early 1990s). However, the most intriguing piece in the pavilion was, for me, the one dedicated to *The Internet Project* (1997), hosted by the internet art gallery äda'web (http://www.adaweb.com/influx/muntadas/). The idea behind the work is that of the children's game 'Chinese whispers/telephone arabe/telefono senza fili, Stille Post.' The web page follows the process of translation of a single phrase, originally given in English, into Japanese, then German, up to a total of twenty-three languages during the artistic event. The sentence "Communication systems provide the possibility of developing a better understanding between people: in which language?" changes its meaning along the process, and the advancement of the translation process is indicated on the screen by a growing spiral. This project makes evident the problems intrinsic in any act of communication across cultural and linguistic differences: there are changes, loss of meaning, and illegibility involved, all of which point to the fact that, even on the networked system of the World Wide Web, miscommunication is more common than we may think. Because languages are all but transparent *media* of communication.

The general effect of the phrase going through the translation process over and over again presents an uncanny quality: on the one hand, it suggests a corporate, United Nations/European Union-speak to which we have grown increasingly accustomed, in which every message is beamed in simultaneous translation around the world, devoid of context and deceptively 'neutral'; yet, on the other hand, following the sentence's metamorphoses on the screen reveals how politically *un*neutral the rules of grammar and translation are (Apter 2001). The cultural and political weight of a language is shown to be socially and historically specific, site specific, like the theme of Muntadas's *On Translation. I Giardini* exhibition. As an outcome, translation is conceptualized as something more than a series of techniques or skills to be learned and applied to a text: it is a fact—and a crucial one—of our culture.

What we are looking at in Muntadas's art is a reflection on a phenomenon that surrounds us every single day—language contact. Languages lead plurilingual existences: they live and die in constant contact, or friction, with other idioms. Muntadas's works remind us that we all live, to a different extent, in more than one language and more than one culture, and that it is high time we explored this aspect of our lives critically. Bi- and multilingual people learn early on that—*pace* Princeton scholar David Bellos, who, in his book *Is That a Fish in Your Ear? Translation and the Meaning of Everything* (2011) argues that nothing is really *un*translatable—not everything can be translated. What can be said in one language may be inexpressible in another (Bassnett 2004: 49). And they negotiate such differences in a variety of ways: by developing techniques of code-switching according to the speaking environment, by translating or mixing languages, by letting interferences from one language 'color' their way of using the other, and so forth. When these techniques are used in art and literature, as happens in Muntadas's installations as well as in many postcolonial literary works, language steps out of its ordinary function and becomes exhibitionist and intensive.

What kind of critical reflections can be offered to interpret these phenomena, and where they can lead the field of postcolonial studies, is the topic of this book. This volume addresses the issue of language and translation in postcolonial literatures. In particular it offers two contributions to the current discourses of "the postcolonial" (Huggan 2001): (i) it insists on a return to a closer attention to the formal—and linguistic *in primis*—features of the postcolonial literary text in order to address its multilingual concerns; (ii) it aims at showcasing a critical praxis able to relate those aesthetic features to real-world issues, and it does so by focusing on language, the most pervasive, yet invisible, element in our lives. As Mary Louise Pratt writes in an essay aptly entitled 'Planetarity':

> It is impossible to think seriously about intercultural dialogue without coming to grips with the linguistic dimension of today's planetary social, ecological, economic, political and imaginary realignments. It can be hard to see them in part because language is always there; always at work. It is the medium in which both the realigning and the analysis of it are going on. (2004: 29)

A loquacious illustration of how language plays a crucial role in contexts where cultural confrontations take place but goes unnoticed is Alejandro González Iñárritu's 2006 film *Babel*. Interweaving English, Spanish, Japanese, Arabic, and sign language throughout the entire story, the film makes its title self-explanatory. The picture of twenty-first-century society that emerges from *Babel* is dry and distressing: being born on one or the other side of the power barrier still makes a hell of a difference, and the buoyant face that multicultural democracies offer the world is easily crossed, its inner poise discarded, to make room for forms of intolerance and fundamentalism that we like to think belonged to a different age. Language and translation, both within and outside one's national and cultural community, are at stake, and the film unfolds along a complex multilingual pattern. The presence of many languages, but also of sign language, is fundamental for both our perception and our interpretation of the film. Our fruition of the film is in fact made more difficult because the narrative keeps changing its language settings; similarly, the characters' true intentions, their needs or desires, are twisted in the process of communication, especially when a tragic event occurs to the American protagonists. Would the critical assessment of intercultural relationships the film offers bear the same meaning if the film 'spoke' just one language? Clearly not. The film would tell a entirely different story had the director chosen to tell it by homogenizing the languages of the characters for the sake of the viewer's accessibility. What *Babel* shows on the level of aesthetic taste is the extent to which the audience of cinemagoers is considered ready—by the filmmaker at least—to appreciate these kinds of language games. Many other films, from the box-office hit *Lost in Translation* (Sophia Coppola, 2004) to Ang Lee's *Eat, Drink, Man and Woman* (1994) or *The Wedding Banquet* (1993), or even the television series *The Sopranos*, could provide instructive examples of the issue of multilingual, beside multicultural, communities. In these films, however, the role that language plays—that is, the way multilingual identities are portrayed—is very likely to escape the viewer's notice, given how the hierarchy of languages is maintained in a way not to disrupt the reception of the film in the main language.

The statement *Babel* makes is that we need to think twice about the language we all use, and three times when we speak about English as a world language. It takes a critical position within the debate on globalization, portraying the inequalities that keep the global economy afloat and exploding the rhetoric of MacLuhan's 'global village' by giving us, the viewers, the untranslatability of cultures as is, with no safety net. Iñárritu chooses not to choose (Sommer 1998) among the languages of the world and, in doing so, deepens the significance of language as a concrete, indeed vital, part of our experience in this world.

Living and Writing with Untranslatables

In her new book, *Against World Literature: On the Politics of Untranslatability*, Emily Apter offers an argument that is very much in line with the project of this volume. "The aim," she writes, "is to activate untranslatability as a theoretical fulcrum of comparative literature" (2013: 3), and to foster "an approach to literary comparatism that recognizes the importance of non-translation, mistranslation, incomparability and untranslatability" (4). While I find Apter's invitation to pay close attention to the *Realpolitik* of language laws and language wars as a way out of the impasse in which comparative literature finds itself at the present time important—albeit not very palatable in CompLit departments as they are today—I think it points with insightfulness to what can actually be put into practice in the postcolonial field.

The postcolonial outlook on textuality is, in fact, marked by a special attention given to the historical conditions of the production of culture—what Said called the necessary 'worldliness' of texts—but also by a way of understanding the former colonies in textual terms, looking at the ways in which texts translated the ideology of colonialism into their narratives and forms. If the whole colonial enterprise of taking possession and knowing the new lands was performed textually (through maps, edicts, treaties, settlers' journals, letters, travel writing, novels, poems, etc.), one of the major vehicles of anticolonial struggle could not but be the texts themselves—this time read and written by the formerly colonized subjects. In other words, postcolonial literary theory has, since its beginning, favored a notion of textual politics whereby the agency of texts is transposed onto the social and political spheres. In this light, in the past fifty years, there has been a flourishing of what Derek Attridge terms "instrumental approaches" (2004: 12) to postcolonial studies. In academic contexts especially, the postcolonial text is read as a repository of sociological or historical information and its 'aesthetic dimension' put to one side as trivial and not essential to the communication of its social message. Such an interpretive stance seems to contradict the notion of 'textual politics' shaped by postcolonial theory, the idea, that is, that a new critical vocabulary was necessary to deal with the 'revolutionary' textualities of postcolonial literature. Working on textuality implies working on how the text is composed, the way in which words are selected and put together, the lines arranged, and this is rarely found in current studies of postcolonial literatures.

This volume attempts to fill this *lacuna* and takes up the challenge outlined by Emily Apter for world literary studies. The texts mentioned in this volume insist on *not* being read "as the Proust of the Papuans," as Saul Bellow famously put it, in that they 'flaunt' a textuality that speaks its message through an intentionally convoluted structure, marking the distance, not only from ordinary language, but also from ordinary readings. This is a central part of the actual experience of reading postcolonial texts, and it deserves more critical attention than it has so far received. When foreign words or unfamiliar varieties of English are used and mixed together in postcolonial texts, they are the graphs of the presence of "the Untranslatable," a "compositional heterogeneity that disrupts the fictional continuum" (Apter 2013: 17) and adds an important metafunction to the text, a reflection on the linguistic *medium* and its sanctioned usage. Missing the pun in a line because we do not master all the languages or the rhetoric of a text is not the sign of our being unfair to the text as readers; however, failing to notice it, or casting the blame on the text's supposed unintelligibility or lack of complexity, misses the point by far. There are texts that intentionally leave some readers out (Sommer 1999), thereby raising questions of accessibility that are cursorily dismissed or overlooked by an almost exclusive focus on the thematic content of the literary work (Bertacco 2009). Part of the challenges of reading these works has to do with learning to read them, as all the chapters in this volume contend. We need readings that are both textually and contextually specific. As with languages, social differences are not always comprehensible or bridgeable; in other words, "untranslatables" *do* exist, and this aspect of cultures' untranslatability needs to be acknowledged. In a very literal sense—this volume argues—translation is the model, not only for postcolonial writing developing within multiple cultural and linguistic contexts, but also for a critical praxis aware of, and sensitive to, the complexities of contemporary global language politics.

Language and Translation in Postcolonial Literatures

The idea behind this volume is very simple: a single-language approach to postcolonialism is unfaithful to one of the basic constituencies of the postcolonial world—its multilingualism. If the postcolonial is to survive as a viable critical discourse, it will have to become literally a discourse *of* and *on* translation in order to be responsive to the complexity of the textuality, and even the literariness, of postcolonial texts. In a world where bi- and multilingualism have become the norm for huge numbers of people, postcolonial studies should speak more than one language at once, thus pushing its field of inquiry toward the borders between languages and different disciplines. This volume looks at translation as a basic feature of contemporary global culture and argues for a translational model for postcolonial studies. Translation as both a lived experience (many people *do* live in translation) and as an epistemological framework (it implies a comparative perspective) provides an ideal vantage point to forge the discourses of postcolonialism for the new millennium.

The volume is divided into four parts, meant to make the clusters of topics covered more immediately visible to the reader, even though, it needs to be said, several chapters could easily be grouped in more than one part. Part I focuses on 'Translational Texts' and is concerned with the language politics that is showcased in multilingual textualities as well as with providing methodological tools to students and scholars desiring to approach the postcolonial literary text from a multilingual and comparative perspective. In 'Bridging the Silence: Inner Translation and the Metonymic Gap,' Bill Ashcroft explains why the issue of language use is a stridently political topic of discussion in postcolonial studies. It is important, Ashcroft argues, to distinguish between English as a linguistic code and the use to which it has been (and can be) put, and postcolonial literatures offer the ideal case study. Ashcroft looks at the debate on world English(es), pointing to the fact that the inventiveness and innovative skill of postcolonial writers have remained, significantly, left out and unaccounted for. Yet literary language has free rein to use the aesthetic and creative dimensions of language use, and in cross-cultural situations it can be *metonymic* of cultural difference. The 'metonymic gap' is a central feature of the transformation of the literary language of postcolonial texts, and Ashcroft attaches his discussion to his own seminal work, with Griffiths and Tiffin, in *The Empire Writes Back* (1989). An emphasis on translation as a crucial part of the 'materialities of communication' in postcolonial literatures leads Ashcroft to focus his readings on the music, the 'bodily presence' of the words in the text, and to offer the concept of presence, or cultural *Stimmung*, as a new tool to conceptualize both the production and the consumption of the postcolonial literatures.

In her chapter, Chantal Zabus deals with the transfer between cultures and texts in the African context, exploring the phenomenon that she terms 'indigenization': the attempt to write with an accent in the language of former colonizers. This chapter updates and expands on Zabus's important work in *The African Palimpsest* (1991)—where she studied the Francophone West African novel by male writers—by examining French use in West African novels as well as English use in the South African novel, and by adding a critical discussion on language use around issues of sexuality and gender in novels by African female authors in English, French, and Arabic. Zabus examines the 'textual dissidence' of a wide array of writers, from Chinua Achebe, Flora Nwapa, Ngugi wa Thiong'o, to Es'kia Mphahlele, Nkunzi Zandile Kabinde, Ahmadou Kourouma, Nazi Boni, to name but a few. Zabus's chapter provides a rich inventory of textual technics marking untranslatability in African literary texts. Comparing literary and cultural forms in West and South Africa, Francophone and Anglophone traditions, Zabus provides a fine example of a truly comparative and multilingual approach to postcolonial textualities, and her final discussion of the words of gender and sexuality in novels (mostly) by women adds an essential page to the debate on the language of contemporary African literatures.

An equally important and unavoidable lesson on language use in postcolonial literatures is the one contained in the works by Nobel laureate Derek Walcott. Through the close reading of Walcott's early musical play *Ti-Jean and His Brothers* and its recent lyrical version *Moon-Child*, Roberta Cimarosti constructs an intensive course on postcolonial language use. *Ti-Jean and His Brothers*, first performed in 1958, addresses the consequences of the Anglicization of the Caribbean, which caused the 'bad translation' of the territory through inadequate British vocabulary but also, in later times, the inappropriate use of British English in the educational system, which produced a diffused negative attitude toward the possibility to master the official language as well as an impoverishment of the cultural potential of Creole. The phrase in the title, *learning to shant well*, stands for the art of the 'good translation' as conceived by Walcott. It means learning to use English, as stemming from the sounds, names, and rhythms of Creole. And it points to the indirect way in which the 'bad English translations' could only be redressed by going beyond the resentful use of the language typical of anticolonial discourse.

In 'The "Gift" of Translation to Postcolonial Literatures,' Bertacco discusses the theoretical impact of translation on our writing as well as reading practices. She explores the phenomenon of a 'translational poetics' through close readings of two works (by First Nations playwright Tomson Highway and Trinidadian-Canadian poet Dionne Brand) and argues for the recognition of the creative role of translation in shaping the poetics of these texts. Bertacco begins by considering translation a basic feature of postcolonial cultures and in using translation scholarship as a critical tool for approaching postcolonial textuality. She explores the ways in which the poetics of the text is affected by its bilingual or multilingual nature, and what kind of reading is demanded by a textuality that explicitly toys with several languages.

The chapters contained in Part II, 'Translation as Pre-Text,' all look into specific contexts in which living and learning in translation constitutes the norm of everyday life and, therefore, the 'pre-text'—as what comes *before* the text—of innovative forms of cultural engagement and performance. In '"Make a Plan": Pre-Texts in Zimbabwe,' Doris Sommer and Naseemah Mohamed zoom into the multilingual practices that this volume aims at highlighting by analyzing in detail a pilot-arts-based literature program offered in a high school in Bulawayo, Zimbabwe. The frame is a creative pedagogy called "Pre-Texts," Harvard University's most innovative approach to teaching language and literature, as an alternative to colonial practices of rote learning and corporal punishment, often for speaking Ndebele instead of English. The students observed were translating Chinua Achebe's *Things Fall Apart* into music, dance, and Ndebele, the second most widely spoken language native to Zimbabwe. The students wove between the two languages seamlessly, confirming the results of research that document the advantages of multilingual learning. By highlighting the connections between learning, making, and citizenship, this chapter argues for arts-based pedagogy to stimulate new forms of civic engagement.

An insightful look into translation as a material yet unnoticed fact of our culture is offered by Sherry Simon in her chapter 'Postcolonial Cities and the Culture of Translation' in which Simon examines in detail the spaces of colonial and postcolonial cities. As the translation scholar notices, "despite the sensory evidence of multilingualism in today's cities, the scripts on storefronts, the sidewalk conversations, there has been little sustained discussion of language as a vehicle of urban cultural memory and identity, or as a key in the creation of meaningful spaces of contact and civic participation" (Chapter 6 in this volume). Language is an essential part in the life of any city, and Simon's chapter focuses on the history of the city that one can learn by analyzing the areas of contact between different languages, the patterns in terms of demographics and urban planning these language contacts illuminate, and how these patterns leave an indelible mark on the imaginary of the city. Taking Montreal and Calcutta—two 'intensely translational' cities—as case studies, Simon's chapter provides a sophisticated methodological model useful to understand, beyond the binary paradigm opposing colonized to Native we have grown accustomed to, the many variations of the translational city, as a space in which language contacts and language frictions define the pre-text of civic space and of cultural intervention.

Geography also informs the chapter 'Elli, Lella, Elengou: A Vernacular Poetics for the Mediterranean,' by poet, translator, and critic Stephanos Stephanides, who explores the entanglements of language, territory, and history in the context of his native Cyprus. Stephanides revises the famous comparison between the Caribbean and the Mediterranean seas established by Edouard Glissant in *A Poetics of Relation* and moves beyond the dichotomy opposing the dispersal of the Caribbean to the containment of the Mediterranean, by focusing on the diversity of the peoples and the cultures of the Mediterranean. Many languages have been used in Cyprus throughout its history: walking us through the various phases of Cypriot history in the company of the lines of the island's poets, Stephanides offers a historicized understanding of notions of cosmopolitanism, nationalism, and multiculturalism in the context of the history of the Mediterranean. It is a fascinating trip that culminates in his activity as a poet and a translator and that helps us understand the extent to which translation does provide an essential, and intellectually sophisticated, epistemological framework to decipher the world in which we live.

In 'The Politics of Language Choice in the "English-Language" Theater of Malaysia,' Susan Philip looks at the use of language to construct identities and the questioning of these constructed identities through theater pieces that play with multiple languages. The context is that of Malaysia, a complex multicultural, multiracial, and multilingual country in which language and culture are interlinked in ways that complicate common understandings of national and ethnic identity. Philip's chapter provides a instructive introduction to language policies in Malaysia and reflects on the unique role that the English language has assumed after independence, that is, once it lost its connotations of colonial dominance. Because English does not 'belong' to any particular ethnic category, its use is not so culturally and politically loaded as with the other national languages. The plays under discussion (*A Chance Encounter*; the *Break ing Ji Poh Ka Si Pe Cah* production; K. S. Maniam's and Jit Murad's plays; *Parah*) are multilingual and call for a multilingual performance, dramatizing not only the complexity of Malaysia's linguistic framework, but also the mutual incomprehensibility of these languages. Interestingly, Philip notices, they offer a view of language that is based more on everyday practice than on official language policies.

Part III, 'Contexts of Translation,' considers the *Realpolitik* of the translation of postcolonial literatures and its impact on national literary traditions at different historical moments and, especially, in different contexts. In '"Word of Struggle": The Politics of Translation in Indigenous Pacific Literature,' Michelle Keown investigates the politics of translation and multilingualism in postcolonial Pacific literature, analyzing and comparing the translations of Kanak/New Caledonian and Ma'ohi/French Polynesian literature by three different Aotearoa/New Zealand–based translators: Jean Anderson, Raylene Ramsay, and Deborah Walker-Morrison, who have produced commentaries on their translation practices that take into consideration the ethical and political issues surrounding the translation of the work of Indigenous or postcolonial writers. This chapter adds an important contribution to the new area at the intersection of postcolonial studies and translation studies the volume as a whole aims at supporting, and, in line with recent developments in postcolonial studies—which have included increasing recognition of non-Anglophone scholarship—it examines the collaborations between Francophone and Anglophone Pacific writers, as well as the emergence of new traditions originating along the borders between cultures and languages. The Pacific literature scholar provides an introduction to the literary history of the Pacific region and sophisticated close readings exploring the formal and stylistic aspects of both the source texts and the translations discussed. The ethical challenges involved in the translation of the work of Indigenous or postcolonial writers are given central space, as well as issues of untranslatability and unassimilability, that are crucial to the survival of Indigenous Francophone Pacific cultures and the literatures in which they are conveyed.

In 'Translation and Creation in a Postcolonial Context,' Italian writer and translator Franca Cavagnoli explores what she calls "the desire for creativity" in postcolonial literatures, from the point of view of both the writer and the translator. Cavagnoli provides a survey of the issue of language variance in postcolonial literatures in English—spanning from Joyce to Tutuola, from Saro Wiwa to Rushdie. Offering a Gramscian reading of the act of writing in multicultural contexts, Cavagnoli argues that postcolonial authors "are the first [. . .] translators of their own texts" (Chapter 10 in this volume). In the second section of her chapter, Cavagnoli zooms into close readings of postcolonial textualities, examining in detail passages from the works by the writers analyzed in her survey in the first section. Like in Keown's chapter, literary analysis meets translation studies at their best, and the struggle of writers and translators to exploit the creative potential of liminal space while challenging the cultural values of the publishing establishment is put under scrutiny. As Cavagnoli notes, "translations have always been set in history, culture and ideology" (Chapter 10 in this volume), and her chapter provides an important and informed reflection on the dominant trends within the Italian translation industry.

In the last chapter in this part, Biancamaria Rizzardi argues for the necessity to reconceptualize translation in the postcolonial field in terms of exchange and relation. A translation that is attentive to the text, to its rhythms, features, and internal symmetries or asymmetries, offers, Rizzardi argues, an antidote to the 'deforming' tendencies that characterized past attitudes to translation—tendencies such as 'rationalization,' 'clarification,' 'ennoblement,' and 'exoticization' of the vernacular. By offering an insightful analysis of the 'translation decade' in Italian letters—immediately after the end of World War II—which marked a radical turning point in Italian culture thanks to writers and translators such as Emilio Cecchi, Cesare Pavese, Elio Vittorini, and Eugenio Montale, Biancamaria Rizzardi offers the importance of the translation of North American literature to undermine the literary autarchy of the Fascist regime as a model to which today's translators of postcolonial literatures should turn for inspiration. The cultural renewal made possible by this generation of poets and translators in fact left an indelible mark on Italian literary culture as well as on the ordinary language. Opening up to complexity, leading the reader through the act of translating toward a syncretic and multicultural knowledge, is the call to action that the author addresses to readers and translators of postcolonial literatures.

Part IV, 'Colonial Past, Digital Future,' pushes the discussion on the role of language and translation in postcolonial cultures into the future by looking at the globalization context of the new digital ecology. The two chapters included in this part look at the phenomenon from very disparate angles, providing the best conclusion for a volume of this sort. In her chapter, Evelyn Nien-Ming Ch'ien puts the materiality of language in the current processes of globalization at center stage. In the age of the Internet, while borders may be crossed and territorial entitlements erased in the virtual world, cultural differences and assertions of civilizations keep existing and mobilizing people. And theories of postcolonialism can be particularly relevant to understand the complexities of what Ch'ien calls "an era of borg-like cyber-colonialism" (Chapter 12 in this volume). In this new world order, technology, Ch'ien argues, is the culture that colonizes with more reach than other cultures and determines the pace of life, separating the high-speed existence of globalized subjects from the local-speed existence of those who are not wired. However, while technology may seem like the central force, it is really only one *medium*; language and writing remain the colonizers' primary tools, those that change the physical landscape for good. Through her analysis of Peter Greenaway's film *Pillowbook* (1996), Ch'ien explores the issue of postcolonial linguistic confusion: the vernacular literature scholar reads calligraphy as a special case in the study of how linguistic identity and development are disrupted in a postcolonial world, and the anachronistic nature of calligraphy in a technologized and globalized world triggers a highly sophisticated reflection on the consequences of our technological subservience.

In 'Doing the Translation Sums: Colonial Pasts and Digital Futures,' Michael Cronin discusses the role of translation of postcolonial literatures within the new digital ecology. More and more, the question of the production and accessibility of postcolonial literatures in translation must also address the nature of the digital contexts in which they are made available. Even when not explicitly stated, the underlying ideology of many of the online centers that promote national literatures in translation is compatible with a postcolonial view of cultural promotion via a form of digital nationalism. Cronin detects a notion of 'soft power'—influence through attraction or co-option—as typical of postcolonial countries, countries that may lack in economic or military resources and that look at cultural promotion as a means of exercising influence. And translation, Cronin argues, has become a key component in the incorporation of postcolonial literatures into the operation of 'soft power' in the digital age. The translation imperative that is central to the experience of the colonized points to the possibility of a global cybercitizenship, where the role of literature and culture are considered, once again, important, a World Republic of Letters that is going to alter the features of citizenship and of literary taste for the next generations. One of the challenges for students and scholars of postcolonial literatures in translation, then, is to decipher how the global, digital community of writers and readers of translated literatures will enable or will hinder the emergence of new forms of expression.

Taken together, the chapters in this volume point to a new area of development for postcolonial studies that increasingly includes the recognition of non-Anglophone contributions to the field. What is still needed, and what this volume aims at doing, is to theorize language and translation in postcolonial (con)texts in innovative ways by offering new methods and new tools. The methodology employed in the chapters is largely descriptive, in that all contributors ground their reflections on a thorough respect for, and attention to, the ordinary, the everyday, and in doing so provide insightful theories of interpretation for contemporary multilingual, translational, and untranslatable texts. The volume as a whole provides more than just a theory of how postcolonial languages work: it outlines a pragmatics of language and translation of value, we hope, to all scholars with an interest in literature in the age of globalization.

References

Apter, E. (2001) 'On Translation in a Global Market' *Public Culture* 13: 1: 1–12.
Apter, E. (2013) *Against World Literature: On the Politics of Untranslatability* (New York: Verso).
Ashcroft, B., Griffiths, G., and Tiffin, H. (1989) *The Empire Writes Back: Theory and Practice in Post-Colonial Criticism* (London: Routledge).
Attridge D. (2004) *The Singularity of Literature* (London: Routledge).
Bassnett, S. (2004) 'Intercultural Dialogue in a Multilingual World' in *Intercultural Dialogue: Mary Louise Pratt, Ron G. Manley, Susan Bassnett.* With an Introduction by Nick Wadham-Smith (London: British Council), pp. 48–61.
Bellos, D. (2011) *Is That a Fish in Your Ear? Translation and the Meaning of Everything* (Toronto: Penguin Books).
Bertacco, S. (2009) "Postcolonialism" in Oxford Handbook of Philosophy and Literature, edited by Richard Eldridge (Oxford: Oxford University Press), pp. 322–342.
Edwards, V. (2004) *Multilingualism in the English-Speaking World* (Oxford: Blackwell).
Huggan, G. (2001) *The Postcolonial Exotic: Marketing the Margins* (London: Routledge).
Iñárritu, A. G. (2006) *Babel* (USA: Paramount).
Muntadas, A. (2002) *On Translation* (Barcelona: MACBA & Actar).
Ngugi wa Thiong'o. (1993) *Moving the Centre: The Struggle for Cultural Freedoms* (London: James Currey).
Pratt, M. L. (2004) 'Planetarity' in *Intercultural Dialogue: Mary Louise Pratt, Ron G. Manley, Susan Bassnett.* With an Introduction by Nick Wadham-Smith (London: British Council), pp. 10–31.
Sommer, D. (1998) 'Choose and Loose' in *Multilingual America: Transnationalism, Ethnicity, and the Languages of American Literature*, ed. W. Sollors (New York: New York University Press), pp. 297–309.

Sommer, D. (1999) *Proceed with Caution, When Engaged by Minority Writing in the Americas* (Cambridge, MA: Harvard University Press).

Walcott, D. (1972) *Ti-Jean and His Brothers* (New York: Farrar, Strauss and Giroux).

Walcott, D. (2012) *Moon-Child* (New York: Farrar, Strauss and Giroux).

Zabus, C. (1991) *The African Palimpsest: Indigenization of Language in the West African Europhone Novel*. 2nd enlarged ed. (Amsterdam: Rodopi).

Part I

Translational Texts

1 Bridging the Silence
Inner Translation and the Metonymic Gap

Bill Ashcroft

It is a standard assumption that translation represents a deterioration from the original—a deterioration in either meaning or aesthetic value: a translation can be "either beautiful or faithful but not both" as the cliché goes. Salman Rushdie's well-known response to the supposed inferiority of cross-cultural writing is that something is gained in translation:

> The word 'translation' comes, etymologically, from the Latin for 'bearing across.' Having been borne across the world, we are translated men. It is normally supposed that something always gets lost in translation; I cling, obstinately, to the notion that something can also be gained. (1991: 17)

The postcolonial writer faces in two directions, so to speak. The decision he or she makes is not just how to write 'between languages,' but how to make language perform this 'bearing across' (indeed, to 'bear' this particular 'cross') within itself: how to be both 'source' and 'target.' This might be called 'inner translation,' one that occurs when postcolonial writers appropriate English. It provides an added dimension to the debates about translation, and this chapter will discuss the extent to which cultural experience is intentionally withheld, or not fully 'carried across' the translation in the literary appropriation of English.

While colonial education systems privileged the teaching of English and in many cases punished pupils for using vernacular language at school (Ngugi 1981: 11), something occurred among speakers and writers of English in British colonies that imperial administrations, and the institution of English literature itself, could not have foreseen. Postcolonial writers took hold of the language with a vengeance, and in so doing took hold of the means of their self-representation. Appropriating the language, producing a variously hybridized English, and transforming the official genres of English literature, they produced a located form of English and interpolated networks of production and distribution to speak to a world audience. This is of course just one side of the argument. The alternative view is that the explosion of interest in postcolonial writers represented the hunger of global publishing systems to produce new and exotic works (Narayanan 2012: 34). The truth is perhaps a combination of both views. Bourdieu's theory of 'field' in *The Field of Cultural Production* (1993) may be useful for identifying the complex weave of practices that go to make up what we understand as 'literature.' But given this complex interrelation, and the fact that the global publishing industry might have had its own reasons for promoting postcolonial writers, the agency of writers in adopting and adapting the language cannot be denied, as they translated cultural realities into English and represented themselves—translated themselves—to a global audience. This translation changed the field of English literature forever.

The issue of language use is a stridently political topic of debate in postcolonial studies, and the reasons are clear to see. We may regard ourselves as belonging to a certain category of race, or being at home in a certain place, but for some mysterious reason we don't simply *have* a language. We tend to believe that our language *is* us—that it inhabits us and we inhabit it. Our language "is not just *a* language," says Edgar Thompson, "it is *our* language, the language of human beings":

> The language of those outside, or what they call a language, is the language of people who babble and answer to silly names; they are barbarians even when they use much the same vocabulary. But in our language we know ourselves as brothers and sisters or as comrades or as fellow countrymen. In it we make love and say our prayers, and in it, too, is written our poetry, our oratory, and our history. (Thompson and Hughes 1965: 237)

Languages may be held to represent various cultural traits, but *our* language is different; our language is transcendent—it is the language of God Himself. Language is an instrument of communication, but in our heart of hearts, we know God speaks only our language to us, because *our* language is *us*.

The political consequence of this in the spread of a global language is the assumption that the language is in the vanguard of neo-imperialism and global capitalism, leading to accusations of 'linguistic genocide.' The attack on world Englishes began in earnest with Phillipson's *Linguistic Imperialism* (1992). Bruce Moore's *Who's Centric Now?* (2001) explores regional varieties of English in relation to the lively debate about the increasing 'globalization' of English, asserting that a new 'threat' to regional varieties of English had emerged in the spread of 'global English' by electronic communication that has the effect of washing out difference and reducing the cultural diversity of world Englishes. One of the strongest attacks on the spread of world English occurs in many of the essays contained in Mair's *The Politics of English as a World Language* (2003). The volume is wide-ranging and indicates the disciplinary differences in approaches to the question, from accusations of English as a "killer language" destroying the linguistic biodiversity of the planet to discussions of Sri Lankan English literary texts as active in cultural conservation. The protest about the dominance of English continues in a recent book by Pavithra Narayanan: *What Are You Reading: The World Market and Indian Literary Production* (2012).

None of these books says anything about the inventiveness and innovative skill of postcolonial writers in English, who are effectively regarded as mere ciphers for global forces. Beneath the clamorous and overheated political debate around world Englishes is an assumption that is central to the issue of representation and cultural translation: that language itself is culture. Consequently, the argument goes, using a global language alienates you from your culture. Ngugi wa Thiong'o offers the earliest statement of this position in his essay 'Towards a National Culture,' collected in *Decolonizing the Mind* (1981), in which he expresses four general objections to the use of English: (1) the colonial tongue becomes a province of the *élite* and thus the language itself reproduces colonial class distinctions; (2) language embodies the "thought processes and values" of its culture; (3) learning a colonial tongue alienates a speaker from the "values" of the local language and from the values of the masses (which to Ngugi are the same thing); (4) national language should not exist at the expense of regional languages that can enhance national unity "in a socialist economic and political context." To various degrees these objections apply today to the use of a global language. The interesting thing is that when Ngugi decided to write novels in Gikuyu (a form that didn't exist in that culture), he translated them back into English for a world audience.

Chinua Achebe responds to the assertion that African writers will never reach their creative potential till they write in African languages by reiterating the point that a writer's use of a language can be as culturally specific as he or she makes it. If we ask, "Can an African ever learn English well enough to use it effectively in creative writing?" Achebe's answer is yes. But the secret such a writer has at his or her disposal is a healthy disregard for its traditions and rules. All writers have a creative sense of the possibilities of language, but the non-English-speaking postcolonial writer has the added dimension of a different mother tongue, a different linguistic tradition from which to draw. If we ask, "Can he or she ever use it like a native speaker?" Achebe's answer is "I hope not." His point is one that remains as true today as it was then. The appropriation of English by postcolonial writers is not only possible, but extremely effective and enriches the language. "The price a world language must be prepared to pay is submission to many different kinds of use" (Achebe 1975: 61).

These different kinds of use demonstrate, in fact, the amazing subtlety and robust determination of postcolonial writers to keep their distance from Received Standard English. As far back as *The Empire Writes Back* (1989), the combination of abrogation and appropriation were used to describe the post-colonial adoption of English. Writers *abrogated* the centrality and dominance of 'standard' English, "dismantling of its imperialist centralism" (Ashcroft, Griffiths, and Tiffin 1989: 43), while *appropriating* and transforming that language into a culturally relevant vehicle. Rather than being absorbed into the great swamp of English, writers employed techniques of inner translation and transformation to produce an English that was culturally located, culturally specific, and clear in its identification of difference. This rendered the language itself as translation.

The 'Third Space' of Translation

The myth that cultural identity is somehow embodied, 'hard-wired,' in language would present insurmountable problems to translation if it were true. If our language "is us," as we tend to assume, how can our cultural identity be translated? The concept of language as *itself* somehow a 'third space,' a vehicle that is by its very nature interstitial, is suggested in Sherry Simon's discussion of the hybridity and self-doubt characteristic of much contemporary Quebec writing:

> These doubts increasingly take the form of the cohabitation within a single text of multiple languages and heterogeneous codes. In this case, translation can no longer be a single and definitive enterprise of cultural transfer. Translation, it turns out, not only negotiates between languages, but comes to inhabit the space of language itself. (1992: 174)

In other words, language itself is transformative, a space of translation. Translation no longer negotiates between languages, for language *is itself* the site of ceaseless translation. And the critical discovery here is that language—this site of translation—is continually and productively *unstable*. Because language is never a simple correspondence between signs and referents, a simple translation of reality into words, we may say that *all* language occupies what Bhabha calls the "Third Space of enunciation" (1994: 37) in its provisionality and untranslatability. This is the space that postcolonial writers inhabit between the imperial and vernacular cultures. But it is one version of the interstitial space that all language occupies.

In his classic essay 'The Task of the Translator,' Walter Benjamin rejects the notion that translation can or should be faithful to the original text, for, "the task of the translator [. . .] may be regarded as distinct and clearly different from the task of the poet. The intention of the poet is spontaneous, primary, graphic; that of the translator is derivative, ultimate, ideational" (1969: 76–77). Benjamin's point is that it is language that presents the 'problem.' Poets are doomed to be unfaithful to experience just as translators are doomed to be unfaithful to the poet, because language itself is 'unfaithful.'

The complaint that a colonial language is inauthentic to local identity assumes that there can be such an 'authentic' language. But what if *all* writers find themselves subtly displaced from language in one way or another? This is certainly the implication of Benjamin's essay. Postcolonial writers have the added experience of being unfaithful to two languages both of which can only ever be 'unfaithful' to experience. Unfaithfulness is the hyperbole that identifies the instability of language. But perhaps even 'instability' is not quite the right word. All language is *horizonal* in that it offers a horizon of representation to experience—all representation intimates a 'something more' in the horizon of the statement. Within this horizon of possibilities, language can never be perfectly 'faithful' to experience, for experience itself functions in concert with, rather than prior to, language. Without resorting to Whorfian determinism, we can say that the language does not reflect but invents, or 're-presents,' experience. So the postcolonial writer does not exist in a state of suffering and loss, but of an expanded and fluid capacity to re-create experience.

One can therefore never write exactly what one 'intends.' Meaning does not exist *before* the linguistic exchange, but *in* it. Benjamin disperses intention completely: "all suprahistorical kinship of languages rests in the intention underlying each language as a whole—an intention, however, which is realized only by the totality of their intentions supplementing each other: pure language" (1969: 74). His point here is that all writing is already a translation of this "pure language," what he calls *reine Sprache*, or, to put it another way, translation elevates the original into pure language: "the language of a translation can—in fact, must—let itself go, so that it gives voice to the *intentio* of the original not as reproduction but as harmony, as a supplement to the language in which it expresses itself, as its own kind of *intentio*" (Benjamin 1969: 79). There is no metalanguage or transcendental signifier because:

> This movement of the original is a wandering, an errance, and a kind of permanent exile if you wish, but it is not really an exile, for there is no homeland, nothing from which one has been exiled. Least of all is there something like a *reine Sprache*, a pure language, which does not exist except as a permanent disjunction that inhabits all languages as such, including and especially the language one calls one's own. What is one's own language is the most displaced, the most alienated of all. (Benjamin 1969: 92)

The term *reine Sprache*—'pure language'—is ironic then, because it can never be realized. It is the utopian horizon of all communicability. The vessel of

pure language, to use Benjamin's well-known metaphor, is eternally fractured, and translation is but a reenactment of this fragmentation, the emblem
of its own failure to be primary.

The Metonymic Gap

In this absence of a pure language, therefore, not only postcolonial writing, but perhaps *all* writing, as Simon suggests, may be a form of perpetual
translation. Nevertheless in the cross-cultural situation language becomes
particularly strategic because language is *metonymic* of cultural difference.
That is, it doesn't embody culture but stands for it metonymically: it is the
'part that stands for the whole,' and metonymically signifies not identity,
but difference. This metonymic function operates not only in the vernacular
language; it becomes a dynamic feature of language variance in postcolonial
English. The 'third space' of postcolonial language use therefore assumes
intentionality by virtue of the ways in which postcolonial writers maintain
a separation between text and reader. The point is that this is not a failure
of translation or a sign of the inadequacy of English: it is a sign of the subtle
cultural strategies that occur in the postcolonial text.

Variant' English texts may be regarded as transcultural contact zones
offering a unique perspective on the issue of cultural translation. Ethnographers have used the term 'transcultural' to describe how subordinated or
marginal groups select and invent from materials transmitted to them by a
dominant or metropolitan culture (e.g., Taussig 1993). The word was coined
in the 1940s by Cuban sociologist Fernando Ortiz (1978) in relation to Afro-
Cuban culture, and incorporated into literary studies by Uruguayan critic
Angel Rama in the 1970s. Ortiz proposed the term to replace the paired
concepts of acculturation and deculturation that described the transference
of culture in reductive fashion, one imagined from within the interests of the
metropolis (Pratt 1992: 228). The concept of the contact zone in postcolonial
studies has often been framed as a contestatory space because it is marked
by "highly asymmetrical relations of dominance and subordination" (Pratt
1992: 4). However, the concept of transculturality we discover in the postcolonial text proposes a more constructive dialogue, a zone of contact that produces, despite these asymmetrical relations, a new, 'third' cultural space.

The transcultural text is a space of negotiation, a space in which the
boundary between self and Other blurs. The 'cross-cultural' text—a term
that is comparatively static and linear—may be seen to be a 'transcultural'
text once we understand it to be a space in which meaning is negotiated,
where, in a sense, both writer and reader are changed in constitutive collusion. The meaning of the translated text is a negotiation between different
voices, between the writer and reader 'functions.' People living in different
cultures may live in totally different, and even incommensurable, worlds: different worlds of experience, expectation, habit, understanding, and tradition.

Nevertheless, meaning is *accomplished* between writing and reading participants in ways that may confound theories of cultural incommensurability.

Bakhtin's concept of dialogism further expands our understanding of the ways in which the negotiation of multiple voices occurs in the text. While all language may be regarded as translation, Bakhtin is interested in the novel form because it provides a particularly rich medium for the many-voiced— *heteroglossic*—appearance of different languages.

> For the novelist working in prose, the object is always entangled in someone else's discourse about it, it is already present with qualifications, an object of dispute that is conceptualized and evaluated variously, inseparable from the heteroglot social apperception of it. The novelist speaks of this "already qualified world" in a language that is heteroglot and internally dialogized. Thus both object and language are revealed to the novelist in their historical dimension, in the process of social and heteroglot becoming. (Bakhtin 1981: 330)

Significantly, Bakhtin is talking about a putatively monoglossic text, unhampered by issues of cultural communication. For him, such a text is already heteroglossic, already engaged in dialogue *within* the text, a dialogue, which to all intents and purposes, is a *cross-cultural* dialogue between 'belief systems.' All forms involving a narrator:

> signify to one degree or another by their presence the author's freedom from a unitary and singular language, a freedom connected with the relativity of literary and language systems; such forms open up the possibility of never having to define oneself in language, the possibility of translating one's own intentions from one linguistic system to another, of fusing "the language of truth" with "the language of everyday," of saying "I am me" in someone else's language, and in my own language "I am other." (Bakhtin 1981: 314–315)

The dual dynamic of saying "I am me" in another's language and "I am other" in my own language captures precisely the dual achievement of the second-language writer. For such a writer, while emphasizing the way in which the space between author and reader is closed within the demands of *meanability*, also demonstrates in heightened form the writer's negotiation of the forces brought to bear on language:

> Every concrete utterance of a speaking subject serves as a point where centrifugal as well as centripetal forces are brought to bear. The processes of centralization and decentralization, of unification and disunification, intersect in the utterance; the utterance not only answers the requirements of its own language [. . .] but it answers the requirements

of heteroglossia as well; it is in fact an active participant in such speech diversity. (Bakhtin 1981: 272)

For the postcolonial writer these forces are the forces of a culturally ossified way of seeing and the heteroglossia of a world readership. One of the preeminent advantages of postcolonial writing in English is the capacity to translate ways of seeing into the 'bilingual' text without making any concessions to the 'way of seeing' of the reader. This is because the text is already a heteroglot profusion of ways of seeing. But it is also because the postcolonial text manages to extend Bakhtin's view of dialogue with the discovery that *true dialogue can only occur when the difference of the Other is recognized.*

Understanding may not demand a shared experience of the world, but the pressing questions for the postcolonial text are: What is that process by which both recognition and otherness occur? How is a communicable sense of difference *installed* in the English text? This installation demonstrates intentionality in the broadest sense: whether writers actually will it or not, and despite the constitutive nature of transcultural meaning, there is an element in postcolonial literature that introduces what appears to be a gap in the text. This is a 'gap' that exists beyond interpretation, in fact, seems, if not to *resist* interpretation, at least to provide a barrier to the unequivocal determination of meaning. By stressing the distance between the participating writers and readers, the text prevents itself from being so transparent that it is absorbed into the dominant milieu of the reader of English. Such writing, while it provides a path for cultural understanding that overcomes the exclusionary effect of anthropological explanation, also questions easy assumptions about meaning and its transmissibility and actively reinstalls the reality of its own cultural difference in quite explicit ways.

This installation of difference may be called the 'metonymic gap.' This is the cultural gap formed when writers transform English according to the needs of their source culture: by inserting unglossed words, phrases, or passages from a first language; by using concepts, allusions, or references that may be unknown to the reader; by syntactic fusion; by code-switching; by transforming literary language with vernacular syntax or rhythms; or even by generating a particular cultural music in their prosody. Such variations become synecdochic of the writer's culture rather than linguistic signs that somehow embody culture. Thus the inserted language 'stands for' the colonized culture in a metonymic way, and its very resistance to interpretation constructs a 'gap' between the writer's culture and the English reader's understanding. The local writer is thus able to represent his or her world to the colonizer (and others) in the metropolitan language and, at the same time, to signal and emphasize a difference from it. In effect, the writer is saying, "I am using your language so that you will understand my world, but you will also know by the differences in the way I use it that you cannot share my experience." The reader exposed to such language is unequivocally in the presence of an 'Other' culture.

The metonymic gap is a central feature of the transformation of the literary language. The writer concedes the importance of *meanability*, the importance of a situation in which meaning can occur, and at the same time signifies areas of difference that may lie beyond meaning, so to speak, in a realm of cultural experience in which the reader must see himself or herself as Other. The distinctive act of the cross-cultural text is to inscribe *difference* and *absence* as a corollary of cultural identity. Consequently, whenever a 'strategy of transformation' of the dominant language is used, that is, a strategy that appropriates English and inflects it in a way that transforms it into a cultural vehicle for the writer, there is an installation of difference at the site of the meaning event. In this sense such strategies are directly metonymic of that cultural difference that is imputed by the linguistic variation. In fact they are a specific form of metonymic figure—the synecdoche.

This strategy may appear to be a strategy of resistance, and indeed, in response to those critics who see the vernacular culture being swallowed up by English, the metonymic gap is a *refusal* to translate the world of the writer completely. Culture might not be embodied in the language, but it may be *disembodied* in the sense that the presence appearing in the text may lead the reader to engage in a dimension of cultural revelation that occurs through its materiality, its music, and its transformative difference. Linguistic meaning may therefore be seen to be 'negotiated' because it too is a meeting place for the writer and reader functions, but it is a meeting in the space of *silence* within the language.

There are many techniques by which postcolonial writers perform an 'inner translation' and transform the language they use. Perhaps the simplest example of the metonymic gap is the use of untranslated words. These usually do not impede interpretation, because as Wittgenstein explained in *Philosophical Investigations* and *The Blue and Brown Books*: "For a large class of cases—though not all—in which we employ the word 'meaning' it can be defined thus: the meaning of a word is its use in the language" (1975: 43). This may certainly be true for untranslated vernacular words in an English sentence. Refusing to translate words not only registers a sense of cultural distinctiveness, but also forces the reader into an active engagement with the vernacular culture. The refusal to translate is a refusal to be subsidiary. The reader gets some idea about the meaning of these words from the subsequent conversation, but further understanding will require the reader's own expansion of the cultural situation beyond the text. Hence the absence of translation has a particular kind of metonymic function.

Cultural difference is not inherent in the text but is inserted by such strategies. By developing specific ways of both constituting cultural distance and at the same time bridging it, the text indicates that it is the 'gap' rather than the experience (or at least the concept of a gap between experiences) that is created by language. The absence of explanation is therefore first a sign of distinctiveness and it also ensures that meaning is not a matter of definition but of active engagement. In the passage "The day he had come to show her husband sample suitings, he slipped nearly breaking his neck. He had learnt since then to walk like an *ogwumagada*" (Aniebo 1978: 35), we do not need to know exactly what an *ogwumagada* is to know that its walk is significant, that he must walk carefully, with caution, foot after foot. In fact, *ogwumagada* means 'chameleon' in Igbo. Although we can locate the meaning of the word, more or less, by its location in context, the word itself confirms the metonymic gap of cultural difference.

Cultural *Stimmung*

The metonymic gap is far more powerful in signifying cultural difference than most critics of global English acknowledge. But it is also true that this is a particular function of *literary* language because literary language resists that process of which Moore complains, that the spread of global English through the Internet leeches out the cultural specificity of world Englishes. Literature does this because it has free rein to use the aesthetic and creative dimensions of literary writing. This makes the metonymic gap something more than a gap in interpretation because the language variance achieves a culturally different atmosphere, mood, or *Stimmung*.

This is a term investigated by Hans Ulrich Gumbrecht in his *Atmosphere, Mood, Stimmung: On a Hidden Potential of Literature* (2011), which continues the general movement of his earlier *The Production of Presence*, which challenges "a broadly institutionalised tradition according to which interpretation, that is, the identification and/or attribution of meaning, is the core practice, the exclusive core practice indeed, of the humanities" (2004: 3). Gumbrecht's dissatisfaction arose from a sense that 'materialities of communication' were completely ignored in the humanities. Gumbrecht advanced the idea of presence to circumvent the entrapment of literary experience in the ascertainment of meaning. The moods and atmospheres connoted by the term *Stimmung* "undoubtedly belong to the presence-related part of existence, and their articulations count as forms of aesthetic experience" (Gumbrecht 2011: 7). But our everyday being-in-the-world seems to fuse consciousness and software in a way that suspends the experience of presence.

The 'presence' available in the text is related to another dimension of experience beyond hermeneutics. *Stimmung* is difficult to translate into English but offers, according to Gumbrecht, a 'third position' to literary theories broadly ranged around the poles of deconstruction and cultural studies. The word encapsulates the English words 'mood' and 'climate' but also connects with the German words *Stimme*, or voice, and *stimmen*, to 'be correct,' and Gumbrecht is most interested in the meaning that connects *Stimmung* with music and the hearing of sounds:

Hearing is a complex form of behaviour that involves the entire body. Skin and haptic modalities of perception play an important role. Every tone we perceive is, of course, a form of physical reality (if an invisible one) that 'happens' to our body and, at the same time, surrounds it. (2011: 4)

Gumbrecht deploys *Stimmung* to describe the reader's engagement with a number of texts, from the picaresque to Shakespeare's sonnets to popular culture texts of the present. *Stimmung* is particularly useful for detecting affective elements in texts for which the historical and contextual background is sketchy. Similarly it may provide a useful insight into that untranslatable space in the cross-cultural text. The 'atmosphere' of historically distant literary texts may well be applicable to those that are culturally 'distant.'

Gumbrecht first elaborated this idea with a discussion of 'latency,' which is "whatever we believe is in a text without being unproblematically graspable" (2009: 87). That which is latent in a text, which for our purposes is something that remains untranslated, may be available to an experience of *Stimmung*, and "enjoying, resenting, or merely noticing a Stimmung is always and inevitably a psychic move that gives us a sharpened awareness of otherwise often bracketed layers of our physical existence" (Gumbrecht 2009: 90).

Chinua Achebe gives an interesting example of cultural 'presence' that goes beyond the strategies of language variance alone, but that is available to the 'sharpened awareness' of the reader. In his famous debate with Ngugi wa Thiong'o, in *Morning Yet on Creation Day* (1975) Achebe demonstrates the way in which the writer can avoid language "colonizing the mind," arguing, in effect, that style performs an act of cultural translation.

Allow me to quote a small example from *Arrow of God*, which may give some idea of how I approach the use of English. The Chief Priest in the story is telling one of his sons why it is necessary to send him to church:

> I want one of my sons to join these people and be my eyes there. If there is nothing in it you will come back. But if there is something there you will bring home my share. The world is like a Mask, dancing. If you want to see it well you do not stand in one place. My spirit tells me that those who do not befriend the white man today will be saying *had we known* tomorrow.

Now supposing I had put it another way. Like this, for instance:

> I am sending you as my representative among these people—just to be on the safe side in case the new religion develops. One has to move with the times or else one is left behind. I have a hunch that those who fail to come to terms with the white man may well regret their lack of foresight.

The material is the same. But the form of one is *in character* and the other is not (Achebe 1975: 61–62).

Achebe is arguing here the very important fact that the appropriation and transformation of English can adopt a culturally felicitous form, keeping the language in character with a source culture. He compares his passage with a very prosaic rendition that supports his case, but his case is an aesthetic one as well as a cultural one as his choice of an alternative makes clear. Achebe may have compared his passage with a more aesthetically pleasing one than he chooses, but there is no doubt that in moving into the English the writer carries with him a command of the rhythm and tonal cadence of the original language, thus laying stress on metrical regularity and the music of the lines. This cadence is metonymic of Igbo culture and in this respect establishes a much more subtle cultural gap than mere linguistic variance alone. The English carries with it the proverbial character of the original Igbo in a way that produces both cultural veracity and poetic resonance. The transcultural space lies in the materiality of the language, for this is the space of contact between cultures, a space of recognition of difference. The Igbo is transformed into English, but the English is transformed by the Igbo cadence—the language might be English, but the cultural resonance is Igbo.

Language operating in this way achieves something a simple translation might never achieve: it foregrounds the various forms of language use in the text and constructs difference in two ways. On the one hand, the linguistic features simultaneously install and bridge a cultural gap between African subject and English-speaking reader by replicating the rhythms of oral language in literary English. On the other, the reader, simply by opening the 'African novel,' makes an unspoken commitment to accept this formal, highly structured, metrically measured, and tonally smooth writing as African English. This dialectic is the essential feature of the literature of linguistic intersection, and its particular facility in this context is its capacity to intimate a cultural reality through the music, the 'bodily presence' of the words. The important fact here is that the aesthetic, whether consciously or not, is a feature of both the production and consumption of the text.

But *Stimmung* may be a better word than 'aesthetic' to describe that sense of culture conveyed in the music of the lines. The concept of *Stimmung* like the concept of presence is of particular interest to the cross-cultural English variant text because both signify an engagement by the reader beyond the purely hermeneutic—an engagement even beyond something we might regard as 'understanding.' The 'atmosphere' of the Igbo culture present in Achebe's text above is not available to interpretation and therefore occupies the metonymic gap by which the cultural distinctiveness of the text is maintained. Here I am extending the sense of 'mood' or 'atmosphere' to include that difficult to define sense of cultural difference made available through the sound and rhythm of the prosody. Even Achebe's explanation must fall short of delivering the experience of Igbo culture to the reader. Such a text

is transcultural in the sense that despite the space of untranslatable difference between text and reader, an engagement with cultural difference occurs
for which words like 'presence' or *Stimmung* may be very appropriate. The
related term *Stimme*, or voice, connects *Stimmung* to the 'sound,' texture, or
materiality of the appropriated English. Indeed, this is a matter of music,
and the music of the text conveys something powerful about the culture, but
something beyond translation. The music of a text like Achebe's resonates
across the silence between cultures in a way that confirms the difference
between them.

This can be seen everywhere in the postcolonial text once we are alert to
it. Take the example of a verse from the poem by the Caribbean poet Linton
Kwesi Johnson:

> di lan is like a rack
> slowly shattahrin to san
> sinkin in a sea of calamity
> where fear breeds shadows daak
> where people fraid fi waak
> fraid fi tink fraid fi taak
> where di present is haunted by di paas
> Donnell and Welsh 1996: 375)

While the poem transcribes the sound of the local dialect, its orthography
still 'constructs' a reader for whom its variations pose no serious obstacle.
Rather, the code variations become a part of the enjoyment of the poem. At
first reading the poem might be formidable to a monolingual speaker, but the
secret of the poem is its orality and its *performance* of a cultural reality that
resists easy interpretation. There is much more *meaning* in the poem than an
interpretative gloss would encompass, and, by balancing the requirements of
meanability and difference, the poem *insists* on presence. The 'cultural atmosphere' of the poem lends itself to the experience of *Stimmung*. The 'much
more' that constitutes cultural presence is in fact beyond meaning for it exists
in the *sound*, the music, of the lines, a dimension also very aptly described by
Gadamer's term—'volume':

> But, can we really assume that the reading of such texts is a reading
> exclusively concentrated on meaning? Do we not sing these texts [*Ist es
> nicht ein Singen*]? Should the process in which a poem speaks only be car-
> ried by a meaning intention? Is there not, at the same time, a truth that
> lies in its performance [*eine Vollzugswahrheit*]? This, I think, is the task
> with which the poem confronts us. (Gumbrecht 2004: 66)

The 'volume' of Johnson's poem is encompassed in the 'performance' of the
sound and shape of the lines, a materiality that opens up the nonhermeneutic

dimension of reading. This is not an aesthetic volume alone: it is an extension, a 'beyond' of cultural difference, as well. Gumbrecht makes the point
that this tension between the semantic and nonsemantic dimensions of the
poem reflects the distinction between 'earth' and 'world' that Heidegger
makes in his essay "The Origin of the Work of Art." "It is the component of
'earth' that enables the work of art, or the poem, to 'stand in itself'; it is 'earth'
that gives the work of art existence in space" (Heidegger 1971: 34). We must
imagine the cultural earth of the poem, then, to be that which is adumbrated
by the physical texture of the lines. In the cross-cultural text, the earth is that
which is approached through the world, but because the 'world' of the text
is hybrid, the earth is engaged in a transcultural negotiation, a constitutive
negotiation of writer and reader functions.

The conclusion we can make from this is that, far from remaining colonized by writing in the colonizing language, the postcolonial writer may
convey cultural reality, and cultural difference, more effectively than a translation might—indeed remain 'truer' to the source culture. This is achieved,
paradoxically, by the writer installing a gap that some might assume to be
an inevitable 'problem' for translation. The metonymic gap operates directly
when the writer employs any of the multiple strategies of language variance
in providing a form of inner translation. But there is, in the music of the prosody, the potential for the text to provide a cultural 'atmosphere' or *Stimmung*
that exists beyond the hermeneutic requirements of meaning. This deictic
engagement with the text operates across the metonymic gap, so to speak,
while acknowledging its presence. In this acknowledgment of the space of
untranslatability between cultures, the reader enters what Bakhtin calls
'true dialogue' by recognizing the difference of the Other. While English
is undoubtedly a language of the elite in formerly colonized countries, we
might make the same accusation of literature everywhere. But it has been the
achievement of literary writers to transform English into a cultural vehicle.
Far from being dominated by a global language, postcolonial writers have
translated their cultural realities in a transformed language that has changed
the field of English literature forever.

References

Achebe, C. (1975) *Morning Yet on Creation Day* (London: Heinemann).
Aniebo, I. N. C. (1978) *The Journey Within* (London: Heinemann).
Ashcroft, B., Griffiths, G., and Tiffin, H. (1989) *The Empire Writes Back: Theory and Practice in Post-Colonial Criticism* (London: Routledge).
Bakhtin, M. (1981) *The Dialogic Imagination: Four Essays*. Ed. M. Holquist, trans. C. Emerson and M. Holquist (Austin: University of Texas Press).
Benjamin, W. (1969) 'The Task of the Translator' in his *Illuminations*. Trans. H. Zohn (New York: Schocken), pp. 69–82.
Bhabha, H. (1994) *The Location of Culture* (London: Routledge).
Bourdieu, P. (1993) *The Field of Cultural Production* (New York: Columbia University Press).

Donnell, A., and Welsh S.L. (1996) *The Routledge Reader in Caribbean Literature* (London: Routledge).

Gumbrecht, H. U. (2004) *Production of Presence: What Meaning Cannot Convey* (Stanford, CA: Stanford University Press).

Gumbrecht, H. U. (2009) 'How (If at All) Can We Encounter What Remains Latent in Texts?' *Journal of Literature and the History of Ideas* 7: 1: 87–96.

Gumbrecht, H. U. (2011) *Atmosphere, Mood, Stimmung: On a Hidden Potential of Literature* (Stanford, CA: Stanford University Press).

Heidegger, M. (1971) *Poetry, Language, Thought.* Trans. A. Hofstadter (New York: Harper and Row).

Mair, C. (ed) (2003) *The Politics of English as a World Language: New Horizons in Postcolonial Cultural Studies Asnel Papers 7* (Amsterdam: Rodopi).

Moore, B. (ed) (2001) *Who's Centric Now? The Present State of Postcolonial Englishes* (Melbourne: Oxford University Press).

Narayanan, P. (2012) *What Are You Reading: The World Market and Indian Literary Production* (New Delhi: Routledge).

Ngugi wa Thiong'o. (1981) *Decolonizing the Mind: The Politics of Language in African Literature* (London: James Curry).

Ortiz, F. (1978) *Contrapunto Cubano (1947–1963)* (Caracas: Biblioteca Ayacucho).

Phillipson, R. (1992) *Linguistic Imperialism* (Oxford: Oxford University Press).

Pratt, M. L. (1992) *Imperial Eyes: Travel Writing and Transculturation* (London: Routledge).

Rushdie, S. (1991) *Imaginary Homelands: Essays and Criticism 1981–91* (London: Granta).

Simon, S. (1992) "The Language of Cultural Difference: Figures of Alterity in Canadian Translation", in L. Venuti (ed.) *Rethinking Translation: Discourse Subjectivity, Ideology,* London: Routledge: pp. 159–176

Simon, S. (1999) 'Translating and Interlingual Creation in the Contact Zone: Border Writing in Quebec' in *Post-Colonial Translation: Theory and Practice*, ed. S. Bassnett and H. Trivedi (London: Routledge), pp. 58–74.

Taussig, M. (1993) *Mimesis and Alterity* (New York: Routledge).

Thompson, E., and Hughes, E. C. (eds) (1965) *Race: Individual and Collective Behavior* (New York: Free Press).

Wittgenstein, L. (1975) *Philosophical Investigations.* Trans. G. E. M. Anscombe (Oxford: Blackwell).

Zabus, C. (1991) *The African Palimpsest: Indigenization of Language in the West African Europhone Novel.* 2nd enlarged ed. 2007 (Amsterdam: Rodopi).

2 'Writing with an Accent'

From Early Decolonization to Contemporary Gender Issues in the African Novel in French, English, and Arabic

Chantal Zabus

The issue of translation and of transfer between cultures and texts is more problematic when the transfer, as refracted in texts, occurs between a dominant culture and a subordinate culture. This is the case with postcolonial societies affected by colonization and its indelible aftereffects. I addressed these issues in relation to sub-Saharan African texts in *The African Palimpsest* (1991), where I was concerned with the mechanisms in conveying African thought patterns into the language of the ex-colonizer, principally English and French. Even though much work went into my retrieving the African language in filigree in the sub-Saharan Europhone novel, I realize with hindsight that I had omitted three areas of critical inquiry: (1) I had focused on sub-Saharan, mostly West African, languages; (2) my corpus was made of novels by male African authors; and (3) Arabic fell out of my purview. My aim, therefore, is to suggest ways in which these lacunae can be filled by expanding on French use in West African novels, providing examples of English use in the South African novel and then moving on to consider language use around issues of sexuality and gender in novels by African female authors, which I briefly extend to the novel in Arabic.

Unlike translation, which happens between two texts, indigenization takes place within one text. Faced with the historical inevitability of writing in the colonizer's language while wishing to 'indigenize' their texts, writers from formerly colonized countries have sought to convey concepts, thought patterns, and even linguistic features of their mother tongues or first languages in the European language. Indigenization is an attempt to "write with an accent," which is how the Iranian-born, US-based Taqi Modarressi described his "translation" into English of his Persian novel, *Ādāb-e ziārat, The Pilgrim's Rules of Etiquette* (1989). Such Persian phrases as "nobody chopped any chives for him" or "[he was] trying to be the bean in every soup" (Modarressi 1992: 7–9) clearly suggest a language other than English; they have a different tempo, a different rhythm.

Bound to Violence: Writing Back and the Beginnings of Textual Decolonization

Among the sub-Saharan African writers who "write with an accent," Nigerian Gabriel Okara is probably the most daring of all experimenters. His experimentation is linguistically verifiable in his one and only novel, *The Voice* (1964), which captures the disillusionment following the independence of Nigeria in 1960. Like, for instance, *Fragments* (1969) by the Ghanaian Ayi Kwei Armah, *The Voice* starts with the return to the native land of travel-worn Okolo ("the voice" in Ijǫ). Our "been-to" (for he has "been to" the West) is jolted by Nigeria's moral bankruptcy. As a result, he starts his hallucinatory wandering through the corrupt city of Sologa (an anagram of Lagos, Nigeria's first capital) until he is set adrift down the river, bound back-to-back to an alleged witch.

Okara's linguistic experimentation in *The Voice* is sustained by the metaphorical fight between "the crooked words" of political propaganda said, for the most part, in English, and Okolo's ideology of "the straight words" said in Ijǫ (Okara 1964: 117). Okara intimates that ultimately, Okolo's straight words will triumph over the crooked words of corrupt politics, imported ideology, and the British word order, that is, the logocentric relation between word and referent in the English language.

Okolo's English is imbued with Ijǫ thought patterns, word order, and concepts, which account for the novel's quaint, pseudo-naïve lingo that *consciously* achieves what Amos Tutuola, a decade earlier, had stumbled on with the inadvertently botched Yoruba-informed English of *The Palm-Wine Drinkard* [*sic*] (1952). Okara has, for instance, rendered the English—"he is timid"—through its Ijǫ equivalent "he has no chest" or "he has no shadow" (1964: 23). Double- and triple-barreled coinages like "making-people-handsome-day" (70) can be traced to Ijǫ: *kémé mién èbimò èréin*. When such lexical and semantic innovations are extended to the syntax, the result may be both stilted and alluring as in "Who are you people be?" (26) or "everybody surface-water-things tells" (34). The postponement of the verb and/or of the negative can be traced to Ijǫ syntactical patterns: "To every person's said thing listen not" (7) is from *Kęmę gbá yémǫ sę póù kúmǫ*, that is, literally, "Man-say-things-all-listen-not," whereas "He always of change speaks" (66) comes from *Yémǫ détmìnìù bárá sèrìmósę érí ęrémìnì*, that is, literally, "Things-changing-how-always-he-(is)-speaking."

Okara's art is also permeated with indigenous rhetoric like the hyperbolic statements characteristic of the *copia* of oral narrative and of drum language, the ample use of epic eulogies characteristic of heroic poetry, such as "I am unless-you-provoke-me!" (Okara 1964: 99). He also makes use of reification, as in "two chunks of darkness" (40), of the epistrophe by ending sentences or clauses with the same word; and the anaphora by repeating the word or phrase in successive clauses, as in "Okolo ran, Okolo ran." Such a degree of language experimentation as Okara's recalls other rhetoric worldwide, such as the reiterative technique used in the black spoken church sermon or in jazz improvisation, as well as the traditional Shona songs of Zimbabwe. But the main source remains Ijǫ, the fourth registered language in Nigeria after Yoruba, Hausa, and Igbo, excepting the official language, English, and Arabic.

Even though Okara claimed that his aim was "to translate [African ideas] almost literally from the African language native to the writer" (1963: 15), he does not translate in that he neither seeks equivalency nor aims to recode the original according to the norms of the dominant language; he *relexifies*. Relexification thus occurs when there is an attempt at simulating the indigenous tongue. It is the making of a new register out of the givens of an alien lexicon.

Okara's experiment led to an artistic impasse, and *The Voice* had no substantial following. But Okara's reliance on the indigenous linguistic heritage rather than on the exogenous English one helped oust English from "its ancestral home," to use Chinua Achebe's phrase (Achebe 1975: 102). In *Things Fall Apart* (1958), the celebrated Nigerian writer grafted onto the novel form several discursive elements that constitute "the Igbo ethno-text" (Zabus 2007: 148). This ethno-text comprises rules of address, riddles, praise-names, dirges, and, most notably, Igbo proverbs or *ílú*, such as the prayer over the cola nut, variants of which can be found in other English-language novels by Igbo novelists such as Onuora Nzekwu in *Blade among the Boys* (1962) or Nkem Nwankwo in *Danda* (1964). This process of embedding proverbs into the very texture of the novel is at times carried to unprecedented lengths: Achebe's *Arrow of God* (1964; 1974) contains as many as 129 proverbs.

In his seminal essay, "The African Writer and the English Language," Achebe has argued that, in order to recapture the patterns of traditional speech, he had to forge a "new English" that must be "in character" (1975: 102) with its new surroundings, away from its ancestral home. He proceeds to quote a passage from *Arrow of God* in which Oduche, the son of a Chief Priest, reports his father's words upon sending him to the Christian school: "I want one of my sons to join these people and be my eye there" (Achebe 1964: 45). This corresponds to the Igbo: *Áchọlu m ka ofú n'ime umụ m sònyélu ndi-à ka ó bụlu anya m n'ebe afù*, which, calqued or transliterated verbatim back into English, reads: "I want me that one inside children my join people these that he becomes eyes my inside place-that" (Obiechina 1974: 17). Achebe settled for this intermediary stage—"Be my eye there"—according to the discursive norms of English when in fact he could have written, as he himself showed: "I am sending you as my representative among those people just to be on the safe side [in case the new religion develops]" (1975: 102). The intermediary form of semantic relexification in proverbial rhetoric proves to be more viable than what Okara attempted when exploring the relexification of syntax. Characteristically, the struggle between English and Ijọ in Okara's *The Voice* left no room for Pidgin, even though the novel is set primarily in the emblematic city of Lagos, where ẸnPi or Nigerian Pidgin is rife.

Not all writers have opted to relexify their texts, but they have resorted to other methods like 'cushioning' and 'contextualization,' which, along with the glossary, antedate relexification. They will presumably outlive it because the African novelist will always be compelled to provide areas of immediate context ('contextualization') or to tag an explanatory word or phrase ('cushioning') onto the African word. Cushioning *obi* with 'hut,' to take the commonest example from *Things Fall Apart*, is effective in preventing the use of culturally misleading expressions like 'sitting room' introduced in, for instance, Elechi Amadi's *The Concubine* (1966) and *The Great Ponds* (1969) without the element *obi*, as well as "reception room" in Kazuo Ishiguro's *An Artist of the Floating World* (1986) to designate the Japanese room for receiving important guests and paying one's respects at the Buddhist altar—the *tokonoma*. Conversely, 'hut' might wrongly connote preindustrial 'primitiveness' in the Western reader's mind. The main drawback to cushioning is that the brief tag may not encompass the full cultural significance of the transferred item and that it may defer understanding and break up the connectability of the text. To remedy this problem, the African writer often contextualizes the African-language word by explaining it to the lay reader by either inserting the unfamiliar word or phrase within a dialogue or by having the reader infer from the context or the syntax or both what the African word means. This riddling device, which involves the often Euro-American reader in a guessing game, is proof that the time has not come yet when the African novelists can insert an African word or refer to an African cultural event in the same manner as European novelists can throw into their texts German, English, or Latin locutions and refer to Jupiter, Mozart, and Nietzsche without any explanation.

Writing Sideways: Twist-and-Turn in South Africa and Francophone West Africa

Short of resorting to these strategies of "writing back" (Ashcroft, Griffiths, and Tiffin 1989), African authors have alternatively devised ways of writing sideways. The ways of writing sideways or of twisting a medium and turning it to one's aesthetic advantage differ, depending on the particular brand of colonialism. In her *Emerging Traditions* (2011), Vicki Briault Manus reports on how South African writer-activists took part in resistance, after the 1910 Act of Union, through journalism and pamphleteering but also fiction while township lingoes emerged from the Babel along with the "first signs of indigenization" (Briault 2011: 39). It is, however, only in the 1990s, in the post-Apartheid era, that writing by indigenous writers shifted from a protest literature of powerlessness to a literature of struggle in English marbled with other South African languages. Like his West African counterparts, South African novelist Es'kia Mphahlele uses glossed or untranslated words, relexified proverbs, metaphors, and expressions from Sesotho, as in his early piece *In Corner B* (1967) or *Father Come Home* (1984): "the child of my brother has been vomited by sleep" meaning "the child's sleep has been disturbed by a nightmare"; "do not come into my mouth" meaning "do not interrupt me"; or "I'll come out of the grave and breathe maggots into your life" meaning "I will come to haunt you." Mphahlele called this gap between English and Sesotho a resounding gap or "resonance" (1979: 1).

Although South African and West African authors have both experienced in their writing what I have designated as the metonymic gap (Zabus 1991:

175–193), there is no syntactic experimentation in the South African novel. Any attempt at relexification is confined to such units as proverbs, as in the South African (Xhosa) Sindiwe Magona's autobiography *To My Children's Children* (1990) and her *Forced to Grow* (1998), where proverbs are relexified from Xhosa into English, and sometimes tagged by the Xhosa source.

About his mother tongue, Afrikaans, South African novelist Breyten Breytenbach lamented that it is still stigmatized as "the language of Apartheid": "Does a language, of itself, have only one political meaning? Surely not. [. . .] A language is what you make of it" (Breytenbach 1994: 85). Both Mphahlele and Breytenbach base their craft on the inherent plasticity of the colonizers' language—whether it is English or Afrikaans, which were admittedly the only two official languages before the official end of Apartheid in 1994. With the new 1996 South African Constitution, the nine indigenous languages (i.e., Zulu, Xhosa, Pedi, Tsonga, Venda, Sotho, Ndebele, Swati, and Tswana) were raised to the status of official languages, alongside English and Afrikaans. However, this unusual equation—"2 + 9 = 1," used by Kamwangamalu (2003), points to unplanned unilingualism in South Africa at the outset of the twenty-first century: '1' is the English language at the expense of the other official languages, including Afrikaans and the above nine African languages, which are likely to face the fate of the KhoeSan (Xhoisan) and Indian languages, that is, attrition and eventual death. As Briault has demonstrated (2011), KhoeSan languages like Nama and Xiri have resisted the South African linguicide, but their use is confined to dialogues, as in Zoe Wicomb's *David's Story* (2000). Moreover, Creoles and Pidgins such as Fanagolo, Tsotsitaal or Flaaital, and Iscamtho do not have official status, and there are no novels written in *tsotsitaal* or a Creolized form like Nguni-Sotho (Briault 2011: 216–219). Briault, however, speculates on the possible convergence of Black South African English and White South African English, while evoking the recently identified phenomenon of People's English. Meanwhile, however, a language like Xhosa is very much alive, both in the social arena and in the novel, even though in filigree. Zakes Mda's third novel, *The Heart of Redness* (2000), depicts the cultural traditions and performances of the amaXhosa, the southernmost Bantu-speaking people, who inherited their click consonants from the Xhoisan. The novel, which shuttles between the great Xhosa cattle killing of 1856–1857 and the year 1998, taps into the South African storytelling tradition and has been interpreted as "the fictional equivalent of Xhosa overtone singing" or *umngqokolo* (Jacobs 2002: 227).

Tellingly, gender roles are defined in isiXhosa terms—*xhego* (an old woman); *intombi* (a young woman); *makoti* (a daughter-in-law)—whereas a cultural practice such as *ukukrexeza* is cushioned or tagged by the parenthetical "(having lovers outside marriage)." So are the circumcision rites involving *abakhwetha* (the initiates) or rituals such as *ukurhuda* in which sacred enemas and emetics are administered (Jacobs 2002: 229). Significantly, these ways of "shadowing" cultural artifacts and practices are contained in the dialectic between *ubuqaba* ("backwardness and heathenism") and *ubugqobokha* ("enlightenment and civilization"), which in turn reflects on the novel's two main narrative periods, the nineteenth-century forebears and their post-Apartheid inheritors (Mda 2000: 20–21, 98). This "split-tone song"–style novel (Jacobs 2002: 229) returns us to the metonymic gap between English and the African-language words that here "stand for" the colonized culture.

Even if West Africa and South Africa share the same harrowing history of slavery, dispossession, and colonization, none of the West African countries experienced the legal straightjacket that the Apartheid regime (1948–1994) foisted on the Black African population. While both West African authors and indigenous South African authors discussed meeting halfway through the similar techniques of contextualization, cushioning, code-switching, and the use of Pidgins, the tooling and honing of the English-language weapon to present an indigenous worldview is less sharp in South African than in Anglophone West African texts. Indeed, no strategies involving deep lexico-semantic or morpho-syntactical transformations are deployed with the will to textual violence that is present in the West African texts in English.

Possibly as a result of French assimilation policies, Francophone West African texts have deployed less daring strategies than their Anglophone counterparts under British indirect rule. However, Ivorian Ahmadou Kour-ouma, for instance, has dared experiment with the sacrosanct French lan-guage. In his *Les Soleils des indépendances* (1968), which hinges partly on the virulent denunciation of corrupt postindependence regimes in West Africa, Kourouma echoes Okara and Achebe when he evokes the "translation" of Mandinka expressions into French. But the idea of rupture with, or sever-ance from, the French rhythm will only partly materialize, presumably as a result of a Francophile abidance by the correct usage prescribed by the Académie Française.

The breach with the starchiness of French results in heavy reliance on lexico-semantic (vs. morpho-syntactic) relexification from Mandinka and orature-based devices such as Mandinka proverbs; collages of *ngóni dɔn kili* (hunters' songs); accounts based on the oral *kókóró*, the historico-mystical chronicles of Malinke extended families; as well as questions addressed by the griot-like narrator to the audience. In stark Mandinka rhythm, *Suns of Independence* opens with the death of Koné Ibrahima: "Il y avait une semaine qu'avait fini dans la capitale Koné Ibrahima, de race malinké, ou disons-le en malinké: il n'avait pas soutenu un petit rhume. 'Ibrahima Koné a fini, c'est son ombre,' s'était-on dit" (Kourouma 1968: 1). Literally, "A week ago Koné Ibrahima, of Madinka blood, had finished in the capital city, or, to put it in Mandinka, he had not sustained a small cold. 'Ibrahima had finished; it was his shadow,' it was said." The Mandinka concept of *djă* pops up in its shad-owy guise ("ombre") with Koné's death: "[il] a fini" is from the Mandinka: *à bánna* (from the verb *ban* ['finir'] + *-rà* in the present perfect) to mean 'he has died.' The coined expression "il n'avait pas soutenu un petit rhume" is relexified from *mòla má kùn á rò* or *mùra má kun à rɔ* (cold [did] not have [post-position]). This familiar expression corresponds to the slang "to peg out" or "to kick the bucket." The text is padded with similar phrases like "refroidissez le coeur" from Mandinka: *Í jùsú súmā* or *Í dùsú súmā* (your heart cool down) instead of 'calme-toi' (calm down).

In Kourouma's later novel, *Monné* (1990), the following greetings—"Oui, je suis bien votre fils Kélétigui" / "A vous la bienvenue, Télétigui" / " Et j'ai marché les longues excursions et vécu les grandes souffrances" (1990: 212)—could be traced to Mandinka: "*Òwò, me/nde le i denke Keletigi di.*"/ "*I bisimila, Keletigi!*"/ "*N ka/N bara taana/toòna kosòbè, ka sèkèn/sègèn hali.*" From "I (auxiliary or -na suffix) have walked, I got tired a lot / or have seen a lot of places." These specifically Mandinka rules of address, relexified into French, could conjure up any other polite formula, especially with the Arabic phrase *bi-smililāhi* (literally: in the name of God), which is used all over the Arab world. Likewise, even if *Suns of Independence* reeks of the Mandinka of *Woro-dugu*, the land of the cola nut in Ivory Coast, Kourouma's native land, other devices taken from Mandinka orature belong to the vast corpus of African traditional oral material. For instance, the use of "soleil" in *Le soleil des indépendances* may be traced to Mandinka *télé*, which means 'day,' or, with a plural maker, 'era' or 'time' but Burkinabe novelist Nazi Boni, who made use of his native Bwamu in *Le Crépuscule des temps anciens* (1962), used "finir" and "soleil" in the same way as Kourouma does. So, for instance, we read: "Des générations étaient nées, avaient fait leur soleil et disparu" to signify that "generations had been born, had lived and died" (Boni 1962: 19).

Le crépuscule des temps anciens also shares with Anglophone texts such as Achebe's early novels the use of proverbs, and makes use of the technique of tagging or cushioning as in "*Hanwa*, les femmes" where the Bwa word *hanwa* is directly tagged by "women" (Boni 1962: 53). In another instance, Boni dwells on "His Excellency the muddy *Mb'woa Gnoudjoa*," which he tags with the phrase "cheval aquatique" or "aquatic horse" (25). Louis Millogo notes that the Bwa title *Mb'woa* could be translated into French as "grand-père" or "ancêtre," that is, "grandfather" or "ancestor," which conveys the respect due to the advanced years of the elderly, anthropomorphized hippopotamus (2002: 261). As a result, a French critic, writing in 1966, found Boni guilty of vilifying the French language (Pageard 1966: 74). Likewise, Kourouma's novel was first turned down in France and then published in Montreal to be later recuperated by the Parisian publishing house Seuil. But even so, it failed to get the *Grand Prix des Lectrices* for *Elle* magazine on account of its most unorthodox use of the *langue de Molière*.

Writing Rites

In *Crépuscule des temps anciens*, Nazi Boni uses the Bwa word *Dô* to refer to a rite of passage without any further specification. On one occasion, one reads,

"Vous savez qu'on n'affronte pas ces épreuves en nombre impair sous peine de voir le plus jeune de la promotion avalé par le Dô" (1962: 137), implying, if I paraphrase, that initiates do not undergo the rite serially in an odd number for fear that the youngest initiate in his age-group gets "swallowed up by the Dô." In Bwa culture, the concerned age-group is between twenty-five and thirty years of age and one can only infer that this rite of passage entails the transfer of power from the *yenissa* or "initiates" to the *bruwa* or "non-initiates" after the rite of circumcision performed on grown men (163, 118, 111). The rite can lead to death, we surmise, through hemorrhage.

Death by excision, the controversial counterpart to male circumcision, is central to an early novel by Kenyan Ngugi wa Thiong'o, *The River Between* (1965), in which the nubile female body is presented as a site of contest between the new converts to Christianity and the conservative "tribalists," that is, the future Mau Mau fighters during the 1952–1956 Kenyan Emergency. Male circumcision is also central to the plot's development. The main protagonist, Waiyaki, has reportedly been "cleansed" (14–15) before "the biggest of all rituals, circumcision [, which] would mark his final initiation into manhood" and forever remove his identity as *kihii*, or "uncircumcised boy" (45), in a form of cultural castration. In Kikuyu culture, as Jomo Kenyatta has made amply clear in his *Facing Mount Kenya* (1938), the word for circumcision for boys and excision for girls is conveyed through one word: *irua*. The reader is therefore not surprised to be told of the Presbyterian preacher's daughter Muthoni's oracular decision "to be circumcised" (27–28), which corresponds to wa Thiongo's rendering of *irua*. Her subsequent death by hemorrhage is a sacrificial one, the martyrdom of a "Christian in the tribe" (61). Wa Thiong'o ventriloquizes through Muthoni and has her die at peace, "a woman, beautiful in the manner of the tribe" (53), thereby providing the first positive account of death by excision in excision-related literature.

Muthoni's excision, which involves clitoridectomy and labiadectomy, is clouded in mystery, whereas Waiyaki's circumcision is described in minute detail. It covers a whole panoply of sensations: from the numbing of his muscles by the cold water of the Honia river, and the ensuing shrinking of his penis through the "thin sharp pain" produced by the knife as it cuts through his flesh, to his communion with the earth through the dripping of his blood "on to his fingers, falling to the ground, while a white calico sheet covered him" (Ngugi 1965: 53). Wa Thiong'o's narration around Waiyaki's swelling wound is in inverse proportion to the laconic mention of Muthoni's wound, which is "getting bigger and worse" (55) but is shrunk to italics. This narrative asymmetry may also reflect wa Thiong'o's autobiographical vestment of the ceremony, which he underwent at fifteen before he became a Christian.

If the rendering of female *irua* by the term "circumcision" obscures the dire reality of genital excision among girls, wa Thiong'o's short-circuiting of the operation also belittles the events leading to Kenya's independence.

Indeed, the en masse excisions in the late 1930s in Meru, Central Kenya, were a response to the vocal campaigning of Protestant missionaries who, during the 1929–1931 controversy, preached against excision and enlisted the help of London-based humanitarian and feminist groups and gradually medicalized the practice. This controversy foreshadowed the later forcible excision of Christian girls, as in this foreboding prediction in wa Thiong'o's *The River Between* that "the day would come when all these *Irigu* [unexcised girls] would be circumcised by force, to rid the land of all impurities" (149). Kenya's coming to independence therefore cannot be understood without the Kikuyu ideological alignment of excision or *irua* with purity and anticolonial sentiments.

The metonymic gap between *irua* and excision in *The River Between* points to the erasure of gender issues in the male craft of writing rites and to the need for women to indigenize their text by make it "a text of one's own." Although the language of post-patriarchy is not linguistically tangible as yet, African women writers have tried to reconnect with the tongue of the "mother-culture" and develop some sort of "voice-print" within a system that denied their sisters access to functional literacy (Zabus 1996). Alternatively, they have come up with linguistic strategies that attempt to name and speak the unspeakable.

The eponymous character in the debut novel *Efuru* (1966), by Flora Nwapa, the first Nigerian woman writer to be published, is reminded of the primary function of genital excision: a young woman must "have her bath" before she has a baby (14). The reader senses from the immediate context that "to have a bath" is different from, say, a later authorial statement: "One day [Efuru] returned from the market [and] had her bath" (83). The Western reader is indeed perplexed until the narrator in *Efuru* refers to "circumcision"—"Efuru's husband returned home and was told about his wife's circumcision" (12). "Bath" as in "[she must] have her bath" is relexified from Igbo, more specifically, from *isa aru* or *iwu aru*, which is the Oguta variant of Igbo (in Eastern Nigeria). It refers to the ritual of genital excision, which entails cleansing or purification, in the same way in which Bambara *bolo koli* refers to "the washing of one's hands" (Zabus 2007: 87).

Nwapa opted for "bath" to describe the culture-specific practice that was to be labeled female genital mutilation (FGM) or female genital cutting (FGC) by various organizations, including the World Health Organization, in the wake of the 1975–1985 United Nations Decade for Women. Nwapa was in the 1960s trying to bridge the metonymic gap between Igbo and English and between the ancestral rite and human rights; she was writing from a liminal position "between rites and rights" (Zabus 2007). Nwapa was also telling the previously untold story of African women while writing with their accent. The Igbo noun *Nkali*, which roughly translates as "being greater than another," alludes to power in storytelling: *who* tells the story of another person. Using Achebe's reference to the necessity for the "balance of stories," third-generation Nigerian author Chimamanda Ngozi Adichie, whose much

acclaimed novel *Purple Hibiscus* came out in 2004, acknowledged that reading Achebe and Guinean Camara Laye had "saved [her] from the danger of
a single story."[1] Women writers are now empowered to radically challenge
this "single story" and to redress the wrongs in the rite.

Gender and Sexual Dissidence

If indigenization was a useful strategy of linguistic decolonization, very
much akin to the political process of Africanization, despite some of its aber-
rant applications, one should warn against overreading for indigenization. A
case in point is the seemingly Yoruba-inflected novels of Beninese novelist
Adelaïde Fassinou in two of her French-language novels, *Modukpé: le rêve
brisé* (2000) and *Enfant d'autrui, fille de personne* (2003). Whereas the Yoruba
language has been invariably associated with prominent Nigerian and therefore Anglophone authors such as Amos Tutuola or Wole Soyinka, it is at first
refreshing to see that Yoruba can also be in filigree in West African writing
in French.

In *Le rêve brisé* ("The Broken Dream"), Fassinou does use Yoruba rules
of address such as the mother addressing her daughter as "Dukpé ma fille"
(2000: 64) from the Yoruba "Dukpé, *omo ni*." Some Yoruba words are "cushioned" with their French translations of the type "sara: aumône" (32), that
is, alms-giving after *sàárá* in standard Yoruba. In her later novel, *Enfant
d'autrui*, words like "boba" to refer to a kind of shirt, after *bùbá* in standard
Yoruba, are left untranslated and unexplained. However, as Babatunde Ayeleru has demonstrated, this later novel is imbued with the typical reserve
and sense of modesty when referring to sexual matters and, specifically, the
sex organs, so that a man's stomach and private parts are referred to, respectively, as "le ventre," that is, "the belly," and "le bas-ventre" (37), that is,
"below the belly." Likewise, "le sentier qui mène à son intimité" (47), that is,
"the path that leads to her intimate parts," is clearly euphemistic; "goûter au
fruit défendu" (81), that is, "to taste the forbidden fruit," with its inescapably
Biblical innuendoes, to refer to both the sexual act and female genitalia, is
ascertained in Yoruba parlance, where to "eat the forbidden fruit" signifies
"to sleep with a woman," itself an admittedly euphemistic expression to refer
to having sexual intercourse with a woman.

Ayeleru also traces the expression "quitter le sein" to the Yoruba *fi oyon
si* (literally: drop or abandon the breast) to refer to weaning. Even though
the French phrase is patterned after "donner le sein" to render "breast-feed,"
it is neither Yoruba nor French and is rather an attempt at relexification.
However, "faire sa toilette intime" (76) to refer to washing oneself does not
so much render the Yoruba reluctance to dwell on anatomical details, as
Ayeleru argues, as it is a typically standard French idiom, however bashful.
Such texts as Fassinou's command our attention for their laudable attempts at
indigenization with the proviso that not all French use harks back to Yoruba,

but they are also valuable in that Fassinou broaches questions of gender and sexuality more boldly in French that she would have presumably in Yoruba.

The language of post-patriarchy in Africa would indeed be inchoate if sexual minorities were not busy forging a language that captures their sexual dissidence, between tongues, in a text that dare not speak its name. In *Embrace* (2000), South African novelist Mark Behr relates the tribulations of Karl de Man, an Afrikaner homosexual child growing up under Apartheid. When questioned by his father about rumors of same-sex activities at the boarding school, Karl acknowledges the difficulty of relaying a sexual vocabulary that could not possibly "translate favourably into [the father's] world: piel, voël, dinges, cock, dick, schlong, John Thomas, willy, penis, dong, ding, tool, horing, bone." Instead, when probed further by his inquisitive father, Karl settles for the Afrikaans word of his early childhood "[We played] with each other's filafoois" (227). In this English-language novel, untranslated Afrikaans pieces of reported dialogue are, if not frequent, occasionally unsettling for the monolingual English reader. African words are also used but are deflected from their actual meaning by bigoted white characters. A case in point is the reference to the word *sangoma* as "heathen witch doctors" (134) when in fact the Zulu word designates a traditional healer.

In her autobiography, *Black Bull, Ancestors and Me: My Life as a Lesbian Sangoma* (2008), South African Nkunzi Zandile Nkabinde explains her initiation as a *sangoma* within the larger system of Zulu gender-differentiated spiritual possession cults involving "female men" and "male women" as well as her coming out as a lesbian. "Lesbian" is a word that she has to look up in an English dictionary at the age of thirteen and that does not quite render the relationship she, as a male-dominated traditional healer, has with her "ancestral wife." Both biowomen, Nkabinde as a "male woman" and her "ancestral wife," are not united in a common identity based on shared sexual orientation, as in the sexual orientation clause in the 1996 South African Constitution, but rather are distinguished from each other according to gender difference, complicated by spirituality. Even though Nkabinde translates her gender identity into "tomboy," "lesbian," and "butch," the Zulu label tagged onto her "ancestral wife" falls off the grid of a global, transnational, and translational vocabulary.

In South Africa, the word 'lesbian' comes with a hurtling conglomerate of indigenous (e.g., Zulu) and other designations and their corollary practices. For instance, same-sex between female "gang bosses" and women inmates in the women's jail is called *snaganaga* but does not qualify as "lesbian" sex (Nkabinde 2008: 134). Bongie, who was sent from Soweto (South West Townships) to Nelspruit in the eastern Transvaal, reports that a girl to whom she had proposed to at the boarding school "asked [her] if [she] was a lesbian." The girl declined Bongie's overtures, refusing to have a lesbian affair, but conceded that "if we could be *amachicken*, then she wouldn't mind. You see, she just meant to kiss and hold hands and nothing further"

(Gevisser and Cameron 1995: 187). *Amachicken* involves foreplay only, whereas the English word "lesbian" is equated with genital sex, without the two terms overlapping. In Kampala, Uganda, where Sections 140 and 141 of the penal code condemn same-sex relations, some Ugandan women identify themselves as "tommy-boys," that is, biological women who see themselves as men, often pass as men, and need to be the dominant partner during sex, rather than "lesbians."

The word 'gay' is also susceptible to a category crisis, as a South African "masculine man" playing the dominant role in a relationship with another man, for instance, is called "a straight man" and is not perceived as "gay" because he acts as penetrator. When, at Heritage Day Celebrations in KwaDukuza on September 26, 2006, Jacob Zuma, who was to become president of South Africa three years later, declared: "When I was growing up an *ungqingili* [a derogatory Zulu term for a gay man] would not have stood in front of me. I would knock him out,"[2] he was presumably threatening a receptor rather than the inserter or penetrator who retains a form of heterosexual identity. Just as not all women who have sex with women (WSW) identify as lesbian, homosexual, bisexual, or queer, not all men who have sex with men (MSM) think of themselves as gay or queer. Both groups are seldom members of activist Lesbian-Gay-Bisexual-Transgender (LGBT) organizations and are not computed in the sexual health literature on HIV/ AIDS. Also, a phrase like "a male lesbian," relexified from *'yan kifi* in Hausa (a language in the Islamized northern parts of Western African countries) to refer to a passive homosexual male, reveals a certain level of translational uneasiness and possibly the incommensurability of African same-sex relations. Such terms covering practices that are recoded into Western palatable jargon are finding their way in the novel form.

The Arabic word *mithliyyah* is a recent invention patterned on the combination of the Greek original word for 'sameness' and the Latin word for 'sex' (i.e., homosexuality), whereas *ghayriyah* renders differentness or heterosexuality. Also, the coinage *al-shudhuudh al-jinsi*, itself a translation from the European, end-of-nineteenth-century medical conception of 'sexual deviance' or 'sexual inversion,' is the most commonly accepted term to refer to the Western conception of homosexuality. Joseph Massad's linguistic forays in *Desiring Arabs* (2007) are part of a larger thesis whereby the word 'homosexuality' does not accurately describe "same-sex contact" in "the Arab world" (172).

To take one instance from the African Mashreq, in Egyptian novelist Najib Mahfuz's *Zuqaq al-Midaq* (1947), the first volume of his Cairo trilogy, the Sufi ascetic Shaykh Darwish tells the married café owner, Kirshah, who is having an affair with a young man: "This is an old evil, which in English they call Homosexuality and is spelled, h-o-m-o-s-e-x-u-a-l-i-t-y, but it is not love. True love is only for the family and descendants of the prophet" (1992: 101). It is worthwhile to note that, with the exception of the English word 'homosexuality,' all the English words that Darwish utters in the novel—"history," "tragedy," "frog," "end," or even "viceroy" and "elopement"—have Arabic equivalents (Massad 2007: 277). Mahfuz does use the term *shudhuudh* to refer to Kirshah's same-sex practices. Admittedly, *shudhuudh*-as-deviance refers to "all nonnormative sex, desires, excess, and general public misconduct" (Massad 2007: 278), whereas Nabil Matar understands "deviance" as an Islamic concept rather than a recent translation from European languages (1994: 78). Whether of Islamic or European origin, *shudhuudh* has a negative import that Massad in his castigation of the purveyors of Western gayness and its liberation strategies (e.g., 2007: 340, 369) and Mahfuz endorse; the latter's *Al-Sukkariyyah* (*Sugar Street*, 1957) indeed reintroduces male same-sex desire but this time as an "illness" combined with a "disgust" for women (304).

In his novel *Sharaf* (1997), Egyptian novelist Sun'allah Ibrahim stages the attempted rape of a young man called Sharaf (which means 'honor') by an Australian, which functions as the West's symbolic rape of Egypt. The colloquial Egyptian term used in the novel, *yatasakhmat*, is used as a euphemism to refer to "being buggered," which is Massad's translation to support his argument that "in a globalized world, being buggered [. . .] becomes the only fate awaiting all oppressed men, including the majority of Egyptian men" (2007: 377). As *yatasakhmat* is derived from the word *sukhmah* (blackness) and *sukham* (coal or soot), "the Egyptian colloquial verb *sakhmata* is the colloquial rendering of *sakhkhama* (in classical Arabic), which means blacken," the use of the term aligns blacks and penetratees "in one stroke" (2007: 378–379). Massad concludes his analysis of "deviant fiction" by casting "globalization as sodomy/castration" (385). 'Ala' Al-Aswani in *'Imarat Ya'qubyan* (*The Yacoubian Building*, 2002) completes this decadent process by linking "sexual deviance" to "postcolonial degeneration" (389).

In his discursive resistance to the imposition of Western vocabularies, Massad has targeted the white male European or American gay scholars' "missionary" explanations of what they mean by "homosexuality" (2007: 184) in Arab and Muslim history. In the process, he has also taken a few stabs at the "Gay International's" obsession with romantic coupling and its discursive transformation of practitioners of same-sex contact into homosexual or gay subjects. The process of naming homosexuality matters, if only for the inclusions and the exclusions that it fosters. In an African context, homosexual men and men who imitate women may be socially accepted as long as they are slotted as social jesters who entertain the crowds. As Guinean moviemaker Mohamed Camara has said about his film *Dakan* (1997), "the minute that you say that a homosexual is a man who makes love with another man or a woman who makes love to another woman that is when the problem starts" (Ellerson 2005: 62) on the grounds that "homosexuality" was and is still thought to be quintessentially un-African. The term 'un-African' is often used as a means of controlling variant gender performance or sexualities, and punitive behavior includes beating, rape, and, in some contexts, aversion therapy, forcible sex change, and even murder.

In 2008, eighty-six United Nation member countries had laws that criminalized same-sex relations. Thirty-seven African countries, along with Middle Eastern countries, constituted a majority of those. Even if, as Massad argues, the insertion of "deviants" into "discourse of liberation, identities, and rights have made their lives much worse" (2007: 376), the visibility of same-sex relations and their discursive representation outside the vocabulary of deviance are bound to help shatter African epistemic blindness to a desire that is universal, even if it is culturally relativized. The novel can register this shift by accenting homosexuality in a culture-specific yet positive way.

As a crisscrossing of universalism and cultural relativism, indigenization can dispel the seeming incommensurability, as well as the untranslatability, of gender- and sex-related terms. This can be observed linguistically in new coinages such as *magai* to refer to 'gay' in Kenya. Sex, like the language-contact situations resulting in Pidgins and Creoles, can produce hybrid forms, which, far from being degenerate, reflect both the argumentative frenzy around the very instability of sex and gender. Like linguistic indigenization, the indigenization of sex should make us aware that intercourse between a dominant and a dominated partner, like the linguistic transfer from a dominated to a dominant culture and language, can interpenetrate and thus yield creative mistranslations and harmonious misconducts.

Notes

1. See Chimamanda Adichie, 'The Danger of a Single Story,' www.youtube.com/ watch?v=D9Ihs24lzeg (accessed October 7, 2009).
2. See 'Zuma Earns Wrath of Gays and Lesbians,' *Mail and Guardian*, www.mg.co. za/article/2006–09–26–zuma-earns-wrath-of-gays-and-lesbians (accessed June 23, 2012).

References

Achebe, C. (1958) *Things Fall Apart* (London: Heinemann).
Achebe, C. (1964) *Arrow of God* (London: Heinemann).
Achebe, C. (1975) 'The African Writer and the English Language' in *Morning Yet on Creation Day*, ed. C. Achebe (Garden City, NY: Doubleday), pp. 91–103.
Adichie, Chimamanda Ngozi (2004). *Purple Hibiscus* (London & New York: Fourth Estate).
Al-Aswani, 'Ala' (2002). *The Yacoubian Building* (Cairo: Mirit Lil-Nashr wa al Ma'humat).
Amadi, Elechi (1966). *The Concubine* (London: Heinemann).
Amadi, Elechi (1969). *The Great Ponds* (London: Heinemann).
Armah, Ayi Kwei (1969). *Fragments* (London: Heinemann).
Ashcroft, B., Griffiths, G. and Tiffin, H. (1989) *The Empire Writes Back: Theory and Practice in Post-Colonial Criticism* (London: Routledge).
Ayeleru, Babatunde (nd). 'Indigenization as Sexuality in Adelaïde Fassinou's *Le rêve brisé* and *Enfant d'Autrui, fille de personne.*' Unpublished manuscript.
Behr, M. (2000) *Embrace* (London: Abacus/Little, Brown, and Cy).
Boni, N. (1962) *Le crépuscule des temps anciens* (Paris: Présence africaine).

Breytenbach, B. (1994) *The True Confessions of an Albino Terrorist* (San Diego: Harcourt Brace).

Briault Manus, V. (2011) *Emerging Traditions: Towards a Postcolonial Stylistics of Black South African Fiction in English* (Lanham, MD: Lexington Books/Rowman and Littlefield).

Camara, Mohamed (1997). *Dakan.* Film produced by René Feret. May 1987; 87 minutes.

Ellerson, B. (2005) 'Visualizing Homosexualities in Africa–*Dakan*: An Interview with Filmmaker Mohamed Camara' in *African Masculinities: Men in Africa from the Late Nineteenth Century to the Present*, ed. L. Ouzgane and R. Morrell (New York: Palgrave MacMillan and University of KwaZulu-Natal Press), pp. 61–74.

Fassinou, A. (2000) *Modukpé: Le rêve brisé* (Paris: L'Harmattan).

Fassinou, A. (2003) *Enfant d'autrui, fille de personne* (Cotonou: Editions du Flamboyant).

Gevisser, M., and Cameron, E. (eds) (1995) 'Five Women: Black Lesbian Life on the Reef' in *Defiant Desire: Gay and Lesbian Lives in South Africa* (London: Routledge), pp. 186–192.

Ibrahim, Sun'Allah (1997). *Sharaf* (Cairo: al-Hilal).

Ishiguro, Kazuo (1986). *An Artist of the Floating World* (London: Faber & Faber).

Jacobs, J. U. (2002) 'Zakes Mda's *The Heart of Redness*: The Novel as *Umngqokolo*' *Kunapipi* 24: 1/2: 224–236.

Kamwangamalu, N. M. (2003) 'When 2 + 9 = 1: English and the Politics of Language Planning' in *The Politics of English as a World Language: New Horizons in Postcolonial Cultural Studies*, ed. C. Mair (Amsterdam: Rodopi), pp. 235–246.

Kourouma, A. (1968) *Les Soleils des indépendances* (Montreal: University of Montreal Press).

Kourouma, A. (1990) *Monné* (Paris: Seuil).

Mahfuz, N. (1947) *Zuqaq al-Midaq* (Cairo: Maktabat Misr).

Mahfuz, N. (1957) *Sugar Street.* Trans. W. Hutchins and A .B. Samaan (New York: Doubleday).

Mahfuz, N. (1992) *Al-Sukkariyah* (Cairo: Maktabat Misr).

Massad, J. A. (2007) *Desiring Arabs* (Chicago: University of Chicago Press).

Matar, N. (1994) 'Homosexuality in the Early Novels of Nageeb Mahfouz' *Journal of Homosexuality* 26: 4: 77–90.

Mda, Z. (2000) *The Heart of Redness* (New York: Farrar, Straus and Giroux).

Millogo, L. (2002) *Nazi Boni, premier écrivain du Burkina Faso: La langue bwamu dans Crépuscule des temps anciens* (Limoges: Presses universitaires de Limoges).

Modarressi, T. (1992) 'Writing with an Accent' *Chanteh* 1: 7–9.

Modarressi, T. (1989) *The Pilgrim's Rules of Etiquette* (New York: Doubleday).

Mphahlele, E. (1979) 'South African Writers Talking: Nadine Gordimer, Es'kia Mphahlele, André Brink' *English in Africa* 6: 2: 1–23.

Mphahlele, E. (1984) *Father Come Home* (Johannesburg: Ravan).

Ngugi wa Thiong'o. (1965) *The River Between* (London: Heinemann).

Nkabinde, N. Z. (2008) *Black Bull, Ancestors and Me: My Life as a Lesbian Sangoma* (Johannesburg: Fanele).

Nwankwo, Nkem. (1964). *Danda* (London: Heinemann/André Deutsch).

Nwapa, F. (1966) *Efuru* (London: Heinemann).

Nzekwu, Onuora. (1962). *Blade Among the Boys* (London: Hutchinson).

Obiechina, E. N. (1974) 'The Problem of Language in African Writing: The Example of the Novel' *Conch* 5: 1–2: 17–20.

Okara, G. (1963) 'African Speech . . . English Words' *Transition* 10: 15–16.

Okara, G. (1964) *The Voice* (London: Heinemann).

Pageard, R. (1966) *Littérature négro-africaine* (Paris: Le livre africain).

Tutuola, Amos. (1952) *The Palm-Wine Drinkard* (London: Faber & Faber).

Wicomb, Zoe. (2000) *David's Story* (Cape Town: Kwela Books).

Zabus, C. (1991) *The African Palimpsest: Indigenization of Language in the West African Europhone Novel.* 2nd enlarged ed. 2007 (Amsterdam: Rodopi).

Zabus, C. (1996) 'Language, Orality, and Literature' in *New National and Post-Colonial Literatures.* Ed. Bruce King (Oxford: Clarendon Press).

Zabus, C. (2007). *Between Rites and Rights: Excision in Women's Experiential Texts and Human Contexts* (Stanford, CA: Stanford University Press).

3 Learning to *Shant Well* and the Art of the Good Translator

Roberta Cimarosti

Was evil brought to this place with language?

—Derek Walcott, *Midsummer* (1984)

Lead-In

In this chapter, I will sustain that Derek Walcott's early musical play *Ti-Jean and His Brothers* (1972) and its recent lyrical version in concert *Moon-Child* (2012) may be read as two master classes on the way English and Creole can be translated into a Creolized form of English to better suit the needs of Caribbean society; *Ti-Jean* teaches how to avoid impulsive slippery turns that may impede the felicitous passage into a localized full-fledged English and *Moon-Child* thoroughly displays and celebrates its accomplishment. *Ti-Jean and His Brothers*, first performed in 1958, addresses the consequences of the Anglicization of the Caribbean, the 'bad translation' of the territory through inadequate British vocabulary, but also, in later times, diffusion of British English through the education system, resulting in a general negative attitude toward the possibility to master the official language and in the diminishment of the Creole mother tongue.[1] In *Ti-Jean* three basic conditions for undertaking a 'good translation' of the local reality are established: (a) the choice of the right 'source text,' both the Creole and the British cultures and languages present in the territory; (b) adoption of a good 'translational' method, a metaphoric process by which things and names are reimagined and rearticulated according to new associations based on local use; (c) the consequential shaping and command of a new hybrid English, which becomes the established language.[2]

In this respect the phrase in the title, *learning to shant well*, stands for the art of the 'good translation' as conceived by Walcott. First, it means learning to use English, as stemming from the sounds, names, and rhythms of the Creole, as rooted in the history of the islands, and as represented by the name and the practices of the *shantwells*, street-singers and storytellers that roamed the villages in colonial times. Their oral narrations could be made up of a mix of European languages into which fragments of African grammars, rhythms, and contents were also transferred, and whose music was produced through songs, vocal rhythms, and European and African instruments as well as new ones made from scratch. (Hill 1997: 74) It was a performative mixed language sprouting from partial memory and creative transformation of all the inherited legacies, and characterized by a proximity of voice and music that produced the empowering songs of the spirituals, and out of which, in later times, blues and jazz, calypso, and reggae would grow.[3]

Second, *learning to shant well* hints at the indirect way in which the 'bad English translations' needed to be redressed beyond any rancorous use of the language typical of colonial discourse, whose notorious spokesman has long been Shakespeare's cursing Caliban (Ashcroft 2009). Clichéd Caliban is the icon of the English-speaking colonial, whose language is shaped through responses to material and psychological subaltern situations, and whose creative potentials remain subdued, comparable to Caliban's conspiracy, a failure engraved in Caliban's very name, notoriously an anagram of 'cannibal,' an earliest European coinage inaugurating the Manichean translations of the New World to come (Hulme 1992: 16–17). *Ti-Jean* and *Moon-Child* drop out of Caliban's facile revengeful course: *Ti-Jean* indicates how to overcome the devil, the resentment rising in the articulation of discourse, by resorting to one's knowledge of the oral mother tongue—its musical tradition, its fatalistic but genuine faith, including superstitions. And *Moon-Child* exhibits the triumphant passage into Caribbean English, so good a translation as to also contain the bad one with its redeemable terms on display, and make both Englishes work together as well, on the same page, through rhymes that point out the electrical tension wherefrom ever new expressive possibilities may come:

> In moonlight, walk with caution
> on the bright country road
> and you will meet this abortion
> hopping there like a toad,
> hopping with feet reversed
> still unbaptized, still cursed. (Walcott 2012: 20)

Lesson One: *Ti-Jean* and Getting the Language Right

Ti-Jean and His Brothers, with music and songs by André Tanker, was written and first staged over the years of national independence, when what is today called 'Creole Continuum' was then far from being an ideal language situation. The gap dividing the Creole mother tongue from the official language was a source of anguish, as people fell victims to their own way of speaking because of an unresolved tension between desire for self-expression and its denial. It was also a period in which national independence was leading the local intelligentsia to claim a highly representative role for Creole and its main art form, the calypso, hence posing a most insidious threat to the creation of an official local standard of English. (King 2000: 29–35)

These specific socio- and psycho-linguistic circumstances Edouard Glissant has lucidly analyzed and ascribed to the effects of an unnatural relation to one's culture and language, which he has defined as a "forced poetics" typical of peoples with Creolized histories and traditions. "Forced poetics exist where a need for expression confronts an inability to achieve expression. It can happen that this confrontation is fixed in an opposition between the content to be expressed and the language suggested or imposed" (Glissant 1992: 120). The constraining circumstances characterizing such forced poetics are generated through a combination of negative components that scholars have been thoroughly examined: First, the paralysis that had characterized the history of the Caribbean societies since the second half of the eighteenth century, when the elites preferred not to claim independence from Britain, refusing to follow the example of the North American colonies and hence abandoning the islands to a future of cultural and economic stagnation (Brathwaite 2005). Second, the diffused mixed feelings about English and the frustration for the unacknowledged status of the Creole in spite of the fact that it was used by the vast majority of the population, which resulted in a barrier between the two languages and the formation of an inferiority complex in Creole speakers. A state of inferiority that had also been scholarly theorized since the middle of the nineteenth century in European studies that ascribed the use of Pidgins and Creoles to 'primitive races' (Ansaldo, Matthews, and Lim 2007). Third, a still economy that did not renovate itself after emancipation but remained based on the plantation system, where Creole continued to have no functional use and people became exploited peasants with no active role in productivity and no possibility to employ skills other than those assigned to them by the neocolonial system (Heuman and Trotman 2005: 104–128).

Such is the scenario against which *Ti-Jean* is set from its prologue. It's a rainy evening in the island forest and the moon with the mythic figure of Ti-Jean, symbol of clarity of vision and expression, cannot be seen. "Greek-Croak, Greek-Croak" (Walcott 1972: 85). A frog, amazed that a passing bird ignores Ti-Jean's story, starts narrating it, emitting the typical 'crick-crack' sound framing Creole storytelling but also revealing the aspiration of the croaky voice to produce, one day, a wider, more sophisticated orchestration of sounds:

FROG: If you look in the moon,
         though no moon is here tonight,
         there is a man, no, a boy,
         [...]

God put him in that height
to be the sun's right hand
and light the evil dark,
but as the bird is so ignorant
I will start the tale truly. (86)

The storytelling frame with the talking animals has the main function of creating a buffer zone between the tragic story of Ti-Jean and the audience, hence to modulate the impact of its pathos.

BIRD: How poor the family was? [*Sad music on flute*]
FROG: Oh that was poverty, bird!
    Old hands dried up like claws
    heaping old sticks,
    too weak to protect her nest. (88)

The house, actually a hut, is surrounded by a hostile environment haunted by terrifying evil spirits, squealing devils, grave percussions, howls of wind, and thunder rumbles, whose paralyzing effect on the household, along with its deadly ambience and the illiterate pointlessness of its dwellers, is an image of the way society maintains the status quo.

    [*Light shows the hut*]
    Look, the four of that family
    lived in a little house, [. . .]
    where night and day was rain, [. . .]
GROS-JEAN: One time again it have nothing to eat [. . .]
MI-JEAN: I went out to do fishing [. . .]
    yet I cannot catch no fish
    without I first have bait, [. . .]
TI-JEAN: Maman, m'a fait un rien. (88, 90–91)

Evidently, the play is set within constraints that strongly impact self-expression and inhibit actions, intending to engage the people's imagination in its most popular mouthpiece: the Creole folktale, the very means by which the local mentality acquires a voice, gets articulated, and propagates, as well as being the place where, for Walcott, the local epic of the people has been compressed (Walcott 1997a: 48). Glissant has explained at length the entrapping mechanism characterizing this popular genre and the main negative features that he points out seem to correspond to those we find in *Ti-Jean*:

  a. the centrality of the master's world, implying the lack or the renunciation of one's own;

b. the absence or the rejection of work ethics, as if one did not have the right to rely on any;

c. the entrapping cycle of fear and misery containing the illusion of hope which regularly becomes frustration;

d. the absence of references to the local environment, indicating a problematic bond between language and place, determining both a diffused poor sense of belonging, and a scarce vocabulary to describe the territory. (Glissant 1992: 125–132)

For Glissant, in the Creole folktale, the landscape is an anonymous space where characters simply pass through, mirroring the fact that the land is neither possessed nor claimed and no affective bond is there that joins people and the surrounding nature. It has always been Walcott's view, however, that such overwhelming emptiness must be read as a fortunate blank space that colonial topographers were unable to fill, and whose apparent silence hid a still unauthorized local language with new coinages provided by use, which would find the way to freely manifest outside its 'safe houses' or 'actually its huts.'[4]

One night, an unborn creature called Bolom breaks into Ti-Jean's house, claiming to be sent by the devil to announce a mortal challenge: the three brothers should make the devil feel human weakness and if they succeed, they will inherit all his riches, but if they get vexed while talking with him, they will die. The Bolom is Creolized English still in embryo, a malformed Calibanesque creature murdered by the same colonial history that generated him and whose life is now in the hands, and mouths, of the three brothers: will they manage to face the devil without losing their temper and give the Bolom another life?

> This is the shriek
> of a child which was strangled,
> [. . .] strangled by a woman,
> who hated my birth,
> twisted out of shape,
> deformed past recognition,
> tell me, Mother,
> would you care to see me? [Bolom moves out of the light, shrieking] (97)

In birth order, Gros-Jean, Mi-Jean, and Ti-Jean set out to meet the devil's challenge, crossing the symbolic spaces of the folktale. They leave their mother's *house*, pass through the *forest*, and then reach the *plantation*, where they are challenged by a double-faced devil manifesting first as Papa Bois, the mythic African figure protector of the forest, and then as Planter, a typical mulatto landowner, whose talk is all nostalgia for a lost Africa and a faraway Europe. As they pass from *hut*, through *forest*, and on to *plantation* talking with mother, animals, and devil, the brothers are also undertaking a journey through language, traversing its long-established relations with place and people, and the challenge consists in avoiding stumbling on the intricate interstices of self-expression, where language works in tight contact with identity, and rather to see where the wrong connections lie in order to make them right.

One by one we are presented the three brothers in transit and are asked to compare and learn from their performances. Gros-Jean takes fast leave from his mother, passes through the forest, behaving cruelly toward the animals, and is bold and rude to Papa Bois, failing to see he's a devil:

GROS JEAN: *Bon jour, vieux papa.*
OLD MAN: *Bon matin, Gros Jean.*
[. . .]
GROS JEAN: Is man I am now, and looking for success. Which way, papa?
OLD MAN: I cannot tell you the way to success;
          I can only show you one path through the forest.
GROS JEAN: I have no time to waste.
          It have nothing, I fraid, man, or beast man,
          and more quick I get what I want, more better.
          (105–106; my emphasis)

Gros-Jean's use of French and sloppy English betrays not only a poor adherence to both his mother tongues, Creole and Creolized English, but also an ungrammatical use of the comparative, revealing his profound unawareness of the wrong way taken, which makes him an easy prey for the Planter, who calls him several names except the right one, until enraged Gros-Jean loses his patience and gets eaten: "*Boi Diable-là manger un 'ti mamaille / Un!* (Give the devil a child for dinner / One!)" (114).

Mi-Jean shows even less attachment to country and language, and his journey significantly begins right in the forest, where he abuses its creatures—"Is animal you are, so please know your place" (115)—and tells Papa Bois of his plans to become a rich sea captain and then to settle in the States and become a lawyer. Full of himself and lost in his future, he slips on his own passion for legalese once the devil drops the word 'hence' in the conversation, knowing that in the case that Mi-Jean ignored that term, shame would trigger his judgmental attitude against his own insecurity.

MI JEAN: I on my way to the sea
          To become a rich captain,
          The land work too hard.
          Then to become a lawyer. [. . .]
OLD MAN: [. . .] Hence the net, the net and the book.
MI JEAN: What?
OLD MAN: I say hence the book,
          Hence the net and the book.

MI JEAN: *Ça c'est hence?* (What is "hence"?)
OLD MAN: Same as whereas, and hereunto affixed. (118–119)

Once in the plantation, Mi-Jean receives the coup de grâce as soon as the Planter compares his wordy arguments to a goat bleating and the offensive equation makes him burst out in anger and miserably fall to pieces, a trap he could have avoided had he turned down the bait in the forest, had he renounced debating altogether. "I don't mind talking to you, but don't insult me, telling me a goat have *more sense than I, than me. Than both of we*!" (129; my emphasis).

Ti-Jean's journey begins with full acknowledgment of his mother's values and the appreciation of the beauty of the territory, both solid sources of his use of English, giving him the force to disagree with Papa Bois's negative assessment of the Caribbean climate and to see he's a devil:

OLD MAN: It's a damp, mournful walk through the forest, isn't it [. . .]
TI-JEAN: *Bon jour, vieux cor,'* I find the world pleasant in the early light. (138)
            [. . .]
            If evil exists, let it come forward.
            Human, or beast, let me see it plain. (142)

Similarly, once under the Planter's rule, Ti-Jean feels legitimated to pretend to carry out his orders while following his own goal instead, so he liberates the laborers working in the cane fields and burns the plantation together with its great house. The commonsense values acquired at home and the work songs learned from the human environment shape Ti-Jean's vernacular, endowing his words with a pathos that serves his actions:

[Drums. Cries. Caneburners' chorus.]
TI-JEAN: The man say Burn, burn, burn the cane!
CHORUS: Burn, burn, burn the cane!
TI-JEAN: You tired work for de man in vain!
CHORUS: Burn, burn, burn the cane! (149)

The happy ending sees the ascendance of Ti-Jean to new English master because he has established the new rules for the use of the language, whose right tone and translingual range now gives access to self-expression, as conveyed in the image of the finally found "key to the door of breath" (162). The achievement stems from Ti-Jean's rectification of a historically wrong sentence that condemned colonial generations to use English within gradations of curse; the mistake lay in an unfair representation of the command of English allowed, as portrayed in European masterpieces like *The Tempest*, in which even the most creative use of the inherited language binds its user to colonial discourse by assuming his subaltern position, a pronouncement extending to praise of proficiency and even to the inclusion of excellences in the British canon.

In the play, the moment of rectification is made to pass unnoticed, since its accomplishment very much depends on discretion and on action undertaken without egotistic clamor.[5] A completely drunk Planter, still unaware that all his properties have been destroyed, has just got back from a party and while in the middle of a tirade about the misery of life in the tropics, bumps into Ti-Jean, who, in cunning sympathy, declares himself "as drunk," actually as "drunk as a fish." The simile, a significant loan from *The Tempest* connoting Caliban's failed conspiracy, is a fake comparison of equality, hiding centuries of crimes still at work in the mechanisms of the language, and its purpose is to reassure the Planter about the persistent hopelessness of Ti-Jean's situation. Except that a revolution that changed the course of events has already taken place.

DEVIL: Oh, nobody loves me, nobody loves me. [. . .] I had the only love of God once but I lost that. I had a host of burnished helmets once, and a forest of soldiery waited on my cough, on my very belch. [. . .]

TI-JEAN: [*Enters, also with a bottle*] Oh, it's you, you're back late. Had a good dinner?

DEVIL: You nearly scared me. How long you been hiding there?

TI-JEAN: Oh, I just came through. *Drunk as a fish.* (152; my emphasis)

Lesson Two: *Moon-Child* and Making the Language Sound

The second master class starts where the first one ends, as a lyrical application of the rules learned from *Ti-Jean*. Center stage is a *conteur*, a narrator speaking in rhymed and very musical verse, interweaving English and French Creole, a contemporary sophisticated version of the *shantwell*. The storytelling frame is now a cabaret belonging to a villager called Félix Prospère, where a Carnival party will soon take place, as it's the eve of Boxing Day when, just as in the past, people gather to play, sing, and dance in public places and parades to perform historical traditions and contemporary events.

Here is the *conteur* presenting the wide, expressive range of Creole: its obscure components that produce only noise, confusing stories either of the fruit of superstition or of colonial inhibitions; its meaningful featured voices comparable to the characters and traditions of the folklore; and, among these, outstanding elements allowing the language to go beyond itself, as when, for instance, it comes across unexpected meanings produced by its translingual roots, as in the case of the Bolom discovering itself to be a *beau l'homme*, a French-derived lexeme that reconnotes its previous monstrosity.

The night is full of noises,
the country people say;

the moonlit leaves have voices,
Loupgarou, gens-gagé,
Dovens, but where precisely
is this creature from,
a voice that sings so nicely,
who answers to "Beau l'homme?" (Walcott 2012: 19)

One such transformative power fueled by French, Creole, and English cross-couplings and lexical metaphors moves the *conteur*'s performance of retelling the story of Ti-Jean, whom he now calls *Moon-Child*. He orchestrates the beauty of the isle in all possible details, explicates the moral of the fable, explains the psychology of the characters, and updates the theme of work and exploitation by introducing the damages caused and the robberies committed through the growing tourist industry. All previous themes that had been taboos or causes of distress he gives voice to by using a repertoire ranging from opaque Creole words and sentences to a highly refined form of hybrid English whose words and syntax resound with Creole pace and rhythm.

The local environment that had previously seemed to be an anonymous empty space has acquired full vitality as the conteur's lyricism joyously traverses *home, forest,* and *plantation,* undertaking the journey with his characters. The *house* extends over the whole of the surrounding nature, reverberating in its own mother tongue, as portrayed in the opening scene of the washerwomen chanting by the riverside among whom is a jolly mother full of fun, singing her love for an absent husband and curiously asking her companions to believe her, as if her repertoire were variable and vast.

[THE MOTHER *and* WASHERWOMEN, *washing by the river stones.*]
THE MOTHER: If you tell me "You lie!" you
                can trust me, I'll understand;
                that man pulling a canoe on the cold morning sand
                at Bouton with one hand
                was Alcindor, my husband,
                Soufrière born and bred.
                Is twelve years since he dead. (9)

In the forest the conteur escorts the brothers by reciting the names and qualities of flowers and plants, which even Gros-Jean now is made to know:

Climbing up through the forest
he passed trees that he knew,
bois-canot, cedar, the blest
laurier-canelles, acajou; [. . .]
the *belisier*'s bright torch. (25–26)

And with his characters he x-rays the double nature of the devil, showing how his bad words contribute to enrich the language. As when in expressing his wish to avenge the loss of Africa, Papa Bois resorts to words that evoke the revengeful spirit of King Hamlet and gets trapped in the web of his mixed hybrid heritage, the translational or metaphoric process whereby new meanings are created to describe novel situations thereby renewing the inherited traditions.

PAPA BOIS: For fifty years I have lived here,
      just listen and I'll tell you, [. . .]
      I sniff the air and smell you
      I am, if you believe me
      the prophet of protection. (28)

The Planter too speaks a mixed vocabulary that makes him a Caribbean Hamlet stuck in a state of paralysis between British and African legacies, translating him into an irresolute stoic deeply involved in the bacchanal of carnival and the calypso. "Then my white father died, / who, from guilt, left me an immense / estate and with it the pride / that corrupts innocence" (61). It's a hybridized idiom that transforms its own bad meanings by recycling their colonial inferences, things of darkness brought to light in acknowledgment of all the language components:

      The names that we are given
      are who we will become: [. . .]
      So there were names for each son:
      big, medium, and small.
      Gros-Jean, Mi-Jean, and Ti-Jean
      will answer if you call.
      Some tall me were called *Shorty*!
      The nickname passes on
      Some big men over forty
      will answer to *GARÇON*!
      But Gros-Jean couldn't take it
      if you forgot his name. (31–32)

A sort of calypso competition between Planter and Narrator stages a duel between the two ways taken by Creole into English: the Planter's is a corrupted opportunistic language, accommodating to tourism and the Carnival show business, just as in the past it had followed the dicta and diction of the colonial master.

      The master had a mission
      [. . .] a calypso competition
      where he would be the winner.

[. . .] The lyrics getting harder,
the singers have no option,
like this khaki-voiced cicada,
than to condemn corruption. (90)

Instead, the Narrator's parlance is rooted in the history of the *shantwell* underlying the story of *Ti-Jean* from its beginning, although it is now in *Moon-Child*
where that heritage is fully claimed, as represented in two types of characters
dating back to the earliest ballads and masquerades. The first is found in
'Gros-Jean,' the name of the legendary *shantwell* whose French Creole verse
was translated into English at the end of the nineteenth century and whose
fables have been handed down in fragments, like this one: "Gros Jean, you
have a voice like thunder, / your voice can raise my mother from the dead"
(Hill 1997: 56). The second is found in the forest creatures, including Papa
Bois, reminiscent of the legend of the vampire-serpent that dressed like a
devil and left his skin and dissolved into the air to look for prey and then was
surprised by sunrise and died screaming Hamletic Creole words, "jouvay,
you paka ou vay?" ("Is it dawn or is it not?"), explaining why to this day this
ancient part of Carnival is called 'Jouvay' and is performed before daybreak
(Hill 1997: 85). And such is in fact the way Papa Bois leaves the stage in
Moon-Child, in the wake of the local beginnings of English:

Farewell, little fool! Come, then, my legions! My bands!
Stretch your wings and soar, pass over the fields
like the last shadow of night, imps, devils, bats!
Soleil-la! Soleil-la! / The sun, the sun! (107)

The lyrical play ends with a song and a prayer, the LALALALALALA joy-
ful chant that has patterned *Moon-Child* from the start and a hymn of praise
to both mother tongues, representing a language composed of a chorus of
distinct voices happily interweaving across the aisle:

Gloria pour	*A Gloria for*
Tout ça nous connaître	*Everything we know*
Gloria botay, la comette	*Gloria botay, la comette*
Gloria Choiseul	*Gloria Choiseul*
Gloria Soufrière	*Gloria Soufrière*
Gloria plus belle	*Gloria plus belle*
Pour tout ça nous ka weh	*In everything we see*
Gloria	*In everything we hear*
Gloria	*Gloria*
Gloria	*Gloria* (113)

Coda

A form of translation takes place in the work of writers from the ex-colonies,
whose English idioms contain a transcription of the local and the inherited

mother tongues that has immensely enhanced the scope of the ex-colonial languages, endowing them with new visions, uses, and flexibilities:

> the green oak of English is a murmurous cathedral
> where some took umbrage some peace, but every shade, all,
> helped widen its shadow. (Walcott 1984: 72)

Walcott, for one, has lingered several times on the translational quality of his art both in his prose and his poetry, this latter occasionally hinting at what is going on in the lines as they are being written on the page, where we are made to see the liaison or the staccato of the voice traversing distant geographies, translingual memories, while hanging fast all along on the strength of the inner tone across which both source texts and languages travel.

> I heard them marching the leaf-wet road of my head,
> the sucked vowels of a syntax trampled to mud,
> a division of dictions, one troop black, barefooted,
> the other in redcoats bright as the sovereign's blood;
> their feet scuffled like rain, the bare soles with the shod.
> One fought for a queen, the other was chained in her service
> but both, in bitterness, travelled the same road. (Walcott 1984: 72)

And how this longest, vociferous, two-sided *road* finally unifies under the one standard and is made to chant the same hymn, is illustrated in a poem from the same collection, *Midsummer*, where the road becomes a diviner's *rod*, a conductor's baton, whose authority and power is compared to that of a stroke of lightning touching earth, and to a dot-like swallow on the wires. The transition of voice and sign, of oral and written cultures, of the popular and the courtly, is powerfully unified in a terrific masterstroke embodied in the monosyllable "God," with its manifold sense of Lord, author, and—last but not least—the spontaneous exclamation that utters a desire mixed with disheartened disappointment at the arduous task. And it is this triple sense of the word 'God' that brings about the concrete vision of an exclamation mark in all its terrible force, as a momentary hieroglyph that translates the lightning that is finally made to land in the space of a page!

> It touches earth, that branched diviner's rod
> the lightening, like the sweet note of a swallow on the staff
> of four electric wires, while everything I read
> or write goes on too long. Ah, to have
> a tone colloquial and stiff,
> the brevity of that short syllable, God,
> all synthesis in one heraldic stroke. (Walcott 1984: 19)

Walcott's critical essays explain that a similar numinous force characterizing the act of naming in the New World marks the end of the battle
against history and its bad translations, as a new literal link is established
between heaven and earth, unifying signifier and signified and forming
the new language.

> It is this awe of the numinous, this elemental privilege of naming the
> New World which annihilates history in our great poets [. . .] the phe-
> nomenon is the zeal with which the slave accepted both the Christian
> and the Hebraic, resigned his gaze at the death of his pantheon, and
> yet deliberately began to invest a decaying faith with a political belief.
> (Walcott 1997a: 40, 45)

The essays also explain the reason why the passage from English and Creole into the new standard is necessary and should accept no compromise
with any other less complete language form, including written Creole, whose
orthography cannot match its subtle range of sounds.

> Today still in many islands, the West Indian poet is faced with a lan-
> guage which he hears but cannot write because there are no symbols for
> such a language and because the closer he brings hand and word to the
> precise inflections of the inner language and to the subtlest accuracies
> of his ear, the more chaotic his symbols will appear on the page [. . .] so
> his function remains the old one of being filter and purifier, never losing
> the tone and strength of the common speech as he uses the hieroglyphs,
> symbols or alphabet of the official one. (Walcott 1997a: 49)

Any less rigorous expressive form would make the language gross and limp-
ing, disfigure the mixed original, and impede its metaphoric transformations
into localized English. This explains an essay that pays homage to Chamoiseau's narrative masterpiece in Creolized French, *Texaco*, whose linguistic perfection is contrasted with the principles proclaimed in the manifesto
advocating the use of written Creole, the *Eloge de la Creolité* written by Chamoiseau, Bonfiant, and Bernabé:

> My hatred of the current way of writing down Creole ("orthography")
> is a lost battle, but my rage continues in defeat. Coarsely phonetic, it is
> visually crass, its aural range is limited to a concept of peasant or artisan
> belligerence that denies its own subtleties of pronunciation, denying its
> almost completely French roots in the ex-colonies. (Walcott 1997c: 228)

The only alternative to be contemplated is that of using the two languages
side by side, like a facing-text translation whose source is Creole, as in the
previously quoted concluding part of *Moon-Child*.

This way of conceiving language and literature as forms of translations substantially differs from that theorized in postcolonial critique to date, which has accounted for the way English varies in the literatures of the ex-colonies in terms of creative responses to colonial diatribes whose dominating discourse the texts would transform into revised domestic versions, yet elaborated in such a way as to keep open, and even privilege, the dialogue with the metropolises that run the literary market. The texts would traverse the gulf between some central embankment and the several oceans and, once landed, their messages would become localized varieties of the official language. No wonder the 'new Englishes' become assemblages of metonymic and synecdochic fragments, and Caliban is their fittest metaphor. The pivotal point of these theories granting validity to language differences and variations in English is a post-structuralist view that sees language as structurally devoid of any essence, a self-standing combination of empty signs adaptable and adoptable to all forms and contexts, and certainly not a dwelling place for identities.

One of the troubles with such principles is that they forcibly bind the new literatures to anachronistic colonial discussions that constitute but one remote component of their overall complex sources. In a desperate attempt to get traditional Standard English and its classics back to the limelight, these theories not only assign them the role of the 'lever' that sets the translation works into motion; they have to forget to notice the kind of 'rod' handled by Walcott, which has thoroughly changed the scenario of English *belle lettres*. In a well-known essay, talking about critics of contemporary Commonwealth verse, Walcott singles out the figure of the radical liberal critic whose emphasis on difference and originality has reproduced old colonizing arguments: "Certain performances are called for, including the fashionable incoherence of revolutionary anger, and everyone is again appeased, the masochistic critic by the required attack on his 'values,' the masochistic poet by the approval of his victim." Part of the problem being that "the benignity of the liberal critic perpetuates the sociological condition of that speech, despite his access to anger" (Walcott 1997a: 54, 55).

On a similar note, David Dabydeen has pointed out the patronizing interpretative practices of postmodern and postcolonial criticism, to which, he underlines, outstanding writers from the ex-colonies have strongly responded, among whom is Wole Soyinka: "We have been blindly invited to submit ourselves to a second epoch of colonization—this time by universal-humanoid abstraction defined and conducted by individuals whose theories and prescriptions are derived from the apprehension of *their* world and *their* history, *their* social neurosis and *their* value systems. It is time, clearly, to respond to this new threat" (Dabydeen 2011: 45). It is hard not to agree that Western theory has been largely unable to understand Caribbean and the literatures in the new Englishes away from the historical pattern that assigns them the role of victims, and has steadily fastened on the old known dialectics—master and slave, colonizer and colonized

(Dabydeen 2011: 45). In order to put an end to such trends of 'bad translators,' Dabydeen makes a twofold proposal. That creative writing itself be the source of both history and culture of the Caribbean region: "The priority of the writing must be restored, otherwise the centuries-old struggle for self-expression will be denied" (Dabydeen 2011: 45). And that one, whether affected or not by contacts with the Europeans, returns to local sources to explain the "nature of West Indianness," as only real sources can grant language its strongest claim to presence and the sacredness of naming alongside the linguistic alchemy that renewably leads to it (Dabydeen 2011: 51).

Finally, let's go back to the type of translation taking place in the two Ti-Jean texts to observe the way it is comparable to a form of relearning of a local English from scratch, in the guise illustrated in the following poetic passage:

> You were distressed by your habitat, you shall not find peace
> till you and your origins reconcile; your jaw must droop
> and your knuckle scrape the ground of your native place.
> Squat on a damp rock round which white lilies stiffen,
> pricking their ears; count as the syllables drop
> like dew from primeval ferns; note how the earth drinks
> language as precious, depending upon the race.
> Then, on dank ground, using a twig for a pen,
> write Genesis and watch the Word begin. (Walcott 1984: 71)

Specialists in second-language acquisition and Creole languages have recently agreed that the three main stages characterizing linguistic development in both domains are very similar, so that a language beginner may be comparable to a first-generation Creole speaker (Siegel 2008: 15–49).

At an initial level, grammar transfer and rewording (or relexification) take place, the former typical of second-language beginners and the latter of Creole first users, in order that substantial parts of the mother tongue get transferred into the target language (Lefebvre, White, and Jourdan 2006: 1–15). Of course, such elementary forms of transference took place centuries ago in the Anglophone Caribbean, where both mother tongues, English and Creole, have long been established, so in Walcott's texts the question at stake has been the creation of a fully grown English stemming from a fusion of its main bilingual sources. It is this translation that risked going from bad to worse in *Ti-Jean*, had the devil also managed to swallow the smallest brother.

The devil, in its dual manifestation of Papa Bois and Planter, is the image of 'fossilization,' characterizing a third stage of 'development' in both language acquisition and Creole formation. This is well illustrated in the brothers' inaccurate use of English, the lack of inflectional morphology, and the missing verbal and pronoun conjugations. Among the causes for linguistic atrophy, linguists have indicated insufficient exposure to the official lexifier, lack of motivation, and resistance to the target language, all of which prove that such debilitating liaisons with the mother tongues may become permanent damages characterizing one's language for 'good' (actually for worse)—unless the psycholinguistic difficulties are found and solved. So it is not by chance that the brothers' performance precipitates when they find themselves contending face-to-face with the devil's intended meanings that lever at their sense of inferiority.

In a blend of literacy and literary planes, Gros-Jean, Mi-Jean, and Ti-Jean could be seen as the three types of writing that Walcott cites to illustrate the linguistic choices of local writers. The first one claims, "I will write in the language of the people however gross or incomprehensible"; the second vaguely attempts a use of English, "'nobody else go' understand this, you hear, so le' me write English"; the third is the good translator, "dedicated to purifying the language of the tribe [. . .] the mulatto of style, the traitor" (Walcott 1997b: 9). For the gulf to be traversed and the good translator to victoriously emerge on the other side, the sense of lack needs to be reconceived for what it has always been: a lucky chance of shaping a whole new language.

This realization and will to make the effort can be compared to the second level of language learning and Creole genesis, when the decisive turn that leads to accomplished forms of translingualism may still occur, as illustrated by Ti-Jean's enterprise and his getting hold of the 'key to the door of breath,' the LALALALALALA note by which *Moon-Child* sets off and goes on and on, framing Ti-Jean's story and engaging the audience so deeply that when the show is over they take the tune back home with them.

To fully see the accomplished translation at work, we only need to look at the way all previously fossilized words are being stirred to life, a fact illustrated at the incipit of *Moon-Child*, where the washerwomen's work songs are listened to and responded by the eared stones: "WASHERWOMEN: The white stones by the river—/ Everyone believe her" (10). Such a regenerative impulse is exposed throughout as a property of the self-translating text that lives by the light of the original one, of which it is claimed to be but a pale reflection, "as this story is better in Creole" (14), refracting in the mixed compounds and single words in French that work very well together—"black pudding, *pain épice*," "malheureux and vagrants" (12, 139). And when the Creole disappears into the rhythm and tone that move English or relexifies into words discovering their previous localized French—as in the case of the Bolom turned into a *beau l'homme*—thus making sense where none seemed to be there before, they *shant* even better, the comparison entirely their own.

Notes

1. "The weird, raggedly inaccurate, infantile maps of the old explorers, in school, were more fearful than comic. The wrongly real outlines were perhaps more terrifying than their blank confessions: Terra Incognita. If what they knew was so inaccurate, how accurate was what they did not? [. . .] The root of evil may come from the wrong or casual naming of things" (Walcott 2005: 51–57).

2. "Take the arrogance of an Old World botanist naming this plant then, [. . .] I now believe that my ignorance is more correct than his knowledge, that my privilege makes it correct [. . .], and that what it reminds me of, its metaphor, is more important than the family it springs from" (Walcott 2005: 56).

3. "I come from a very musical culture whose aim is to be as direct and popular as possible. Calypso and reggae are like this; it's not chamber music, but music made to be staged for a public. [. . .] It's also a very local tradition whose music has a narrative element, a story to tell with a rhythm, no matter how tragic. [. . .] The root of culture lies in the melody of the person who did not receive an education, in formal sense. And the people who mostly hear this melody are the greatest writers. [. . .] If you lose this melody, then you are in trouble: you find yourself in an academic limbo, where your identity gets lost, whereas acquiring an ever-stronger emphasis, not in a patriotic sense, but in the awareness of what your voice is, well, this is the goal for which poets work all life long" (Walcott 2011: 12; my translation).

4. "Eventually, the botanically correct and Latin-tagged label or, even worse, the tag with the name of the 'discoverer,' disappears; it keeps its Creole or country name according to its properties, and without properties medicinal, magical, or edible, without use, it remains anonymous" (Walcott 2005: 56).

5. "The answer is not to boast, 'We could be as subtle as you'; we have a kind of autumn in the coloring of the sea almond; we have mist too, [. . .] but if you were brought up on Odes to the Season, [. . .] if your childhood imagination went by the Shepherd Calendar, [. . .] it is still hard not to fear that your hard-edged vision isn't as primal and basic and barbarous as ABC and the three primary colours. This affects speech, syntax, customs, politics as well as the attempts at an indigenous art. To the extent where the self-assertion does become barbarous and aggressive, to the self-pity of the new nationalism, in those, to some extent, we represent our two seasons. Darkly impulsive and violent, then stretches of dry desolation. [. . .] Not all of us though" (Walcott 2005: 56).

References

Ansaldo U., Matthews, S., and Lim, L. (eds) (2007) *Deconstructing Creole* (Amsterdam: John Benjamin).

Ashcroft, B. (2009) *Caliban's Voice* (London: Routledge).

Brathwaite, K. E. (2005) *The Development of Creole Society in Jamaica, 1770–1820*. Rev. ed. (Kingston: Ian Randle).

Dabydeen, D. (2011) *Pak's Britannica*. Ed. L. Machedo (Mona, Jamaica: University of the West Indies Press).

Glissant, E. (1992) *Caribbean Discourse: Selected Essays* (Charlottesville: University of Virginia Press).

Heuman, G., and Trotman, D. V. (eds) (2005) *Contesting Freedom: Control and Resistance in the Post-Emancipation Caribbean* (Oxford: Macmillan Caribbean).

Hill, E. (1997) *The Trinidad Carnival: Mandate for a National Theatre* (London: New Beacon Books).

Hulme, P. (1992) *Colonial Encounters* (London: Routledge).

King, B. (2000) *Derek Walcott: A Caribbean Life* (Oxford: Oxford University Press).

Kouwenberg, S., and Singler, J. V. (eds) (2008) *The Handbook of Pidgin and Creole Studies* (Oxford: Wiley-Blackwell).

Lefebvre, C., White, L., and Jourdan, C. (eds) (2006) *L2 Acquisition and Creole Genesis* (Amsterdam: John Benjamin).

Siegel, J. (2008) *The Emergence of Pidgin & Creole Languages* (Oxford: Oxford University Press).

Walcott, D. (1972) *Ti-Jean and His Brothers* (New York: Farrar, Strauss and Giroux).

Walcott, D. (1984) *Midsummer* (London: Faber and Faber).

Walcott, D. (1997a) 'The Muse of History' in *What the Twilight Says* (London: Faber and Faber), pp. 36–64.

Walcott, D. (1997b) 'What the Twilight Says' in *What the Twilight Says* (London: Faber and Faber), pp. 3–35.

Walcott, D. (1997c) 'A Letter to Chamoiseau' in *What the Twilight Says* (London: Faber and Faber), pp. 213–32.

Walcott, D. (2005) 'Isla Incognita' in *Caribbean Literature and the Environment*, ed. E. M. DeLoughrey, R. K. Gosson, and G. B. Handley (Charlottesville: University of Virginia Press, 2005), pp. 51–57.

Walcott, D. (2011), 'Walcott in Concerto', interview by Jennifer Scoppettone, *Il Manifesto*, 3 aprile 2011: 11.

Walcott, D. (2012) *Moon-Child* (New York: Farrar, Strauss and Giroux).

4   The 'Gift' of Translation to Postcolonial Literatures

Simona Bertacco

> *It is a gift to know more than one language, more than one culture. It is a*
> *challenge to be able to fly with the 'gift.'*
>
> —Emma LaRoque, 'Preface: Here Are Our Voices—
> Who Will Hear?', 1990

As far as postcolonial literatures are concerned, the 'language issue'—that is, the acknowledgment of the multilingual nature of all postcolonial texts—has fed a lively debate in the early days of the discipline (especially in respect to African literatures) but has quite surprisingly never achieved extensive visibility in literary studies. Part of the reason for what one might call 'the invisibility of language' in postcolonial studies has to do with the fact that postcolonialism, as a scholarly field, has almost always been studied from within the boundaries of *one* colonial empire, *one* language, *one* cultural framework, and *one* academic discipline. Yet postcolonial countries are, by definition, multicultural and multilingual. And postcolonial literature has contributed to shape a new or different use of language for itself. Starting from one of the earliest Anglophone novels to be published, Amos Tutuola's *The Palm-Wine Drinkard* (1952), we could compile an endless list of texts that challenge Standard English, and they do so systematically. Yet, as Sandra Bermann writes in her excellent introduction to the volume *Nation, Language, and the Ethics of Translation*, "if language and translation have become increasingly important in national and international relations, and in the processes of 'globalization' more generally, their role as *cultural* as well as *linguistic entities* is only beginning to be theorized" (Bermann and Wood 2005: 1–2; my emphasis). And this is, to say the least, unfortunate.

My argument in this chapter is that a new space for inquiry under the rubric of postcolonial studies can be projected from here, from a reflection on the critical and theoretical impact that translation has in our increasingly multicultural societies, but especially—for my purpose here—on our writing and reading practices. I shall explore the phenomenon of what I call a 'translational poetics' through close readings of the works of Tomson Highway and Dionne Brand and shall argue for the recognition of the central and creative role of translation in shaping the poetics of these specific texts and of a large number of postcolonial texts. But before proceeding with my argument, let me very briefly discuss the indissoluble link binding translation and colonialism together since it is instrumental to my approach to translation in the context of postcolonial textuality.

Postcolonialism and Translation

A colony, Robert Young writes, "starts as a translation, a copy of the original located elsewhere on the map. New England, New Spain, New Amsterdam" (2003: 139). As a consequence, postcolonial discourse analysis has been centrally concerned with redressing, or retranslating, this kind of linguistic, geographic, and cultural transformation of one thing into something else so much so that, Young goes on to argue, "nothing comes closer to the central activity and political dynamic of postcolonialism than the concept of translation" (2003: 38). In other words, the best place to look for a study of the importance of language in postcolonial textualities is in the work that has been produced at the intersection of postcolonial studies and translation studies. And, in fact, the scholarship that I need to quote as constituting the backbone of my research begins in the chapter in *The Empire Writes Back* (1989) that Ashcroft, Griffiths, and Tiffin dedicated to the language of postcolonial literature, introducing the concept of the 'Creole continuum' to the literary world, and propounding the paired concepts of 'abrogation' and 'appropriation' to outline the various strategies by which colonial languages were being transformed by the native languages of postcolonial writers. And it continues in the exploration of translation as a central experience for the postcolonial literary sensibility that we find in the seminal volume *Post-Colonial Translation*, edited by Bassnett and Trivedi in 1999.

While it is undeniable that there are some excellent texts out there that deal with this aspect of postcolonial literatures (Ashcroft's *Caliban's Voice: The Transformation of English in Post-Colonial Literatures* [2009]; Ch'ien's *Weird English* [2004]; Bahri's *Native Intelligence* [2003]; Talib's *The Language of Post-colonial Literatures* [2002]; and Zabus's *The African Palimpsest* [1991], just to mention a few titles), it is also true that their messages have not had the effect of getting the field in general to change its bad habits. And I think it might be worth looking at the reasons why this is so.

What is it that makes books about postcolonial languages sound not sexy to the critical audience? Again, part of the reason has to be found in the disciplinary division between literary and language studies. There are many excellent works on linguistic imperialism (Phillipson 1992) and on English and the discourse of colonialism (Pennycook 1994, 1998) as there are important books, from the literary side, demanding a closer reading of postcolonial textuality (Bahri 2003; McLeod 2007; Ashcroft 2009). Yet there are no works combining the two disciplinary approaches and different colonial languages together, and this is where I think more work needs to be done.

The way I suggest to approach postcolonial textualities that play with multiple languages is by using, for the literary analysis, a mixed methodology: part linguistic, part literary in nature, following the model established by translation studies, and in particular, within the subfield of postcolonial translation theory, following the lesson of scholars such as Harish Trivedi and Susan Bassnett (1999), Tejaswini Niranjana (1992), Gayatri Spivak (1993), and Maria Tymoczko (2002), all of whom in different ways approach postcolonial questions from a translation perspective. A border discipline itself, translation studies has produced some of the most cutting-edge work in the humanities in the past thirty years or so. I need only mention Lawrence Venuti's groundbreaking study *The Translator's Invisibility: A History of Translation* (1995) on our 'trained' inability to consider translation as a cultural phenomenon, or Michael Cronin's (2002) work on translation as a survival tool for dying languages, or the names of Sherry Simon (1996) working on issues of gender and/in translation, and Emily Apter (2005) in the field of comparative literature, to give an idea of the broad range of issues that the field has covered in an endeavor to rethink comparative literary and cultural studies in such ways as to bring them closer to problems of world literacy, language politics, and language policies.

When we start looking carefully at the language of postcolonial texts, the question of translation comes along as one of the most crucial issues in world literature today, as David Damrosh argues when he describes world literature as "intimately linked to translation" (2003: 212). The global domination of English as the international language of the arts has enabled, on the one hand, the rise of postcolonialism as an international aesthetics defined by Emily Apter as a "specialized niche market within the 'global'" (2001: 2) and, on the other hand, its institutionalization within formal disciplines and educational syllabi. Growing out of the older field of Commonwealth literature studies, which took as its primary subject the new literatures in English written by former colonized peoples, postcolonialism established from the start an Anglophone center of gravity, or an Anglophone bias, as John McLeod writes in the *Routledge Companion to Postcolonial Studies* (2007). In *The Postcolonial Exotic*, Graham Huggan points out that "English is, almost exclusively, the language of this critical industry, reinforcing the view that postcolonialism is a discourse of translation, rerouting cultural products from marginal areas towards audiences that see themselves as coming from the centre" (2001: 4).

Now, even though a new trend is making itself visible in the field, a trend that considers with attention the work that has appeared in Francophone, Hispanic, and Lusophone intellectual contexts (see, for instance, McLeod 2007; Poddar, Patke & Jensen 2009), I think it is fair to say that the real challenge facing postcolonialism today is to become literally and crucially a discourse *of* and *on* translation in an endeavor to rethink comparative literary and cultural studies in such a way as to bring them closer to problems of world literacy and language politics. A translation-oriented approach would ground our theories "in the unavoidable complexities, the historically ingrained prejudices and the day-to-day negotiations that occupy our global communities" (Bermann and Wood 2005: 2). Through a multilingual comparative perspective, we would be able to promote new engagements with theory in the same way as the material translation of a text from source language to target language forces the host literature to make room for a new book, a new genre or style, new ideas. Such an approach would be crucial in two main respects. First, a postcolonial comparative approach would keep the field at bay from critiques of linguistic ignorance or homologation aimed in particular at the category of 'world literature,' a discipline that is taught, in CompLit departments, through an often narrow selection of texts written in or translated into English and elevated to the status of 'World Literature.' The language in which many of these texts were originally written becomes, once again, invisible or inessential, and it is indeed unclear how such a topic can be taught from within an exclusively Anglophone, albeit heavily theory-based, perspective. Second comes the issue of the indebtedness of the postcolonial as a field to European theory. A translation-based approach would represent a fresh start for postcolonial scholarship: after decades in which the (de) constructive principles of European theory offered extremely useful tools to decipher postcolonial textual practices and to shape a critical literacy that made room for the postcolonial experience, the discipline is more than mature now for critical approaches and theories originating in the various postcolonial contexts, theories that imply a detailed and careful knowledge of the contexts being discussed and that feel at ease in dealing with what is non-European or non-Western in the texts.

When we start examing the language of postcolonial texts, the relationship between minority languages and translation takes center stage. As Michael Cronin writes, "minority language cultures are translation cultures *par excellence*" (2002: 139) in that they must translate continually in order to stay alive as viable and real languages. When a people lose their language, they haven't lost language altogether. The speaker is in fact translated, transposed, into another language. In these cases, translation, Cronin argues, "is both predator and deliverer, enemy and friend" (2002: 139). Right here is the contribution that translation studies can give to the postcolonial debate, both in conceptual and methodological terms: by acknowledging the existence of 'translation cultures,' we are led to make room for the centrality of the language issue in the postcolonial field, which implies, to start with, the need to create forums of discussion, outside traditional disciplinary boundaries, where critical vocabularies in different intellectual and linguistic traditions can intersect. In Doris Sommer's words:

To pose the bilingual question to aesthetics, politics, and philosophy is to ask how the disciplines change when we hear more than one language constitute their games. In a world where lingering colonial arrangements and mass migrations make bi- or multilingualism normal, it remains almost inaudible for theoretical interventions because disciplines press on in one language at a time. (2003: 10)

A Poetics Based on Translation

The interrelated issues of language, interpretation, and translation have been a subject for postcolonial writers for a long time. A cursory look at the book titles can be helpful to get an idea: Wole Soyinka, *The Interpreters* (1965); Lola Tostevin, *Color of Her Speech* (1982); M. N. Philip, *She Tries Her Tongue: Her Silence Softly Breaks* (1989); Dionne Brand, *No Language Is Neutral* (1990); Chang-rae Lee, *Native Speaker* (1995); Jumpa Lahiri, *The Interpreter of Maladies* (1999). Most of the times, however, it is in the way language is used that we can detect the work of a translational poetics. And here the list of titles could easily go on for pages: Ken Saro Wiwa's *Sozaboy*; the dub poetry by Lindon Kwesi Johnson and Grace Nichols; the fiction by Merle Hodge, V. S. Naipaul, Salman Rushdie, or Maxine Hong Kingston; the drama by Derek Walcott. Indeed, I will argue that it is the visibility given to 'weird English' (Ch'ien 2004) by postcolonial writers in recent years, rather than the learned use of foreign languages by European modernist writers, that has affected non-postcolonial writers as well, so that the phenomenon is now even more pervasive.

What follows is definitely an incomplete, but I hope exemplary, list of texts that illustrate the phenomenon I am referring to. My starting point is a bilingual collection of poems by the Franco-Ontarian poet Lola Lemire Tostevin that reflects critically on Canada's bilingual policy:

> '*tu déparles*'
> my mother says
> *je déparle*
>   yes
> I unspeak. (np)

Other interesting, and controversial, instances of this literary phenomenon are provided by the great success of Irvine Welsh's novel *Trainspotting* in the early 1990s:

> It's nae good blamin it oan the English for colonising us. Ah don't hate the English. [. . .] They just git oan wi the shite thuv goat. Ah hate the Scots. (94)

Another instance is the huge controversy surrounding the Booker Prize award given to James Kelman's *How Late It Was, How Late*, in 1994:

> Ye wake up in a corner and stay there hoping yer body will disappear, the thoughts smothering ye; these thoughts; but ye want to remember and face up to things, just something keeps ye from doing it, why can ye no do it; the words filling yer head: then the other words; there's something wrong; there's something far far wrong; ye're no a good man, ye're just no a good man. (1)

But also in a market traditionally seen as unwelcoming to multilingualism—the US book market—we are assisting at an interesting change. Jonathan Safran Foer's *Everything Is Illuminated* and Junot Díaz's *The Wondrous Life of Oscar Wao* are just two of the most notable examples of ways in which multilingual textualities have achieved great success among the American reading public:

> I have a miniature brother who dubs me Alli. I do not dig this name very much, but I dig him very much, so OK, I permit him to dub me Alli. As for his name, it is Little Igor, but Father dubs him Clumsy One, because he is always promenading into things. It was only four days previous that he made his eye blue from a mismanagement with a brick wall. If you're wondering what my bitch's name is, it is Sammy Davis, Junior, Junior. (Foer 2002: 1)

> Bad move, cap'n. For Kennedy's intelligence experts failed to tell him what every single Dominican, from the richest jabao in Mao to the poorest güey in El Buey, from the oldest anciano sanmacorisano to the littlest carajito in San Francisco, knew: that whoever killed Trujillo, their family would suffer a fukú so dreadful it would make the one that attached itself to the Admiral jojote in comparison. (Díaz 2007: 3)

To conclude, then, the phenomenon of a literary language that explicitly toys with several languages or dialects is in my view undeniably out there in the world. What is still missing is a literary analysis able to respond to these kind of language games, a literary analysis that puts at the center of its practice a close attention to the techniques and crafts of writing.

The texts I am going to look at can all be read as translational texts, in the sense that their poetics is premised on an act of linguistic or cultural translation. By calling them 'translational,' I don't mean that they are mere transference in the colonial language of a concept in a vernacular language or vice versa, or that this is even the main concern of their authors. Rather, if translation is a bearing across of meaning, postcolonial textualities that toy with more than one language showcase this bearing across on their surface, as Ashcroft claims in *Caliban's Voice* (2009: 163). What I argue is that while these texts are not and should not be seen as translations, translation affects—and functions as—their poetics. Calling these texts translational makes sense precisely because their language (we may call it weird, broken, junk English) involves a foreign language and refuses to hide it.

In immigrant communities all over the world, this kind of 'linguistic overload' is an exclusively oral phenomenon, and misspellings, mispronunciations, and Pidgin forms are interpreted as signs of a lack: in education, in fluency, in social status. However, for multilingual writers, using those forms in writing becomes "an active way of taking the community back" (Ch'ien 2004: 6). The use of a translational textuality is intentional, a playful subversion of the power dynamics in language use in polyglossic contexts and a creative experimentation with spelling and grammar rules.

Translational Textualities

Tomson Highway's *The Rez Sisters*

First Nations writing constitutes a good starting point for a discussion of translational poetics. The text I have selected is a play by Canadian Native playwright Tomson Highway, and here one should notice the special importance of the oral mode when trying to convey different dialects or languages within the same work. *The Rez Sisters*, performed for the first time in 1986, tells the story of seven women on the reservation—all sisters in varying degrees—who like bingo and who hope to solve their problems by winning the jackpot at the biggest bingo in the world in Toronto.

The play illuminates the issue of cultural survival—of Native cultural communities and languages—through a strategy that can be described as "survivance" as used in Gerald Vizenor's work *Manifest Manners* (1994, 1999). According to Vizenor, "survivance" describes those Indigenous literary works that challenge conventional power structures by creatively reimagining Indigenous culture and identity in contemporary times. In the play, in fact, the bingo, while being the most obvious symbol of cultural colonization, also becomes the means for the rebellion of the seven 'rez sisters' against the abuses of Indigenous patriarchal society as well as against the violence of Canadian mainstream society. In Sam McKegney's words: "By controlling the self-image and imaginatively reinventing viable ways of being Native through narrative, postindian warriors defy the impositions of the dominant culture and, most importantly, define their identities for themselves" (2005: 80).

The action takes place at the Wasy, short for Wasyachigan Indian Hill Reserve on Manitoulin Island, Ontario. The play opens with one of the seven women, Pelajia Patchnose, nailing shingles on the roof of her house, from where she looks at the dire state of the reservation and of Indigenous culture:

Everyone here's crazy. No jobs. Nothing to do but drink and screw each other's wives and husbands and forget about our Nanabush. (Highway 1988: 6)

And the old stories, the old language. Almost all gone . . . was a time Nanabush and Windigo and everyone here could **rattle away in Indian** fast as Bingo Betty could lay her bingo chips down on a hot night. (5; my emphasis)

The Rez Sisters is a translational text on several levels. First and foremost, it provides a clear example of translation as a tool of survival for minority language cultures, as Cronin argues. For Native writers, the creation of a dramatic or literary idiom different from the national or standard one represents a crucial political statement of self-assertion: it establishes the speech of the community in a permanent way (Ch'ien 2004: 4). Choice of language there is and it is important to interpret this work. This is a text mostly written in English, but its translational poetics makes a lively performance of what Evelyn Ch'ien calls "postcolonial poverty" (2004: 12).

In *The Rez Sisters*, the translational poetics works in several ways:

1. The names of the characters constitute the first example of what is generally called the 'translation effect' in Native texts, that is, the translation in English of the Native way of naming people, which is the manifest sign of cultural assimilation:

   > PELAJIA *PATCHNOSE*
   > PHILOMENA *MOOSETAIL*
   > MARIE-ADELE *STARBLANKET*
   > ANNIE *COOK*
   > EMILY *DICTIONARY*
   > VERONIQUE ST. PIERRE
   > ZHABOONIGHAN PETERSON

2. The translation of Cree or Ojibway terms is provided in a footnote only at the first occurrence of the word/idiom (*Neeh* ['Oh you,' Cree], *Astum* ['Come,' Cree], *Aw-ni-gi-naw-ee-dick* ['Oh, go on,' Ojibway]), and never occurs in the body of the text.
3. Whole exchanges in Cree and Ojibway are in the original language in the body of the text and translated only in footnote.[1] There are only three instances of this textual effect, and their functions seem to be to serve as markers of dramatic moments and as chorus.
4. Code-switching and code-mixing with 'village English' and Cree or Ojibway.
5. The play is written mostly in broken English, or 'village English,' as the kind of English used on the Native reservations is generally called.[2]

6.Standard English is maintained in one key point (i.e., used by the Bingo
   Master in the climax scene).

Code-switching is "the alternating use of two languages in the same stretch
of discourse by a bilingual speaker" (Bullock and Toribio 2009). Gumperz
lists six discourse-related functions of code-switching (1982: 75–94), and it
might be useful to list them briefly before proceeding with the analysis of
Highway's text.
   Code-switching:

   a. is used in quotations or reported speech;
   b. creates speakers as well as relationships among them;
   c. enables addressee specification: it directs the message to one of several
      possible addressees;
   d. appears in the form of interjections or sentence fillers;
   e. can be used for clarification or emphasis, or to add information about
      the main part of the message;
   f. enables the individualization of a speech versus objectivization.

In all these functions, what code-switching enables is the expressive connotation of speech. In *The Rez Sisters*, we can easily find examples of code-
switching responding to Gumpertz's schematization. In the following
quotation, we see how the speakers and their relationships are signified
by their code-switching between the Native and the English languages (b.
above): "MARIE-ADELE: Come on Zha. You and I can name the **koo-koos-
suk** (Cree for little pigs). All 14 of them" (Highway 1988: 24, henceforth *RS*;
my emphasis).[3]
   The use of code-switching that is most recurrent in the play is type c. and
relates to the addressee specification function, as we can see in the following
example:

ZHABOONIGAN: Marie-Adele. How's your cancer?
          Giggles and scurries off laughing.
VERONIQUE: Shkanah, Zhaboonigan, sna-ma-bah.
          And the footnote read: 'Shush, Z., don't say that.' (Ojibway) (30)

In another instance, the same use of code-switching creates communicative
ambiguity and a comic effect. Marie-Adele is speaking to Veronique and
sees Nanabush as a seagull signaling that he's coming for her (i.e., that she is
about to die), and she shoos him away, saying *Awus!*, while Veronique thinks
she is being shooed away.
   In the play, the Native tongues are often used as 'dramatic markers,' to
signal the apex of the heated debates among the seven sisters, or to counterpoint the tales of pain and despair each of them tells at some point. The

following example is of how code-mixing conveys emotional emphasis in one character's (Marie Adele who is dying of cancer) monologue:

> *MARIE-ADELE:* **Awus!** Ka-tha-pu-g'wun-ta oo-ta pee-wee-sta-ta-gu-mik-si. **Awus! Neee.** U-wi-nuk oo-ma kee-tha ee-tee-thi-mi-soo-yin holy spirit chee? **Awus! Hey,** maw ma-a oop-mee tay-si-thow u-wu **seagull bird.** I goo-ta poo-goo ta-poo. Nu-gu-na-wa-pa-mik. Nu-gu-na-wa-pa-mik
>
> *NANABUSH:* **As-tum.**
>
> *MARIE-ADELE:* **Nee.** Moo-tha ni-gus-kee-tan tu-pi-mi-tha-an. Moo-tha oo-ta-ta-gwu-na n'tay-yan. Chees-kwa. Pause. Mati poo-ni-mee-see i-goo-ta wee-chi-gi-**seagull bird come shit on my fence one more time and you and anybody else look like you cook like stew on my stove. Awus!**

Note:

> *M-A:* Go away! You stinking thing. Don't coming messing around here for nothing. Go away! Nee. Who the hell do you think you are, the Holy Spirit? Go away! Hey, but he won't fly away, this seagull bird. He just sits there. And watches me. Watches me.
>
> *NANABUSH:* Come.
>
> *M-A:* Nee. I can't fly away. I have no wings. Pause. Will you stop shit-ting all over the place . . . *Cree.* (19; my emphasis)

The way code-mixing works here is interesting in two respects: when they are caught speaking to Nanabush, the older women, especially Marie-Adele and Pelajia, shift to Cree or Ojibway. English percolates in these dialogues, since it is the language the characters speak in their ordinary lives. However, the Native words exert what we could call a 'trigger' effect: they summon the Native heritage and its cultural legacy. Moreover, by keeping Standard English almost entirely out of the play, village English is upgraded to the literary language for this community. In an interesting reversal of what often happens in immigrant religious communities, when English is kept outside the ritual because it is seen as a "polluted" language, here village English with its material and scatological emphasis is elevated above Standard English.

Yet, with a final *coup de théâtre*, Nanabush, the central hero of Native mythology, shows up onstage as the only character who speaks Standard English, and he speaks it beautifully:[4]

> *BINGO MASTER:* Welcome, ladies and gentlemen, to the biggest bingo the world has ever seen! Yes, ladies and gentlemen, tonight we have a very, very special treat for you. Tonight, ladies and gentlemen, you will be witness to events of such gargantuan proportions, such cataclysmic ramifications, such masterly and magnificent

manifestations that your minds will reel, your eyes will nicti-
tate, and your hearts will palpitate erratically. (100)

'Bingo,' a loaded word when applied to Native communities today, is the
word of death for Marie-Adele, and marks her return to the spirit world, as
we discover as the game unfolds:

> *And out of this chaos emerges the calm, silent figure of Marie-Adele waltz-*
> *ing romantically in the arms of the Bingo Master. The Bingo Master says*
> *"Bingo" into her ear. And the Bingo Master changes, with sudden bird-*
> *like movements, into the nighthawk, Nanabush in dark feathers. Marie-*
> *Adele meets Nanabush.* (103)

Known as Weesageechack in Cree, Nanabush in Ojibway, but also as Raven,
Coyote, and Trickster, in the play we see Nanabush embodied at first as a
seagull, later as a nighthawk (onstage), and as the Bingo Master (offstage) at
the end of the play who speaks in perfect Standard English. Nanabush, as the
note in the text reads, "goes by many names and many guises" (xii). Nanabush is the perfect embodiment of translation: neither animal nor human,
neither God nor Man, the Trickster, or Great Translator, puts with his own
presence the issue of untranslatability at the very center of the play.

Dionne Brand's *No Language Is Neutral*

Caribbean literature is another ideal place to look for textualities predicated
on a translational poetics, because of the multilingual and multicultural environment these texts emerge out of. The second work I am going to consider
is the poetry of Trinidadian writer Dionne Brand. *No Language Is Neutral*
was published in 1990 and marked the beginning of Brand's international
recognition. *No Language Is Neutral* is divided into four sections, leading the
poet along an exploration of her linguistic heritage and of the history that
she wants to bear witness to. I'm going to look only at the title section of the
book, "no language is neutral," which is made up of one single long poem
consisting of the genealogy, in the feminine, of the poetic persona as well as
of a revisitation of the native landscape. The opening lines draw us into the
scenery and set the rhythm of the long poem as a whole:

> No language is neutral. I used to haunt the beach at
> Guaya, two rivers sentinel the country sand, not
> **backra** white but nigger brown sand, one river dead
> and teeming from waste and alligators, the other
> rumbling to the ocean in tumult, the swift undertow
> blocking the crossing of little girls except on the tied
> up dress hips of big women, then, the taste of leaving

was already on my tongue and cut deep into my
skinny pigeon toed way, language here was strict
description and teeth edging truth. Here was beauty
and here was nowhere. (Brand 1990: 22; my emphasis)

In the Jamaican English Dictionary, *backra* is defined as "white man, he who
surrounds or govern" (Cassidy and Le Page 2002: 18). The island's beauty,
its sand the color of its people, its almond leaves "fat as women" cannot dis-
simulate the air that still stinks of slavery, oppression, poverty, and hopelessness. But it is in the analysis of the language that echoes in that place that
the persona's schizophrenic relationship to her native land is conceptually
developed in the book as a whole:

To hate this, they must have been
dragged through the Manzinilla spitting out
the last spun syllables for cruelty, new sound forming,
pushing toward lips made to bubble blood. This road
could match that. Hard-bitten on mangrove and wild
bush, the sea wind heaving any remnants of
consonant curses into choking aspirate. (23)

The 'they' in these lines are the poet's ancestors who have been drawn with
force to abandon their original idioms (*spun syllables*), in order to adopt a new
language, made of new sounds, turning their mouths into holes of blood, an
image propounding the idea of the removal of the tongue. Only after this
tribute paid to her history can the poet proceed and write in Trinidadian
English Creole (it is the first time in the collection and in Brand's poetic
works) in a way that is not belittling or exotic, but poetically necessary:

Silence **done** curse god and beauty here,
people **does** hear things in this heliconia peace
a morphology of rolling chain and copper gong
now shape this twang, falsetto of whip and air
rudiment this grammar. Take what I tell you. When
these barracks held slaves between their stone
halters, talking was left for night and hush was idiom
and hot core. (23; my emphasis)

I would like to point out two things about this stanza:

1. Trinidadian English Creole (henceforth TEC) is inserted in this passage by the use of the stereotypical "done" (as well as TEC "does").
   According to Maria Casas (2009), this insertion is interesting in that it
   does not break the ortographic standard as is normally the case with

dub poetry, where the accented word is marked by a different spelling. Brand's use seems to create a projection of the oral mode into the
standard spelling whose function appears to be a sudden increase in
emotional intensity for a Native Creole speaker/writer, rather than a
projection of a different identity.

2. These lines mix worldviews and cultural orders by simply coupling
together abstract nouns and cultural referents which belong to the
Western tradition (heliconia peace, morphology, falsettos) with ordinary, monosyllabic words, recording the concreteness of the history of
slavery in the West Indies: the morphology of the new idiom is made of
rolling chains and copper gongs; falsettos are produced by the sound
of whips in the air and a derogatory twang is the rudiment of this
grammar.

This is the first work in which Brand uses code-switching as part of her poetics. Another instance is an illustration of the use of code-switches between
Creole and Standard English that re-create speakers as well as define their
relationships:

This time Liney **done see** vision in this green **guava
season**, fly skinless **and turn into river fish, dream
sheself, praise god, without sex and womb when sex
is hell and womb is she to pay.** So dancing an old
man the castilian around this christmas living room
my little sister and me get Ben to tell we any story he
remember, and in between his own trail of conquests
and pretty clothes, in between his never sleeping with
a woman who wasn't clean because he was a
scornful man, in between our absent query were they
scornful women too, Liney smiled on his gold teeth.
The castilian out of breath, the dampness of his
shrunken skin reminding us, Oh god! Laughing,
sister! We will kill uncle dancing! (25; my emphasis)

In her work on multimodality in Black feminist Canadian writing, Maria
Casas provides an excellent and precise linguistic analysis of Brand's lyrical
passage that I am adopting here since it works perfectly for my own purpose
of exploring Brand's translational poetics (2009: 126–128).

In the opening lines, Liney is created as a character in free direct speech
by a passage in Creole, from "This time" to "she to pay." Creole elements
include "done see," "guava season," "sheself," and past tense "fly," "dream,"
and "is." "Womb is she to pay" is both a wordplay in Standard English
and left-focusing of "womb" in Creole: an existential copula is inserted to
transform "she [is] to pay [for] womb" into "womb, [it] is she to pay." In the

second part, a switch to Standard English, from "So dancing" to "living room," signals a change in speaker from Liney to the poetic persona. In the main clause of this sentence, another switch to Creole, from "my little sister" to "remember," establishes a child speaker. Creole markers in this clause are: the first-person object pronoun "we," past tense "get," and third-person past "remember."

This is a schematization of the speech exchange taking place in this stanza:

- children (Creole): ask Ben to tell them a story
- Ben (Creole): tells stories; remarks that he never slept "with a woman who wasn't clean because he was a scornful man"
- children (Standard): ask whether the women were scornful too

In the passage, code-switching takes place as a marked choice: one set of participants, the sisters, puts as much distance as possible between themselves and the other participant, Ben, by switching to a different code. Their reason for creating this distance is embedded in the complexity of these verses. The poet is reconstructing her genealogy and going back to her personal memories: Liney was a crucial nurturing and emotional figure in the author's childhood, it was the author's grandmother, the woman who stays when her own mother disappears, but as a woman poet she realizes she does not know anything about her: the kind of things she liked or disliked, the dreams she had, the men she actually loved. The two sisters try to find out from their uncle, but all he has to share is "she liked to walk about plenty" and "I was she favourite, oh yes." This is the story the girls are chasing by switching to Standard English, as well as the motive behind this collection of poems: to write the true story of women who were seen as nobodies by their own children. For such a story, words have to be picked with extreme care. It is a poetry that warns us that "no/language is neutral seared in the spine's unravelling. / Here is history too" (ibid.), and meaning can only be found in the interconnection of history, experience, and words.

Brand never writes entire poems in Creole. The function of Creole passages in *No Language Is Neutral* is to mark, both emotionally and lyrically, one specific moment in the story being told. In other words, TEC is used as a poetic necessity to amplify the gamut of meaning that her poetry can achieve. In her more recent work, Brand seems to favor the blending of TEC and Standard English in a sort of syntactic fusion (Ashcroft 2009) or code ambiguity, which opens up poetic meaning even more.

Brand's writing, because of the analysis it provides of how her received language was formed, and because it is written reshaping that very language, propounds a metaliterary reflection that attempts to imagine the place of poetry today as "another place, not here," a place located "between beauty and nowhere" (Brand 1990: 34), pointing to the ability that art has to have visions to be rendered in a language freed from the burden of mimetic representation. Her writing records the struggle to write in a different language, drifting away from words learned by heart, and longing for new ones, in the realization that:

> Each sentence realised or
> dreamed jumps like a pulse with history and takes a
> side. What I say in any language is told in faultless
> knowledge of skin, in drunkenness and weeping,
> told as a woman without matches and tinder, not in
> words and in words learned by heart,
> told in secret and not in secret, and listen, does not
> burn out our waste and is plenty and pitiless and loves. (Brand 1990: 34)

The drift and slippage that are inherent in translation are important to read both Highway's and Brand's works, where the literary language is made up by several layers of languages or dialects and of idiosyncratic usages of Standard English. There is a doubling involved in writing in a 'species' of English that is not exactly the writer's mother tongue, a doubling of minds, of worldviews, of ways of moving through languages. The 'gift' of translation for these writers is precious, since it enables them to insert a deep reflection on the language they use, and by extension that we all use, and on how that language can be forced to become a vehicle of self-expression on their own terms. Highway and Brand, then, base their poetics on translation as a direct consequence of the language practices they learned, or were forced to learn. However, when approaching their texts, it is our responsibility to rise to the challenge they pose.

Notes

1. The reason for this language mixture is explained in the production notes: the two languages, belonging to the same linguistic family, are very similar, and the reservation is supposedly inhabited by both Cree and Ojibway residents.
2. "Village English" is described by another Native writer, Maria Campbell, as follows: "A lot of my writing now is in very broken English. I find that I can express myself better that way. I can't write in our language, because who would understand it? So I've been using the way I spoke when I was at home, rather than the way I speak today . . . what linguists call 'village English.' It's very beautiful . . . very lyrical, but it took me a long time to realize that . . . it's more like oral tradition" (Lutz 1992: 48).
3. The pigs' names are interesting: Simon, Andrew, Matthew, Janie, Nicky, Ricky, Ben, Mark, Ron, Don, John, Tom, Pete, and Rose-Marie. Following the observation about the assimilationist way governing the characters' names in the play, it might be useful to notice that all the pigs' names sound quite Western.

4. Linguistically, "The most explicitly distinguishing feature between the North American Indian languages and the European languages is that in Indian, there is no gender. [. . .] So that by this system, the central hero figure from our mythology—our theology, if you will—is theoretically neither exclusively male or exclusively female, or is both simultaneously" (Highway quoted in Preston 1992: 142).

References

Apter, E. (2001) 'On Translation in a Global Market' *Public Culture* 13: 1: 1–12.

Apter, E. (2005) *The Translation Zone: A New Comparative Literature* (Princeton: Princeton University Press).

Ashcroft, B. (2009) *Caliban's Voice: The Transformation of English in Post-Colonial Literatures* (London: Routledge).

Ashcroft, B., Griffiths, G., and Tiffin, H. (1989) *The Empire Writes Back: Theory and Practice in Post-Colonial Criticism* (London: Routledge).

Bahri, D. (2003) *Native Intelligence: Aesthetics, Politics and Postcolonial Literature* (Minneapolis: University of Minnesota Press).

Bassnett, S., and Trivedi, H. (eds) (1999) *Post-Colonial Translation: Theory and Practice* (London: Routledge).

Bermann, S., and Wood, M. (eds) (2005) *Nation, Language, and the Ethics of Translation* (Princeton, NJ: Princeton University Press).

Brand, D. (1990) *No Language Is Neutral* (Toronto: Coach House Press).

Bullock B. E., and Toribio, A.J. (eds) (2009) *The Cambridge Handbook of Linguistic Code-Switching* (Cambridge: Cambridge University Press).

Casas, M. C. (2009) *Multimodality in Canadian Black Feminist Writing: Orality and the Body in the Work of Harris, Philip, Allen and Brand* (Amsterdam: Rodopi).

Cassidy, F. G., and Le Page R. B. (eds) (2002) *Dictionary of Jamaican English* (Kingston: University of the West Indies Press).

Ch'ien, E. N.-M. (2004) *Weird English* (Cambridge, MA: Harvard University Press).

Cronin, M. (2002) *Translation and Globalization* (London: Routledge).

Damrosch, D. (2003) *What Is World Literature?* (Princeton, NJ: Princeton University Press).

Díaz, J. (2007) *The Brief Wondrous Life of Oscar Wao* (New York: Riverhead Hardcover).

Foer, J.S. (2002) *Everything Is Illuminated* (New York: Houghton Mifflin).

Gumperz, J. J. (1982) *Discourse Strategies* (Cambridge: Cambridge University Press).

Highway, T. (1988) *The Rez Sisters* (Toronto: Fifth House Publishers).

Huggan, G. (2001) *The Postcolonial Exotic: Marketing the Margins* (London: Routledge).

Kelman, J. (1994, 1998) *How Late It Was, How Late* (London: Vintage).

LaRocque, Emma. 'Preface or Here Are Our Voices—Who Will Hear?' in Perreault J. and Vance, Sylvia, eds. *Writing the Circle: Native Women of Western Canada* (Edmonton: NeWest Press), 1990, pp. xv–xxx.

Lutz, H. (ed) (1992) *Contemporary Challenges: Conversation with Canadian Natives* (Toronto: Fifth House Publishers).

McKegney, S. (2005) 'From Trickster Poetics to Transgressive Politics: Substantiating Survivance in Tomson Highway's Kiss of the Fur Queen' *SAIL* 17: 4: 79–113.

McLeod, J. (ed) (2007) *The Routledge Companion to Postcolonial Studies* (London: Routledge).

Niranjana, T. (1992) *Siting Translation: History, Post-Structuralism and the Post-Colonial Context* (Berkeley: University of California Press).

Pennycook, A. (1994) *The Cultural Politics of English* (Harlow, Essex: Longman).
Pennycook, A. (1998) *English and the Discourses of Colonialism* (London: Routledge).
Philip, M.N. (1989) *She Tries Her Tongue: Her Silence Softly Breaks* (Charlottetown, P.E.I.: Ragweed Press).
Phillipson, R. (1992) *Linguistic Imperialism* (Oxford: Oxford University Press).
Poddar, P., Patke, R.S., and Jensen, L. (2009) *A Historical Companion to Postcolonial Literatures* (Edinburgh: Edinburgh University Press).
Preston, J. (1992) 'Weesageechak Begins to Dance: Native Earth Performing Arts' *TDR* 36: 1: 135–159.
Lahiri, Jumpa (1999) *Interpreter of Maladies* (New York: Houghton Mifflin).
Lee, Chang-rae (1995) *Native Speaker* (New York: Riverhead Books).
Simon, S. (1996) *Gender in Translation: Cultural Identity and the Politics of Transmission* (London: Routledge).
Sommer, D. (2003) 'Introduction' in *Bilingual Games: Some Literary Investigations*, ed. D. Sommer (New York: Palgrave), pp. 1–18.
Soyinka, W. (1965, 1970) *The Interpreters* (New York: Collier Books).
Talib, I. (2002) *The Language of Postcolonial Literature: An Introduction* (London: Routledge).
Tostevin, L. (1982) *Color of Her Speech* (Toronto: The Coach House Press).
Tutuola, A. (1952) *The Palm-Wine Drinkard* (London: Faber and Faber).
Tymoczko, M., and Gentzler, E. (eds) (2002) *Translation and Power* (Amherst: University of Massachusetts Press).
Venuti, L. (1995) *The Translator's Invisibility: A History of Translation* (London: Routledge).
Vizenor, G. (1994, 1999) *Manifest Manners: Narratives on Post-Indian Survivance* (Lincoln: University of Nebraska Press).
Young, R. (2003) *Postcolonialism. A Very Short Introduction* (Oxford: Oxford University Press).
Zabus, C. (1991) *The African Palimpsest: Indigenization of Language in the West African Europhone Novel*. 2nd enlarged ed. (Amsterdam: Rodopi).
Saro-Wiwa, K. (1995) *Sozaboy* (London: Longman).
Spivak, G.C. (1993) *Outside in the Teaching Machine* (London & New York: Routledge)
Welsh, I. (1993) *Trainspotting*. London: Vintage.

Part II

Translation as Pre-Text

5 'Make a Plan'

Pre-Texts in Zimbabwe

Doris Sommer and Naseemah Mohamed

A Postcolonial Paradox

In Zimbabwe, pedagogy has hardly changed since the crippling colonial era. Students still learn by rote and are frequently beaten for even minor infractions, which include speaking in their native language. The implications of these practices extend far beyond the classroom because the lessons of unquestioned authority and corresponding submission move the country in vicious circles of self-perpetuating despotism that delegitimizes and often punishes initiative. Initiative is 'correctly' understood as divergence from established rules. The deadening effects of authoritarianism on the economy and political life pose a paradox in Zimbabwe, the country with the highest literacy rate in Africa—above 90 percent.[1] By measures that are common among international agencies, Zimbabwe should be flourishing economically and democratically because literacy rates continue to be trusted indicators of development, according to the UN and Oxfam, for example. Yet these same agencies agree that Zimbabwe has fallen into the hands of a dictator and that there are hardly any signs of popular resistance to disturb his rule. In society at large, as in the micro-society of the classroom, obedience is prized as the soul of good citizenship. Evidently, the high literacy rate hasn't created a stir of self-empowerment. The educational statistics that Zimbabwe's government flaunts neglect the difference between literacy that merely recognizes words on a page and literacy that uses those written words critically and creatively.

Outdated pedagogical practices keep literacy at the simple level of recognition; they control students and limit their exercise of critical and creative faculties. This rigidity shows the continuity between today's classroom and the historically racist colonial education system. Repetition and punishment impede learning and block teachers from recognizing available resources for enhanced learning environments, native languages, for example. The social and intellectual advantages of speaking both heritage and acquired languages are by now widely acknowledged. But colonialism considered that monolingual English speakers would be ideal subjects. Before colonialism, education was informally integrated into the daily routine of life, as children worked alongside their parents as apprentices and wards.

From the establishment of colonial Rhodesia in September 1890, Christian missionaries took on responsibility for the education of Black Africans. Part of the missionaries' goal to 'civilize' Africans was to proselytize and teach Africans how to read the Bible, to encourage subjects to adopt the English language, morals, and cultural norms. The other part was overtly to denigrate and to discourage the continuity of African traditions (see Mungazi 1993; Atkinson 1972; Summers 2002). One of the most powerful mechanisms for the creation of this class of obedient individuals was through the use of racially tinged Victorian teaching methods, which worked powerfully to limit student agency. This is the period when rote repetition and physical abuse became standard classroom practices.[2] Logically, the effects were not only a form of violence against individual agency and the self-efficacy of African students, but also against the local traditions that represented alternatives to British authority. Colonialism aimed at creating docile, Christian, English-speaking subjects who would profit the empire. Now the same practices profit a dictator.

One devastating effect of Victorian teaching methods is to disengage students from their studies, a consequence that has been exacerbated over the last two decades during Zimbabwe's economic decline. Before the economic crash in the early 2000s, students could hold on to the incentive of future employment. Their prospects were greatly enhanced if they managed to graduate from high school. But the current unemployment rate of 80–95 percent means that students face the harsh reality that a high school diploma is no guarantee of even a low-level job. The most economically successful individuals are no longer the most educated. While teachers are paid below the poverty line of $500 per month per household, black marketeers thrive. Buying goods from neighboring South Africa and Botswana to sell them on the euphemistically named 'parallel market' is now considered one of the most attractive ventures for members of the middle to lower socioeconomic classes.

Under the authoritarian and corrupt bureaucratic state, the ability to survive, let alone to thrive, depends on an entrepreneurial knack for navigating the deplorable system. The idea that citizens must find illegitimate means to achieve legitimate ends—buying goods, paying someone 'under the table' and generally 'making do'—has become embedded in the Zimbabwean culture. All manner of irregular activity is known in everyday speech as "making a plan." At first blush, under these humiliating economic and sociopolitical constraints, it seems obvious that unorthodox 'black market' transactions are simply signs of a failed state, an embarrassingly corrupt unofficial effect of the large-scale official corruption. But at a deeper blush, as seen under an unofficial lens, the very practices of 'making do' demonstrate a popular nonconformity with authoritarianism and a talent for entrepreneurial activity.

The fact is that alongside the rigid authoritarian culture that paralyzes Zimbabwe's economic and political nerve, there are potentially therapeutic expressions of lively local culture. It's not that illegality can save Zimbabwe from dictatorship, since the expression of contempt for indecent norms may foster contempt for norms even in a legitimate polity. A smuggler's indifference to the rule of law may be plausible under a dictator's disregard for constitutional accords, but it may also become habitual and hobble the prospects of good government. However, even in the limited case of outright illegality, the liberties taken where no liberty is permitted can also be framed as popular resistance enabled by a still thriving culture of resourcefulness. In that frame it is possible to access an energy and creativity in popular practices that don't risk illegality, especially as they refer to unobjectionable reforms in education. These reforms in teaching and learning can fuel liberating undertows of self-authorization and legal collaboration.

In other words, the unofficial culture of achieving legitimate ends through delegitimized creativity, flexibility, and resourcefulness is not simply to be dismissed as training in illegality, as if initiative were limited to ethically questionable economic transactions. Alongside contraband there are countless expressions of everyday entrepreneurship that hold out a promise of social innovation: if you were to walk through the market, you would notice little street boys pushing toy cars made of recycled wire, as well as men who will charge your cell phone for a dollar by attaching electronic cables to an old car battery. To the country's detriment so far, this otherwise ubiquitous creativity, which we can call an 'economy of resourcefulness,' is overlooked in the classrooms where the payoff could be substantial.

Despite students' demonstrated talents for the extracurricular arts of 'making do,' and in contrast to their experience of working—however poor their material resources—they become passive and sometimes even abject when they walk into the classroom. The disconnect between students' academic and everyday lives generates a counterproductive short-circuit between resourceful energy and stifled learning. Popular culture holds creativity in high esteem, while official culture quashes creativity through conveniently authoritarian vestiges of Victorian education. Our challenge as educators and as active citizens is to tap into the unconquered ingenuity of students and teachers in order to stimulate development at all the levels that good education targets: intellectual political, economic, and psychosocial.

This chapter reports on a pilot program that addresses Zimbabwe's paradox of high literacy and relatively low scores on other indexes of social development defined by the Organization for Economic Cooperation and Development as: (i) civic engagement, (ii) interpersonal safety and trust, (iii) intergroup cohesion, (iv) gender equality, and (v) inclusion of minorities.[3] The scholarly purpose here was to refine a hypothesis about the causality and mutual reinforcement between dictatorship and authoritarian education. And the method included an intervention that offered an alternative to authoritarianism and then assessed the micro-political effects of that alternative in a typical school. For socially responsible scholars, it is often not enough, ethically and even intellectually speaking, to observe and to analyze crises, though conventional academic work often stops here. The effect of identifying crises carries a corollary demand to intervene in ways that academic preparation may help to prepare. Scholars and citizens in general have the opportunity—understood here as an obligation—to make contributions to understanding that lead beyond intellectual satisfactions and that speculate toward amelioration.

Pre-Texts

In a typical, low-resourced high school classroom, eight kilometers from the city center of Bulawayo, the second largest city in Zimbabwe, forty-five high school students were engaged in an atypical English class. They were translating Chinua Achebe's *Things Fall Apart* into music, dance, and, most notably, Ndebele, the second most widely spoken language native to Zimbabwe. The students wove between the two languages so seamlessly that one seemed to announce and to expect the other in a necessary relay. Research on language formation in multilingual classrooms would support this practice. A study conducted in Niger[4] and Guinea Bissau[5] (Hovens 2002) comparing (ex-colonial) monolingual primary schools with experimental bilingual primary schools showed that in both countries, bilingual classrooms were more stimulating, interactive, and relaxed.[6] Rural school children and girls benefited the most from participating in bilingual education. The study also emphasized that students who began instruction in their mother tongues could read and write better in the second language than did the control group students.

Despite the documented advantages of multilingual learning, these practices are an unlikely advance in postcolonial Zimbabwe. Speaking one's mother tongue in an English class is considered a distraction from learning, a punishable infraction that justifies physical abuse from teachers. "I don't like English class because if you speak Ndebele in class, Mrs. Chauke slaps you!" reported Jenna Mhlanga,[7] a fifteen-year-old student attending Nkulumane High School in Bulawayo. In an interview with an English teacher who spent those fifteen years accumulating experience while she meted out punishment, it seemed obvious that one of the greatest challenges facing her students with regard to learning English is that they spoke too much "vernacular" at home.

Our pilot program hadn't intended this bilingual benefit, but it did predict generally self-authorizing and constructive behaviors. The frame was a creative pedagogy called "Pre-Texts," Harvard University's most innovative approach to teaching language and literature. With it, we hoped to change the ways in which Zimbabwean students typically learn. And the conventional classrooms in Bulawayo offered an ideal setting for observing the effects of an alternative approach. The underlying innovation of "Pre-Texts" is the integration of visual and performative arts as vehicles for exploring classic literature in a language class. 'Classics' here means works that can withstand many readings without flattening the experience into predictable responses. A text becomes the prompt for creating original work in a range of artistic genres, so that students become self-motivated to understand the lexical and grammatical elements of the text and to speculate about possible interpretations. Teachers, on the other hand, learn to curb their authority and to become facilitators for students' critical readings and creativity rather than masters of fixed material. This abdication of absolute authority allows students to authorize their own work and to appreciate their classmates' divergent responses as prompts for creativity. The workshop environment manages to close up the debilitating gap between students' class work and their entrepreneurial spirit.

"Pre-Texts" is an intentionally naughty name to signal that even the classics can be material for manipulation. Books are not sacred objects; they are invitations to play. Conventional teaching has favored convergent and predictable answers as the first and sometimes only goal of education. This cautious approach privileges data retrieval or 'lower-order thinking.' But a first-things-first philosophy gets stuck in facts and stifles students. Bored early on, they don't get past vocabulary and grammar lessons to reach understanding and interpretation. Teaching for testing has produced unhappy pressures for everyone. Administrators, teachers, students, and parents have generally surrendered to a perceived requirement to focus on facts. They rarely arrive at interpretive levels that develop mental agility. Divergent and critical 'higher-order' thinking has seemed like a luxury for struggling students. However, when they begin from the heights of an artistic challenge, students access several levels of learning as functions of a creative process. Entering at the lower order seldom leads very far, but turning the order upside down works wonderfully. Attention to detail *follows* from higher-order manipulations because creative thinking needs to master the elements at hand.[8] A challenge to make something new of a text drives even reluctant students to develop an interpretation, which requires understanding and therefore leads to learning the vocabulary and grammar that had seemed bothersome or out of reach.

The theoretical underpinnings of Pre-Texts follow from the contributions of Maria Montessori's project-centered pedagogy and from Paulo Freire's *Pedagogy of the Oppressed* (1968), as well as from the aesthetics of Freidrich Schiller and John Dewey's arts-based pragmatism (Sommer 2009). They all understood the role of the teacher as a facilitator of learning rather than technocrat who imparts information and demands it back from students. African humanist authors such as Ngugi wa Thiong'o specifically highlight the stultifying effects of colonial pedagogy and the necessity to return to African art forms to create and receive knowledge.[9] There are five core objectives of our integrating the arts as divergent languages of interpretation:

1. To promote each student's ownership of classical texts
2. To experience creative thinking as critical thinking
3. To recognize that interpretation legitimately involves one's own experience
4. To show that texts need creative intervention in order to make sense
5. To illustrate that language is an art that triggers other artistic processes

After writing, painting, dancing, acting, and so on, participants sit in a Freirean circle to reflect. The question is always the same: what did we do? (Asking what we learned is likely to get unfriendly answers from teens. They sense that teachers want approval or praise and they refuse to comply. But if you ask what they did, students will want to justify their work or else they may look foolish.) One reflection follows another, in no set order, until everyone has spoken. After a few sessions, the dynamic of universal and brief participation feels natural and necessary. The first few interventions, however brilliant, will not exhaust possibilities. While we wait for more, exercising critical thinking and patience with peers, intellectual and civic skills develop. New facilitators learn to expect original comments from one another and then from students. Participants also notice the democratizing effect of collective reflection; it levels the unevenness between forceful people and shy ones who are worth waiting for.

While readings deepen during the series of visual, literary, and performance interpretations of the same selected text, participants also develop breadth by going 'off on a tangent' each week. Choosing a tangential text that they can connect to the shared reading in any way—even if far-fetched—puts students in command and encourages them to read widely. They peruse books, magazines, and the Internet, using their own criteria to select something they are proud to bring in. The combined dynamic of inexhaustible interpretation of one text and the practically limitless reach of tangents produces deep and broad readers.

Critical literacy associated with higher-order thinking, as opposed to the rote literacy that doesn't dare to confront dictatorship, should be on everyone's agenda because it continues to be a reliable indicator for levels of poverty, violence, and disease. Real proficiency is alarmingly low in underserved areas worldwide.[10] Skeptics will question the cause for alarm, alleging that communication increasingly depends on audiovisual stimuli, especially for poor and disenfranchised populations. They'll even say that teaching classic literature reinforces social asymmetries because disadvantaged people lack the background that privileged classes can muster for reading difficult texts. Audiovisual stimuli, on the other hand, don't discriminate between rich and poor and seem more democratic.

Paulo Freire cautioned against this pedagogical populism, arguing that illiteracy precludes full citizenship. His advice to teachers as cultural workers was to stress reading and writing in order to stimulate critical thinking and therefore to promote social inclusion. Freire traces a spiral from reading to thinking about what one reads, and then to writing a response to one's thought, which requires more thinking, in order to read one's response and achieve yet a deeper level of thought (Freire 1998: 2). Teachers democratize by raising the baseline of literacy to a higher common denominator, not by shunning literary sophistication along with elite works of art. The classics are valuable cultural capital and the language skills they require remain foundations for analytical thinking, resourcefulness, and psychosocial development. Without mastery of at least one spoken and written language, youth have little hope for self-realization. Paradoxically, skeptics reinforce the inequality they decry by dismissing a responsibility to foster high-level literacy for all.

Before and After

The pilot of "Pre-Texts" in Bulawayo, Zimbabwe, consisted of six high school teachers collaborating with four artists to teach Chinua Achebe's literary classic *Things Fall Apart* to seventy-five students. The nine-week program focused on literary interpretation through the arts, including music, drama, poetry, and painting. Naseemah Mohamed, a Harvard College student and native of Zimbabwe, designed the implementation and monitored the outcomes of the pilot through ethnographic fieldwork and qualitative pre- and post-program interviews with participants.

The High School, where the program was implemented, exemplifies many of the current economic and educational challenges facing Zimbabwean schools and communities, including a lack of financial resources, high teacher attrition rates, and low student examination pass rates. The high-density urban community has a population of approximately sixty-three thousand and is located eight kilometers from the center of Bulawayo, the second-largest city in Zimbabwe.[11] Once a postindependence beacon of a rising middle class, the closely packed tiny brick houses along the dirt roads have become a symbol of Zimbabwe's economic and social deterioration over the past decade. Between 70 percent and 90 percent of community members are not formally employed,[12] and an officer from the Ministry of Education informed me that tens of thousands of people from the community have emigrated to neighboring South Africa and Botswana in search of employment.[13] The high unemployment rate parallels the current national unemployment average of 95 percent.[14]

The participating students ranged from thirteen to nineteen years old. They were randomly recruited from over two hundred students who were asked to take home consent forms for the program. All the potential participants were students of the teachers who were recruited for the program. Of the eighty students who were not included in the program, fifteen were interviewed as a control group.[15] Participation was voluntary, with no monetary incentives.[16] The six self-selected teachers did get a small stipend, comparable to that of any other enrichment program. The average length of their teaching experience was twenty years. The staff was made up of senior school officials, including the deputy headmistress, who was an English teacher, the head of the English Literature Department, and the head of the History Department, as well as a literature teacher and two English teachers.

Interviews conducted before the program began revealed the authoritarian structure of the classroom. Students reported being beaten as a form of disciplinary punishment, and teachers stressed their own expertise rather than the contributions of students. In anticipation of the difficulties teachers might experience with an alternative pedagogy, we paired them up with local artists. The artists included a spoken word artist, two actors, a dancer, and a musician who were recruited from one of the largest performing arts companies in Zimbabwe, Inkululeko Yabatsha School of Arts (IYASA).[17] Training for the implementation of the pilot lasted five days while teachers and artists were introduced to the practice of "Pre-Texts." It is basically to (1.) take a text, (2.) spin it using a range of available arts, and (3.) reflect on what you did. Among the many activities that they were expected to integrate and expand on during the program, teachers and artists worked on dramatizing the text with the students and having students create and recite poetry based on the text, as well as composing music scores, poems, and dances. The afterschool program ran for three days a week during two to three hours over the nine-week program.

During the course of this short session, student–teacher relationships changed dramatically. Teachers stopped beating their students, while students' fear of their teachers was replaced by respect and admiration. The students began calling one teacher, formerly infamous for her beatings, "NaTembi," an Ndebele title of respect mixed with affection. Students and teachers began discussing English literature in their mother language of Ndebele. And as they became fluent in testing new ways of thinking, they felt sufficiently confident to be bilingual in the classroom, a liberty that has regularly proven to enhance learning, knowledge retention, and the stability of culture in a community. This was an unpredicted outcome of the program. Teachers, not only students, allowed themselves to speak in their shared native language. All classes in the school are taught solely in English and exceptions are rare though students often don't understand the lesson.[18] We suspect that the use of Ndebele emerged spontaneously because of the more relaxed and informal atmosphere of the program, and the fact that it disrupted the standard colonial student–teacher dynamic.

Bi- and multilingualism develop more than these healthy interactions; they also develop higher-order divergent thinking (Sommer 2004). The students were so enthusiastic about reading and spinning interpretations through art that they rarely missed a day of the voluntary program, defying the norm and their teachers' expectations. Fifteen-year-old Betina Malanda remarked, "The program is helping me understand the teacher more easily, to be confident in my singing, acting, dancing, and writing poetry. It is teaching me to be creative, and show the teacher what children like and want—we children can also contribute something."

The egalitarian structure of "Pre-Texts" and the release from the tyranny of one correct answer allowed students the freedom to express themselves without the fear of being punished or ridiculed. Moreover, this newfound freedom was coupled with displays of individual student talents and particularities, which the teachers had underestimated in their regular classrooms. Mrs. Sibanda, when asked to comment about student–teacher interactions, said:

> Right now, I feel more close to the students because it was not only the teacher who was supposed to present and come up with the ideas like you do in the normal lesson. Yes, there was freedom of expression. No answer was wrong, no answer was right, or there was no best answer. All answers we treated with respect. So it's not like—in the classroom, it's like when you give a wrong answer the teacher will either shout back at you or tell you or call you all sorts of names—why didn't you do your work yesterday blah blah blah.[19] But in this program you just have to respect them because out of that answer, there might be something that can come out that is very, very, creative and you can use it for the program. No matter how stupid you might think the answer is, but in this case you have to accept it. Just to see how far the idea will take the student.[20]

Mrs. Sibanda mentioned respect for the creativity of the students as drawing her closer to them. Other teachers also gave examples of students whom they had taught in their regular classrooms as revealing completely different personalities in the program. Mr. Ngwenya commented that he became passionate about the program because of its effect on his pupils. "There are some of my pupils who were in the program. I never thought they could love to sing but the way they were doing it surprised me. Like yesterday, Netsai, she hardly talks in class. But through acting and dancing, she turns into a different personality altogether." All six teachers commented on how the freedom in the program allowed the teachers to appreciate the intellectual and creative talents of their students.

The program ended with an open community performance where students showcased their interpretive poems, artwork, songs, and plays (all based on Achebe's classic novel) to more than 150 people in attendance. Officials of the Ministry of Sports, Arts, and Culture were guests of honor. The school has since maintained the program and has instituted an 'interhouse drama competition' in which various house groups in the school compete by dramatizing their O-level required book. The regional officer of the Ministry of Education and Culture, E. O. Ndlovu, was so impressed with the program that he asked Naseemah to train five of the Sports, Arts, and Cultural officers for the district. One of the officers, Mr. Giyani, had planned to expand the program to another district, Mutare.

This past summer, "Pre-Texts" continued to work in several Latin American cities and in Hong Kong, as well as in Boston, close to Harvard's home. As in the previous year, we trained teachers for Boston public schools' summer program for English-language learners. The training workshops targeted teachers of mostly elementary grades. Despite the difference in the age-groups of students, we were eager to compare Boston classrooms with the postcolonial paradigms of English-language learners in Zimbabwe. Perhaps surprisingly, given the privileged preparation of Boston's teachers, the monolingual instructors tended to be generally less effective, receptive, and creative with their students than were the teachers in Zimbabwe. In part this embrace of "Pre-Texts" in Bulawayo may respond to the constraints exercised by official authoritarian culture, which animates a parallel culture of resourcefulness. "Pre-Texts" taps into the energy of this alternative to authoritarian order. By contrast, several monolingual teachers in Boston seemed quite centered in a single culture and reluctant to acknowledge the potential sophistication of immigrant children.

In Zimbabwe, citizens are normally nonconformist in small or great measure. Dominated and resentful of the domination, they develop skills to reinterpret existing limitations as conditions of creativity. Through "Pre-Texts" this everyday sophistication crosses the threshold of 'making do' into official culture that occupies the legitimate space of public education. In other words, despite the real cultural damage that the postcolonial condition can cause, the malady of split loyalties and conflicting traditions may also breed its own potential antidote through the dynamic bicultural and bilingual nature of everyday practices. 'Postcolonial' is a term for the doubled or multiple codes of behavior that survive simultaneously. But once classrooms admit that a multiplicity of cultural norms and worldviews, through programs like "Pre-Texts," causes authoritarian pedagogy to give way to mutual respect and admiration, can dictatorship survive this kind of training for young citizens?

Notes

1. Actual literacy rate may be lower owing to the volatile economy and the inability of government to fund education programs over the past decade. Current statistics cited are based the UNESCO 2010 projections based on previous years' data; see rhttp://stats.uis.unesco.org/unesco/TableViewer/document.aspx?ReportId=121&IF_Language=eng&BR_Country=7160&BR_Region=40540 (accessed May 7, 2013).
2. For more about corporal punishment in colonial schools across Africa, see Killingray (1994).
3. The program is described below under the heading "Pre-Texts."
4. Source: Indices of Social Development; see http://www.IndSocDev.org/ (accessed March 7, 2013).
5. For both countries the primary languages that students are taught in are Portuguese and French, respectively.
6. According to the study, the vernacular languages were used in Niger to teach students for the first three grades; then French was introduced in the fourth grade orally. In the fifth and sixth grades, French was introduced in its written form.

7. Pseudonyms have been used throughout the chapter to protect the identity of the participants.
8. See 'Evaluation of Amparo Cartonera,' by Liz Gruenfeld: "Museo Amparo Program students were positively impacted in terms of attention to detail, reading comprehension, and student interpretation of stories, as seen by teachers and artists: Students place more attention in details now. As with the 'hypertexts,' they pay more attention to details in the story to be able to reverse the order of events and say what else might happen instead. Another teacher added that program students learned more words, resulting in a richer vocabulary" (18).
9. In Ngugi wa Thiong'o's *Decolonizing the Mind* (1986) he rejects the uprooting of African languages and African literature by colonial languages. He argues that beyond a communication tool, language is a "carrier of culture," thus making native languages the only means of fully expressing the life experiences of local people. He also discusses the complexity and sophistication of African poetry and the theater in the aforementioned book, and specifically refers to colonial pedagogy in *Wizard of the Crow* (2006).
10. See Oxfam International, 'Education: Tackling the Global Crisis,' April 2001. "Today 125 million children do not get any formal education at all; the majority of them are girls. Even more children do not get sufficient schooling because they drop out before they learn basic literacy skills. Children throughout the world are being denied their fundamental right to education. In developing countries, one in four adults—some 900 million people, are illiterate. The human costs of this education crisis are incalculable." http://www.oxfamamerica.org/files/OA-Education_Tackling_Global_Crisis.pdf. (accessed May 7, 2013).
11. The government designates high people to land ratio, 'high-density areas.'
12. This estimate was generated by my interviews with seventy community members, including teachers, students, and community members on the street. The Ministry of Education Arts and Culture officer, E. O. Ndlovu, who is the designated arts and culture minister of the district, confirmed the estimate.
13. An estimated two million Zimbabwean refugees and emigrants currently live in South Africa. 'Regularizing Zimbabwean Immigration to South Africa,' South Africa Migration Policy Brief, last modified May 2009. http://www.cormsa.org.za/wpcontent/uploads/MigrationPolicyBrief/Migration%20Policy%20Brief%201%20-%20Zim%20Special%20Permits.pdf (accessed February 2, 2011).
14. CIA World Factbook, last modified June 2009. https://www.cia.gov/library/publications/the-world factbook/fields/2129.html (accessed February 2, 2011).
15. The fifteen were also chosen with a random number generator.
16. As stipulated by the Harvard Human Subjects Review Board.
17. I had been introduced to the founder of the group by a mutual friend and had contacted him about requesting performers months before implementing the project.
18. In my pre-program interview with the teacher, she told me that despite her reluctance to teach in Ndebele in her regular English classroom, she is often forced to because "students don't understand anything." Interviewed by Naseemah Mohamed, tape recording July, 11, 2011, Bulawayo, Zimbabwe.
19. I am unsure of whether she was speaking of herself in this section. Though I am inclined to believe that she was referring to other teachers.
20. Interviewed by Naseemah Mohamed, tape recording August 25, 2011, Bulawayo, Zimbabwe.

References

Achebe, C. (1994) *Things Fall Apart* (New York: Anchor Books).
Atkinson, N. J. (1972) *Teaching Rhodesians: A History of Educational Policy in Rhodesia* (London: Longman).
Freire, P. (1970) *Pedagogy of the Oppressed* (New York: Herder and Herder).
Freire, P. (1998) *Teachers as Cultural Workers* (Boulder, CO: Westview Press).
Gruenfeld, L. (2009) 'Evaluation of *La Cartonera* Program Program Cycle: Fall 2008' unpublished report produced for *The Cultural Agents Initiative, Harvard University.*
Hovens, M. (2002) 'Bilingual Education in West Africa: Does It Work?' *International Journal of Bilingual Education and Bilingualism* 5: 5: 249–266.
Killingray, D. (1994) 'The "Rod of Empire": The Debate over Corporal Punishment in the British African Colonial Forces, 1888–1946' *Journal of African History* 35: 2: 201–216.
Mungazi, D. A. (1993) *The Fall of the Mantle: The Educational Policy of the Rhodesia Front Government and Conflict in Zimbabwe* (New York: Peter Lang).
Ngugi wa Thiong'o. (1986) *Decolonizing the Mind: The Politics of Language in African Literature* (London: James Currey).
Ngugi wa Thiong'o. (2006) *Wizard of the Crow* (London: Harvill Secker).
Sommer, D. (2004) *Bilingual Aesthetics: A New Sentimental Education* (Durham, NC: Duke University Press).
Sommer, D. (2009) 'Schiller and Company, or How Habermas Makes Us Play' *New Literary History* 40: 1: 85–103.
Summers, C. (2002) *Colonial Lessons: Africans' Education in Southern Rhodesia, 1918–1940* (Portsmouth: Heinemann).

6 Postcolonial Cities and the Culture of Translation

Sherry Simon

All around the world, cities are rediscovering their underground rivers. In Seoul, Korea, the Cheonggyecheon river was rescued from under a six-lane highway and, now the center of an exquisite linear park, flows through six kilometers of the downtown core. London, New York, Toronto, Montreal, all have plans to excavate the rivers that were covered over during the late Victorian period.[1] There are good ecological reasons to free the rivers. But the symbolic significance is also very strong. Citizens who had no idea that they were treading over tamed, bricked-in streams will now be reconnected with the natural history of their cities—and with a literal reminder of the city as a space of circulation.

Cities are given life by what flows through them. What else moves through cities? People, ideas, money, traffic, sewage, gossip, news media, rumor, virtual messages: a mixture of visible and invisible streams, circulating in complex patterns of overlay, some random, some following preestablished pathways. Recognition of this reality has made circulation a powerful figure for studying the cultural life of cities (Straw and Boutros 2010: 4) and for understanding the ways in which 'they [. . .] act as nodes, or clusters, within the circulation of modernizing forces" (5).

Yet in the discussions of circulation in today's city, and indeed in most of the influential writing in urban studies since the 1980s, there has been a striking absence of one of the most important fluid elements of urban life: language. Authors such as David Harvey (2006), Saskia Sassen (1991), Edward Soja (2000), Allan Blum (2003), Richard Sennett (2005), and Iain Chambers (1990) have made the city the focus of issues of democracy and community, of belonging and citizenship. Language, the medium through which public discussion takes place and through which the history of the city is narrated, is often taken for granted. Despite the sensory evidence of multilingualism in today's cities, the scripts on storefronts, the sidewalk conversations, there has been little sustained discussion of language as a vehicle of urban cultural memory and identity, or as a key in the creation of meaningful spaces of contact and civic participation.

This neglect is particularly striking as cities face the challenge of promoting translation practices that will ensure urban cohesion. Translation is the key to citizenship, to the incorporation of languages into the public sphere. Understanding urban space as a translation zone restores language to the picture and offers a corrective to the deafness of much current urban theory. An urban imaginary, writes Andreas Huyssen, marks the way citizens view their city as a site of continuities, traditions, and conflicts, and is an "embodied material fact [. . .] What we think about a city and how we perceive it informs the ways we act within it" (2008: 3). Clearly language, as "the primary social bond [. . .] and a stock exchange of meanings that carry over from previous states of the code, which are newly introduced, negotiated, withdrawn, and overhauled" (Resina 2008: 143) has pride of place in that *imaginaire.*

Much of the abundant writings over recent decades has emphasized the visual aspects of urban life. And yet the audible surface of languages, each city's signature blend of dialects and accents, is an equally crucial element of urban reality. Just as seeing the buildings and streets of an urban aggregation is crucial to understanding its history, its organization into neighborhoods, its systems of circulation, so hearing introduces the observer into layers of social, economic, and cultural complexity. The waves of languages that flow into one another provide the listener with a rich sensory surface. They merge with particular intensity in border areas, like the noisy streets of polyglot neighborhoods, but also in more private zones, such as publishing houses, theaters, translation agencies, or software research firms.

Language is not an accessory to the work of the city, but an integral part. Contact, transfer, and circulation among languages define the sensibility of daily life and the public presence of communities. More specifically, areas of contact and friction between languages are central to the city's identity. Multiple languages on urban terrain interact in patterns that are written into the history of the city, issuing from factors such as its demographic history, its physical layout, its previous conversations. These patterns mark the life of the individual and of the community, shaping the imaginary of the city in ways that are both conflictual and productive.

Postcolonial Cities

While all cities are multilingual, the history and spatial configurations of some cities mark them as intensely translational. This is the case for postcolonial cities. The history of such cities means that languages and memories meet in a productive dissonance; the legacy of colonialism led to charged interconnections across the city. There are two possible understandings of the 'postcolonial city': the first and most common one refers to the cities of former colonial possessions that were once physically occupied by the colonizer and bear the architectural and topographical marks of this period. The less common understanding refers to former imperial capitals like London or Paris, which today have in turn been marked by the presence of intense migration from east to west (King 2012). Both types of cities are marked by colonialism; both are multilingual. But it is the first type that will engage me, in particular because of the characteristic spatial and linguistic divisions that have been the urban legacy of British and French colonialism. In what follows, I will discuss two cities not often drawn into the same conversation and not often considered for their common topographical inheritance. Both are cities marked by British colonialism—a colonial enterprise whose most enduring legacy was perhaps that of city-building:

> Among history's imperialists the British were certainly not the greatest builders, but they were the greatest creators of towns. Conquerors since Alexander the Great had seen the strategic and cultural advantages of establishing their own cities across the world, but as the first modern industrial power, Britain was the chief exporter of municipalities, and through the agency of her empire broadcast them everywhere. Half the cities of the American East owe their genesis to the British Empire, most of the cities of Canada, many of the cities of Africa, all the cities of Australasia and the tremendous city-states of Singapore and Hong Kong. Sporting pastimes apart, and the English language, urbanism was the most lasting of the British imperial legacies. (Morris 1983: 196)

The two cities are Calcutta, a classical colonial city, the capital of the British Empire in India from the reign of the East India Company until 1911 and part of the empire until 1947, and Montreal, a city doubly colonial (occupied first by the French, then by the British), yet that nevertheless falls outside the bounds of what is classically considered postcolonial. Calcutta (which today has become Kolkata) was founded in 1690 by Job Charnock, a representative of the East India Company, as a commercial outpost on the trade routes linking London to the east. Montreal was founded in 1642 by Sieur de Maisonneuve both as a trading center and as a mystical-religious project. In 1763, after the defeat of the French on the Plains of Abraham and the resulting Treaty of Paris, Montreal fell under British rule. What is common to the cities is a pattern of settlement that separated the landscape into two—a north–south division in Calcutta (the European sector in the south, the Indian city in the north), and an east–west division in Montreal (the Anglophones in the west, the Francophones in the east)—geographical divisions that were also language divides. In both cases, this separation gave rise to complex translational relationships and a productive dissonance that came to define the sensibilities of both cities.

The social and cultural forces that drive translational encounters across the city engage a wide range of affects—from resistance to polite acknowledgment to creative interaction. Sometimes the physical proximity of competing languages results in the communities turning their backs on one another, the better to cultivate their relationships with ideal or imagined allies. In what follows, I will evoke two moments in the life of Calcutta and Montreal in which the relationship between translation and the colonial takes on a clearly identifiable form. For Calcutta, I will introduce the Bengali Renaissance, an exceptionally productive long period of interaction between languages on city terrain, for Montreal a shorter period when the consciousness of the colonial was prevalent in the realm of politics and culture. These moments are neither symmetrical nor equivalent; the forces at play in the two cities are distinct. Yet in each case the cross-city encounter gives rise to an important and enduring critical debate about the effects of translation across divided city space and about the models of translation that can best nourish the urban imaginary.

CALCUTTA: 'Imperfectly Divided'

Historic patterns of segregation in the colonial city gave rise to an agglomeration divided between the 'European' town and 'Native' settlement: "the first, modern, spacious, low density, well maintained through the use of town planning, and culturally different from the surrounding environment; the second, usually separated from the first by parks, railway lines, or open space, invariably more densely settled, with traditional housing, social and cultural buildings overcrowded, and lacking in services and infrastructural provision" (King 2012). This description by the urban studies specialist A. D. King, like the descriptions by numerous other commentators in the past,[2] pays careful attention to the visible manifestations of division in Calcutta city life but omits investigation of the concomitant divide of language. Yet in his further comments on the postcolonial city, King notes that recent studies of colonial cities have come to challenge the absoluteness of colonial divides between the 'Indigenous city' and the 'European colonial settlement,' showing that the traditional dualism of colonizer–colonized, traditional–modern, European–Native, and old–new, and the social and spatial divisions that sustained them, was not nearly so clear-cut as has been represented. "Instead, there were charged interconnections between the two spaces. The new colonial settlement offered opportunities for some Indian residents to move between cultures and spaces, constructing new identities, identifying with the new by rejecting the old, and creating indigenous modernities" (King 2012). He mentions in particular studies of Calcutta where by 'making use of local languages,' European perceptions were challenged by narratives in the Bengali language.[3]

This comment is startling if only because it assumes that previous assessments of Calcutta's divisions and their cultural consequences had not made use of 'local languages,' relying only on English-language accounts of Calcutta social history. The archive in the Bengali languages interprets the geographical layout of the colonial city in ways that are markedly different from the English-language version. This is the central perception of the important study of Calcutta by Swati Chattopadhyay, *Representing Calcutta. Modernity, Nationalism and the Colonial Uncanny* (2005). For Chattopadhyay, Calcutta's spaces were not only physical sites, but locations from which representations of the city itself issued. And so the doubleness of the space gave rise to a doubleness of representation. Two separate structures of power and knowledge underlay representations of Calcutta, rendering the city 'uncanny' in the uneven fit between the two (Chattopadhyay 2005: 3). For Chattopadhyay, translation cannot be a "transparent transaction that simply substitutes one sign for another" (2005: 145). There is no single *ground* that guarantees equivalence between the "the modern forms and techniques of governance instituted by colonial authority [. . .] and the nationalist literary, artistic, spatial ambitions cultivated by the Bengali community" (6). Inevitably, the terrain was uneven and indeed "under construction," as the edifice of colonial knowledge was being raised (146). And so the results of interactions would reflect these aporetic conditions, producing constructs that would "insert new meaning into the milieu" (146). Translation across these separate meaning systems could only lead to "improper constructs"—including not only languages, but also forms of visual art, as was the case for the powerful Kalighat paintings, with their combination of Eastern and Western forms and themes (Guha-Thakurta 1992). They were especially striking representations of the kinds of intermixings that were taking place in all aspects of Bengali daily life. The blending of traditional popular art forms and satirical commentaries on the Westernized habits of Bengali babus spoke of the intensity of mediations during this period, the shaping of new definitions of artistic taste, and the emergence of truly hybrid forms of expression.

   That the divides of Calcutta would foster a vast enterprise of translation was a given. Commerce and administration, missionary activity, and the rule of law would require translation, and so too would emerging forms of cultural expression. From its earliest days as a city created by the East India Company, Calcutta was marked by structures of mediation—as the *banians* and *dewans* who played a double role as economic and linguistic mediators became the landed property owners of the Black Town. It was not only commerce that required mediators. Calcutta became a world-renowned center of scientific knowledge—and historians of science emphasize the role of 'go-betweens' in the urban practices of "constructing and managing new forms of knowledge—in geography, cartography, history, linguistics and ethnology" (Raj 2009: 106–116).[4]

   But it is in relation to what has come to be called the Bengali Renaissance that the translational culture of colonial Calcutta revealed itself most fully. For Amit Chaudhuri, the rich array of cultural forms produced during this period is an expression of "one of the most profound and creative cross-fertilizations between two different cultures in the modern age" (2001: 3). This long period extending broadly from the 1830s to the end of the nineteenth century saw the flourishing of religious and social thought and a renewal of forms in literature, architecture, and the visual arts. Language interactions nourished every area of scholarly and artistic activity, from poetry and the novel to the theater, press, popular culture, visual arts, religion, philosophy, and social thought—and a series of remarkable individuals marked the emergent Bengali culture through their interactions with English as well as with Sanskrit. This generalized program of exchange made for a culture of translation, where mediation impinged on a wide range of activities, making the translator a polymorphous figure. Though freighted with references to the European early modern period, the Renaissance has become a key element in the Bengali national narrative, setting words afloat in a stream heading for a final home in Bengali. This narrative defines the history of the city as the progressive reclaiming of divided territory.

Traffic from one side of the physical and conceptual spaces of Calcutta to the other was not a simple transference of terms, not the re-expression in another language of preexisting ideas and styles, but a process that saw the emergence of new forms of expression in Bengali thought. The encounter between White and Black sides of town quickly became a process of inter-traffic and transformation, involving interaction across languages and temporalities, between contemporary English and Bengali cultural forms, but also with preexisting Indian practices and with Sanskrit. The imperfectly divided city was the theater of an intense exchange of ideas and artistic forms.

The long period of intense interaction called the Bengali Renaissance indeed strains all definitions of what translation can be, and makes translation a privileged point of entry into the cultural life of colonial Calcutta. The duality turns out to be both powerful and deceptive, at every turn interrupted by third terms that complicate the pattern of domination and exchange. And indeed entire libraries of scholarship have been devoted to deciphering and evaluating the 'new meanings' introduced by translation during the period of Indian history known as the Bengali Renaissance. Almost from the moment of its introduction, the very term 'Renaissance,' though continuing to be solidly entrenched in usage to this day, has been criticized. The provenance of the word offers a clue: Why name a Bengali movement in terms that define it as an extension of European history? Why confine the turbulence of colonial history to a reproduction of the patterns predefined by the colonizers? What kind of assumptions does the term bring with it, and do these inevitably shape understanding of the movements it names? While its use in non-Western contexts, whether it be China or Turkey or India, brings with it suspicions of buying into a worldview that is exclusively Western, the debates such usage have nourished are revealing of the cultural crises underlying these moments—and in particular of the different functions that translation is called on to play. While some elements of these crises are common, others betray differences as substantial as the geography of the cities where they occurred—the dusty divides of Calcutta or the watery peninsulas of Istanbul. Whose interests were served by the social and intellectual exchanges of nineteenth-century Bengal, and who dictated their terms? What makes these practices and forms of material culture of enduring interest is not only their intrinsic value as hybrid objects, but the debates that were waged around them, the struggles over the *values* ascribed to these interactions and their results. In a history dominated by the final goal of independence, nationalism, and Bengali cultural pride, the interaction with British ideas is variously coded as opportunistic and retrograde or strategic and progressive—the debate dominated by vocabulary opposing imitation and authenticity, subjugation and power, servility and nationalism, tradition and Westernization. Translation becomes a modernizing agent, a stimulant in the production of new cultural forms, most notably through the ennobling of the vernacular as emergent national language. The enormous symbolic weight of this period and its cultural significance is evident in the fact that these controversies continue into the present—as the ideals of Bengali nationalism are themselves now critiqued in the light of postindependence politics—and the Renaissance continually reexamined for clues it can reveal about the present. These debates are at the very heart of postcolonial theory today—for instance, in the work of Partha Chatterjee or Dipesh Charkraborty—and the transactions across colonial Calcutta continue to drive the terms of discussion.

From Calcutta to Montreal

The nature and meaning of transactions across Montreal are similarly the object of lively debate—though the elements of discussion are different. Montreal has had no intracity movement comparable to the Bengali Renaissance—which was in fact a civilizational, cross-continental encounter of global import. While translation has also been a definitional and enduring aspect of Montreal cultural life, it has resulted in distinctive patterns and effects. The dialogue between French and English, entering into conversation today with the many diasporic languages that also participate in city life, has taken on various tonalities—though perhaps the most prevalent has been a kind of 'distancing': translation that accentuates the gaps between communities as it draws attention to the necessity of contact. Much of the modern history of Montreal has been one of resistance to translation, as the emergent national language seeks to establish its autonomy and ability to filter out undesired influences.

How was Montreal colonial, how is Montreal postcolonial—and how do relations across languages confirm or confuse these labels? First occupied by First Nations peoples and successively established as the French settlement of Ville-Marie from 1642 to 1763, then as the British city of Montreal from 1763 to 1867, the city grew as a divided space, with the English-language population occupying areas to the west of the Boulevard Saint-Laurent and the French-language population living in areas east. The spatial division of Montreal long sustained a regime of social exclusion, similar to that which prevailed in classic British and French colonial cities—yet different in two important ways: not only was the 'Indigenous' population of Montreal neither racially defined nor the object of segregation policies; it was itself the remnant of a former colonial occupier. What then is the meaning of postcolonial in Montreal?

It is useful to consider first the assertion by R. Home that "all cities are in a way colonial":

> They are created through the exercise of dominance by some groups over others, to extract agricultural surplus, provide services and exercise political control. Transport improvements then allow one society or state to incorporate other territory and peoples overseas. The city thus becomes an instrument of colonization and (in the case of the European overseas empires) racial dominance. (Home 1997: 2)

Language competition in cities is often a remnant of colonial, proto-colonial, or proto-imperial dynamics. And in this sense, one could indeed make a case for the internal colonialism of many cities—such as the cities of the Habsburg Empire, for instance, with the domination of German, or cities of the Soviet Empire, or the very complex relations between Spanish and Catalan in Barcelona (which one is the colonizing language?). How does the paradigm of the colonial serve as a medium of self-understanding for the city?

In the case of Montreal, the best way to answer this question is to examine the moment at which Montreal adopted the vocabulary of colonialism as a framework for self-understanding. It was during the 1960s, as Sean Mills (2010) shows in his lively study of the period, that Montreal was informed by powerful currents of thought from the colonial world—and defined itself in colonial terms. Mills recalls the dramatic influence of Frantz Fanon among Montreal intellectuals; his powerful critique of colonialism became a model for imagining Quebec as a colony and Montreal as a classic colonial city. In the 1960s, Francophones were two-thirds of the city's population, yet English remained the language of the city's wealthier neighborhoods. It dominated in the shopping districts of Montreal's downtown, and it was the defining language of Montreal's powerful financial and educational institutions. Montreal's Francophone majority seemed to exist on the edge of the city, an unequal citizenry, though it in fact occupied a vast expanse of city space. The image of Montreal as a colonial city became a familiar one, and poets like Gaston Miron and Paul Chamberland, Gerald Godin, and Micheline Lanctôt made their writing a terrain of resistance.

For Robert Schwartzwald, during this period 'Quebec' was figured as a voiceless, disempowered collectivity of Francophones of French ancestry, one in which others sharing its territory were regarded either as invader-occupiers or, if immigrants of non-Anglo-American descent, their potential pawns in an aggressive campaign of assimilationalist design. In the 1960s and 1970s, these views were condensed through an anti-imperialist lens that focused on Quebec as oppressed and overdue for decolonization (Schwartz-wald 2003: 37). This conception of colonialism became the motor for power-ful literary works (for instance, the 1964 issue of 'parti pris,' *Portrait du colonisé québécois*), but also for Sean Mills the basis for a common struggle across overlapping communities—Quebec nationalists, Black political groups, femi-nists, unions, each with its separate agendas and complicated alliances. Mills deemphasizes the power of language, to the point of translating everything in his own book into English and barely mentioning the linguistic distances among the various communities:

> I argue that in Montreal, individuals, groups, and their ideas crossed linguistic and ethnic boundaries, learning from one another, benefit-ing from each other's analyses, and sometimes even joining together in common cause. Historians of Quebec, and especially those who deal with political ideas, have generally written the history of political and intellectual movements in 'French' or 'English' Montreal as if they oper-ated independently of one another. What I propose is a re-reading of the 1960s through a different lens, asking whether there is, or whether there can be, a common intellectual history for a wide variety of dissident political movement in a multi-cultural city. (Mills 2010: 3)

Mills's quest for a "common intellectual history" in the intensely divided city of the 1960s (a city on the brink of the October Crisis of 1970) is grounded in the common anticolonialist paradigms of political struggle on the ground. It is a portrait of the city that emphasizes crosscurrents, providing a counter-story to the received narrative—which tells the story of the 1960s as a struggle between the emerging Francophone national culture and the conservative Anglophone forces. This account could be contrasted with that of Malcolm Reid in his cult classic, *The Shouting Signpainters* (1972), in which translation plays a strong role and in which the city is depicted as dramatically divided.

Was Quebec a colony or not? Was it oppressed in the same way that Indig-enous peoples were oppressed by European colonial powers? Mills readily acknowledges that the concept of decolonization was not without its major contradictions. How could the descendants of European colonizers claim to be fighting the same battle as the liberation movements of Algeria and Cuba? How could they claim victim status when they in turn were in com-petition with the First Nations communities of Quebec for natural resources, and in fact inflicting on these communities their own form of internal colo-nialism? Yet during a period of intense cultural agitation, the identification of Francophone Montrealers as a colonized underclass was a powerful influ-ence in both political thought and cultural creativity. That the precise nature of this 'English' and the powers that expressed itself through the language were difficult to define was part of the tensions and ambiguities of the period.

'English' could designate the power of the English-Canadian financial elites; it could designate the former colonial rulers, the British, who were still active in certain areas of educational, financial, and cultural life; and it could also refer to the Americans, probably the best candidates for the real imperial power, yet not necessarily recognized as such.[5]

That 'English' should come to mean a protean yet solid locus of opposition defines this period as rife with contradiction. The proto-colonial matrix of transfer in Montreal largely provoked an attitude of resistance. Separate cultural worlds persisted within the space of a single city, resulting in an attitude of defiance, a resistance to translation on the part of Francophones. Cultural nationalism defined itself *against* translation, and so this period did not produce a movement of cross-fertilization. Indeed, the turbulent 1960s could be understood as a period of failed translation. (Simon 2006)

The vexed status of the 'postcolonial paradigm' for Quebec studies as a whole has resurfaced in recent years, with new debates now focusing on the ways in which contemporary postcolonial theory might be applied. Responding to pressure that Quebec studies should 'go postcolonial,' Robert Schwartzwald provides convincing grounds for resisting the models of postcolonial theory, suggesting that the dynamics of transculturalism as they have been developed in Quebec—and particularly in Montreal—can productively challenge postcolonial theory:

> This could include a deepened appreciation for the new circuits of global Francophone migration and the cultural practices to which they give rise; or an appreciation for new ways of living in French as taken up by many for whom French is not a mother tongue; or how a "small nation" (one whose permanence and durability, unlike those "large nations," can never be taken for granted) has alternate models to propose for relations between historic and new minorities and a majority for whom nation remains an important ontological marker. (Schwartzwald 2003)

Schwartzwald's comments provide the basis for rethinking the nature of translation in Montreal. No longer a transaction between two languages representing two language communities, as it was configured—problematically—during the 1960s, translation navigates among a plurality of speaking positions *within* each language. Increasingly inhabited by diasporic identities come to rest in a multilingual and cosmopolitan city, both French and English are losing their ability to function as markers of identity. Montreal today is a Francophone city, where French is the matrix of cultural identity. But French has become a bulky envelope, gathering within it the cultural expressions of its various communities. A half century after the turbulent years of colonial Montreal, the city is now defined by its transculturalism—the circuits of exchange that crisscross the city in increasingly complex patterns.

Today's Kolkata and Montreal, like the postcolonial metropolises of Europe, can no longer be understood through the binaries of a colonial paradigm. It has become clear that there are many variations of the translational city, where language frictions define a fractured civic space—from the cities of the Levant (Beirut, Alexandria, Istanbul) to those of erstwhile Mitteleuropa (Trieste, Czernowitz, Vilnius, Lviv), from the cities of European colonization (Kolkata, Dakar) to regional capitals of multilingual nations (Barcelona, Montreal). As models of plurality, all such cities provide insights into the evolution of today's global cosmopolis, contributing to an understanding of the possibilities of interaction among its increasingly diverse communities.

Notes

1.   See the documentary 'Rivières perdues.' http://www.underthecity.ca/ and htttp://www.lostrivers.com. Accessed August 23, 2013. See Pierre Monette (2012) for the underground rivers of Montreal.
2.   The social division overriding all others, the divide between Europeans and Indians, was given concrete geographical expression: "A straight line, drawn from the Howrah Bridge to the east end of Park Street, divided the city in two bodies of very different character," according to E. Richards, 1914, the engineer appointed by the Calcutta Improvement Trust to draw up a plan for rebuilding Calcutta. North and east of that line was "a city mass that contained the best and worst of Indian residential quarters, and housed the bulk of the population of Calcutta"; to the south and west, arranged along wide roads and around Dalhousie Square, lay "the chief business houses of the British, the sterling banks, the seats of government, public offices and the leading hotels of Calcutta." Although there were areas like the "gray zone" where diverse groups gathered, the distinction between north and south was clearly marked by community and language (Ray 1979: 6).
3.   Carl Nightingale's (2012) recent *Segregation. A Global History of Divided Cities* calls Calcutta and "imperfectly divided city," providing arguments drawn mainly from investigation of a comparative study of real estate transactions in London and Calcutta. "Why did the boundaries of the White Town remain so porous? [. . .] The most important reasons for the growing fuzziness of Calcutta's color line, though, was the influence of Indians themselves within the land market" (Nightingale 2012: 103). "Some even had houses in the White Town. Furiously racist as Calcutta's nonofficial Europeans become, they did not succeed in officially zoning off neighbourhoods for whites only" (108). One of the main contributing factors, Nightingale claims, is the small number of British who actually invested in real estate and therefore would have a financial reason to support segregation as a guarantee of land values. A second reason was the sheer size of the service staff in English households. "London's conquest and division of Calcutta thus did not give the world a model for government-coerced racial zoning. What it did was much more important, though: it set into motion the underlying institutions and ideologies needed for the replication—and the increasingly coercive politics—of white and black town systems across the world" (82).

4. For Raj, Calcutta is an "emblematic instantiation" of the dynamics of knowl-edge mediation. Conceived in 1690 as a contact zone between the English East India Company and its suppliers from north and east India, it became the larg-est clearinghouse of trade in Asia, the second most important city of the Brit-ish Empire in the 1820s, the nerve center of British expansion into the Far East and the Pacific, and a world-renowned center of scientific knowledge (Raj 2009: 112). Amitav Ghosh's novel *The Calcutta Chromosome* (1997) suggests that advances in Western science and medicine were products of the cross-cultural exchanges, translations and mutations of Calcutta.

5. The difficulty of actually naming the oppressor is underlined by Mills, and to me most dramatically encapsulated in the fact that the Front de liberation du Québec in 1970 took as its first hostage a British economic attaché—neither an English-Canadian nor an American. Mills emphasizes the idea that conceptions of Quebec's political colonization by English Canada coexisted with under-standings of Quebec's imperial domination by the United States. These ideas did not necessarily cancel one another out, but contributed to the ambiguity and fluid interpretations of Quebec's colonial situation.

References

Blum, A. (2003) *The Imaginative Structure of the City* (Montreal: McGill-Queen's University Press).

Chambers, I. (1990) *Border Dialogues: Journeys in Postmodernity* (London: Routledge).

Chattopadhyay, S. (2005) *Representing Calcutta. Modernity, Nationalism, and the Colonial Uncanny* (London: Routledge).

Chaudhuri, A. (2001) *The Picador Book of Modern Indian Literature* (London: Picador).

Ghosh, Amitav (1997) *The Calcutta Chromosome*. London, Picador.

Guha-Thakurta, T. (1992) *The Making of a New 'Indian' Art. Artists, Aesthetics and Nationalism in Bengal, c. 1850–1920* (Cambridge: Cambridge University Press).

Harvey, D. (2006) *Spaces of Global Capitalism* (London: Verso).

Home, R. (1997) *Of Planting and Planning. The Making of British Colonial Cities* (London: Chapman and Hall).

Huyssen, A. (ed) (2008) *Other Cities, Other Worlds. Urban Imaginaries in a Globalizing Age* (Durham, NC: Duke University Press).

King, A. D. (2012) 'Postcolonial Cities,' online Elsevier encyclopedia. http://www.elsevierdirect.com/brochures/hugy/SampleContent/Postcolonial-Cities.pdf (accessed November 15, 2012).

Mills, S. (2010) *The Empire Within. Postcolonial Thought and Political Activism in Sixties Montreal* (Montreal: McGill-Queen's University Press).

Monette, P. (2012) *Onon:tà: une histoire naturelle du mont Royal* (Montreal: Boréal).

Morris, J. (1983) *Stones of Empire: The Buildings of the Raj* (Oxford: Oxford University Press).

Nightingale, C. (2012) *Segregation. A Global History of Divided Cities* (Chicago: University of Chicago Press).

Raj, K. (2009) 'Mapping Knowledge. Go-Betweens in Calcutta, 1770–1820' in *The Brokered World. Go-Betweens and Global Intelligence, 1770–1820*, ed. Simon Schaffer; Lissa Roberts; Kapil Raj; James Delbourgo, eds. (Sagamore Beach, MA: Science History Publications), pp. 105–150.

Ray, R. (1979) *Urban Roots of Indian Nationalism. Pressure Groups and Conflicts of Inter-ests in Calcutta City Politics, 1875–1939* (Delhi: Vikas Publishing House).

Reid, M. (1972) *The Shouting Signpainters. A Literary and Political Account of Quebec Revolutionary Nationalism.* (Toronto: McClelland and Stewart).

Resina, J. R. (2008) *Barcelona's Vocation of Modernity. Rise and Decline of an Urban Image* (Stanford, CA: Stanford University Press).

Sassen, S. (1991) *The Global City: New York, London, Tokyo* (Princeton, NJ: Princeton University Press).

Schwartzwald, R. (2003) 'Rush to Judgment? Postcolonial Criticism and Québec' *Québec Studies* 35: 31–44. Canadian Periodicals Index Quarterly (accessed November 15, 2012). http://www.questia.com/library/1G1–110220165/rush-to-judgment-postcolonial-criticism-and-quebec

Sennett, R. (2005) 'Civility,' *Urban Age.* http://www.urban-age.net/0_downloads/. . ./ Richard_Sennett-Civility-Bulletin1.pdf (accessed November 15, 2012).

Simon, S. (2006) *Translating Montreal: Episodes in the Life of a Divided City* (Montreal: McGill-Queen's University Press).

Simon, S. (2012) *Cities in Translation. Intersections of Language and Memory* (London & New York: Routledge).

Soja, E. W. (2000) *Postmetropolis: Critical Studies of Cities and Regions* (Malden, MA: Blackwell).

Straw, W., and Boutros, A. (2010) *Circulation and the City: Essays on Urban Culture* (Montreal: McGill-Queen's University Press).

7 Elli, Lella, Elengou
A Vernacular Poetics for the Mediterranean

Stephanos Stephanides

In memory of Niki Marangou (1948–2013).
Great poet. Great friend.

> *Why not see Helen as the sun saw her, with no Homeric shadow.*
> —Derek Walcott, *Omeros* (1990)

It is not unusual for writers in the Caribbean to explore their *poesis* and cultural imaginary in relation to the Mediterranean. Indeed, the Caribbean is sometimes referred to as a New World Mediterranean, and, for example, Glissant has developed his "poetics of relation" by putting the two seas in counterpoint. Translating the cultural geography of the Caribbean against the Mediterranean, which he claims: "is an inner sea surrounded by lands, a sea that concentrates (in Greek, Hebrew, and Latin antiquity and later with the emergence of Islam, imposing the thought of the One), the Caribbean is, in contrast, a sea that explodes the scattered lands into an arc. A sea that diffracts" (Glissant 1997: 33).

This fragmentation is also the process of differentiation in translation and Creole language practice. Glissant points out that in Martinique he has observed more than a dozen Creole translations of the French bumper sticker 'ne roulez pas trop près,' revealing a cultural instinct to constantly defer and differ through translation. He comments that the car owners exhibit an "inability to settle a common way of writing; subversion of the original meaning; opposition to an order originating elsewhere" (1989: 163–165). Glissant's statement may be questionable in that it appears to create an easy dichotomy between the dispersal of the Caribbean and the containment of the Mediterranean, by ignoring the diversity of the peoples that have occupied and shaped the Mediterranean. Nonetheless, there is some truth in Glissant's statement, if we consider that the symbolic power of the cities and monuments of the Mediterranean, Jerusalem, and Alexandria, Hagia Sophia and the Alhambra, the Parthenon and the Coliseum, often overshadow the cross-cultural processes involved in the production of the seas diverse cultures. Glissant's poetics of relation may prompt us to seek out the cross-cultural poetics of the Middle Sea in its osmotic moments of creolization or syncretism. Here it might be worth remembering that the word syncretism has a Greek etymology in *Syn + Cretan* (signifying federation of different groups of Cretans), and according to the *Oxford English Dictionary* was first used by Plutarch to describe an alliance of Cretans who reconcile their differences to defend themselves against a common enemy. In addition, let us recall that the Mediterranean is not completely enclosed, since the straits of Gibraltar, aka the Pillars of Hercules, provide a sea route and exit into the Atlantic, and in the tradition of narratives known as "the second odyssey," Odysseus not wanting to be contained eternally on his island of Ithake, sets out once more to discover unknown worlds "beyond Hesperia" and beyond the pillars of Hercules. Odysseus's Atlantic journey is alluded to by Walcott—as he delves back into transoceanic memory and the supposed etymology of the name of Lisbon: "swifts, launched from the nesting sills of UIlissiboa, / their cries modulated to 'Lisbon' as the Mediterranean / ages into the white Atlantic, their flight, in reverse" (Walcott 1990: 189). In the fantastic liminalities of the seas, Walcott probes the culture's and subject's ability to forget, confront, scrutinize, judge, connect, evaluate, and select in the interplay. He speaks to the multiple constituencies and sensibilities of a world readership while speaking of his own regional culture and his island, "the Helen of the Antilles," both resisting and celebrating the burden of representation as is apparent in the epigraph to this chapter. He asks: "Why not see Helen / as the sun saw her with no Homeric shadow" (Walcott 1990: 271) in a quest for an illuminating moment of originary vision while caught in the *aporia* of whether to metaphor or not to metaphor: "When would it stop, / the echo in the throat, insisting, 'Omeros'; when would I enter that light beyond metaphor?" (271). This tension between the vernacular world and the cosmopolitan imagination is also articulated in the movement of translation along the continuum of Creole-language practice intertwining English verses with French-based and English-based Creoles, as we find in the poem 'Saint Lucie' from *Sea Grapes*: "moi c'est gens Ste Lucie / C'est la moi sorti; / is there that I born" (Walcott 1986: 314).

In his posthumously published text, *Memory and the Mediterranean*, Braudel motions to a beginning before the beginning of human history to intimate our destiny as historical beings, and he refers to the Mediterranean as an ancient scar on the terrestrial globe. He states:

> if the Mediterranean seems so alive, so eternally young in our eyes, "always ready and willing," what point is there in recalling this sea's great age? What does it matter, the traveller may think, what can it possibly matter, that the Mediterranean, an insignificant breach in the earth's crust, narrow enough to be crossed at contemptuous speed in an aeroplane (an hour from Marseille to Algiers, fifteen minutes from Palermo to Tunis, and the rest to match) is an ancient feature of the geology of

the globe? Should we care that the Inland Sea is immeasurably older than the oldest of the human histories it has cradled? Yes, we should: the sea can only be fully understood if we view it in the long perspective of its geological history. To this it owes its shape, its architecture, the basic realities of its life, whether we are thinking of yesterday, today or tomorrow. So let us look at the record. (2001: 3)

He poetically evokes an originary vision of the sea, invoking a memory that takes you into the realm before and beyond human history in a move that will renew the now. Benjamin has particularly shed light on the transmission of cultural memory as he attributes to the translator the possibility of retrieving from one language into another an unknown or forgotten literary idiom and suggests a relationship between story/history and translatability where translatability is glossed as story/history waiting to be passed on. In 'The Storyteller' Benjamin refers to memory as the epic faculty *par excellence* (1968: 97). Epic memory seems like an effort of memory to exceed a neutralizing 'global' culture through its invocation of over-worlds and underworlds. Likewise, in the Antillean epic, Walcott seems to suggest a translation where the original language dissolves and is remade and therefore remembered through a shipwreck of fragments. That is the basis of the Antillean experience (he affirms in his Nobel lecture), this shipment of fragments, these echoes, these shards of a huge tribal vocabulary, these partially remembered customs. They are not decayed, but strong. This effort of memory "wider than the limits made by the map of an island, is the illimitable sea and what it remembers," he tells us in an illuminatory moment as he watches the Ramleela festival in Trinidad, which involves a dramatic enactment of the Hindu epic *The Ramayana*. He reflects that he was polluting the event with doubt and a loss of degenerative mimicry, when all around him was conviction and delight—not loss (Walcott 1992).

In what follows, I will consider the literary landscape of Cyprus as similarly constituted of a multiplicity of linguistic, historic, and cultural fragments. The island of Cyprus has been shaped by a hopelessly complex multicultural history, division, and by a geographical position that has long ambiguated the geopolitical borders of 'Europe,' 'Asia,' and 'the Middle East.' Any discussion of translation, literature, history, and culture in this zone of indeterminate encounter between heterogeneous cultures and populations is intriguing. The literature of Cyprus has been shaped across a spectrum of languages and transcultural relations that may range from confrontation, indifference, or mutual exclusion to creative engagement, depending on the social and cultural processes and historical moments. If I begin with the island of my birth, it is both because I can speak from a position where I am written and from which I write, where I am translated and from which I translate, and because like many writers I am fascinated by island spaces as metonymy of a world. Fernand Braudel observes that islands are subjected to historical pressures that push them at once 'far ahead and far behind [. . .] general history,' dividing them, 'often brutally, between the two opposite poles of archaism and innovation' (1973: 150). This seems to also suggest a situation of not knowing which time one is in, like Bloch's famous concept of *Ungleichzeitigkeit* (temporal incommensurability). Time compressed into space, and the spatialization of the temporal in an island territory, brings dissimilarities next to each other, but also a mode of noncomprehension or charged speechlessness in need of translations that opens up for revision what may have been denied or may seem obsolete. A layered imaginative geography, in other words, governs the cultural differences related to cultural contests and national or ethnic divisions.

Translation, like writing, may serve to replenish the layered intertextual and interlingual resources of a culture—de-territorializing one terrain to map another. Deleuze and Guattari (1986) have used a tetra-lingual model for the spatiotemporal categories: vernacular (here), vehicular (everywhere), referential (over there), and mythical (beyond), which they use to develop the concept of 'minor literature' in terms of territorialization, de-territorialization, and reterritorialization. The distribution of the four functions of language and their interplay will change through time and among different groups and communities, and this interplay is more salient within the cramped space of an island. For example, in the context of Cyprus, languages of territorialization would be Cypriot Greek and Cypriot Turkish, the rural and maternal languages; the language of the island's various colonizers would have been vehicular and de-territorializing, languages of the 'world' that are found 'everywhere,' such as French and English. The referential and reterritorializing languages of sense and culture in the postcolonial nation-state would be Modern Greek and Modern Turkish. Also reterritorializing are the mythic languages of the past, of spirituality and religion, such as Classical and Byzantine Greek, Ottoman Turkish. Translation redistributes these functions of language, shifts their centers of power and blurs their borders. For Deleuze and Guattari, a 'minor literature' is written in a major language affected by a high degree of deterritorialization. It is literature written in a major language but from a minoritarian or marginalized perspective, such as Kafka writing in German or writers in former colonies writing in the 'langue' of the colonizers. Kafka speaks of the predicament of this condition in a letter to Max Brod of June 1921: the impossibility of not writing, the impossibility of writing in German, the impossibility of writing otherwise, and the impossibility of writing (Casanova 1999: 347, 370). A writer in a minor literature is a stranger in the language in which she [or he] writes, making other voices vibrate within. As a writer in English in Cyprus and a translator into English, I have been involved in the process of 'becoming-minor.' I will return to this idea and focus on English and literary transculturation in Cyprus in the twentieth and twenty-first centuries, but I will first provide a brief historical perspective of language relation and exchange on the island through its long history.

Language relations on the island have been marked by inequalities that have arisen because of conquest, colonialism, or changing demographics impinging on a preexisting state. Many languages have been used on the island throughout its history. The Bronze Age Cypriots spoke a language whose script has not been deciphered and may be related to the language of Minoan Crete. Greeks and Phoenicians arrived on the island around the beginning of the first millennium BC and brought their languages with them. The languages of other rulers of antiquity—Assyrians, Egyptians, and Persians—are hardly documented. During the Hellenic and Roman period, there was a large Jewish community on the island that became Greek-speaking. With the division of the Roman Empire, Cyprus became part of the Byzantine Empire until 1191, when it was conquered by the crusader Richard the Lionheart, who sold it to the Knights Templar, who in turn sold it to Guy de Lusignan in 1192. The ensuing French period on the island lasted three centuries. French became the language of the court and the ruling class, while Catholicism became the official religion and Latin the language of the clergy. The Indigenous population retained the Cypriot dialect form of Greek, and the legislation of the Kingdom of Cyprus was written in Cypriot Greek as was the well-known chronicle of Leontios Makhairas during the same period, which was translated into English by Richard Dawkins in 1932 as *Recital Concerning the Sweet Land of Cyprus entitled 'Chronicle'—The Chronicle of Makhairas*. Also in the medieval period, Italian dialects were used for trade in the coastal towns where some Italians settled. The Venetian economic presence became especially strong, and eventually the Venetians took control of the island in 1489. During this period some sonnets were written in the Cypriot dialect after the Petrarchan tradition, although some argue that these may well be translations from the Italian. The Venetians ruled the island until it was conquered by the Ottomans in 1571. With a weakening Ottoman Empire, the island became a British protectorate in 1878 still under Ottoman Rule, and was annexed by Britain at the outbreak of World War I when the Ottomans sided with Germany. It eventually became a Crown Colony in 1925.

One may find a kaleidoscopic perspective of this cultural history by navigating Cobham's *Excerpta Cypriana (1908)*—an anthology of translated writing on Cyprus compiled by the British commissioner of Larnaca and published in 1908. Including excerpts translated from various languages into English from ancient times up to the Ottoman period and evoking the gaze of travelers, settlers, Cypriots, and conquerors, the anthology evokes the cross-cultural gaze on the island through the millennia: Strabo speaks of the temple of Aphrodite, unapproachable and invisible to women; the Spanish Jew, Benjamin of Tudela, speaks of the heretic Cyprian Jews, Epicureans who profane the Sabbath and keep holy Sunday; Neophytus, the twelfth-century hermit, speaks of England, a country beyond Romania out of which a cloud of English came with their sovereign; Capodilista, a fifteenth-century Paduan gentleman, marvels at banana trees with fruits like cucumbers, yellow when ripe and very sweet of savor; and a document of Ottoman law professes tolerance toward Christians.

Colonial Cosmopolitanism in British Cyprus: 1878–1960

During the first decades of British rule, the combination of colonial rule and Cypriot diasporic consciousness yielded a form of colonial cosmopolitanism. It is noteworthy that literary modernity in Cyprus came belatedly, with the advent of British colonialism in the 1880s, the decade that brought the first printing press (a gift from Alexandrian Greeks) and the first newspaper to the island (published in Greek and English). The history of colonialism and print capitalism is crucial in understanding how the nation 'form' has spread and tried to impose periodization and universal schemes of identity in Cyprus as it has elsewhere. The printing press was a catalyst for the production of local literature, translation, and criticism. In his PhD dissertation, Papaleontiou notes that in the period 1880–1930, which coincides approximately with the first half century of British rule, more than nine hundred texts by about four hundred writers were translated by 150 *literati* for local consumption (1997: 274). English education in Cyprus and Cypriots studying in British universities were important catalysts in this literary activity. In addition, there was a Cypriot diaspora in Egypt, Asia Minor, and the Levant that engaged with Eastern languages and cultures. The newly arrived English education and culture, which may have given further impetus to knowledge of the East through British Orientalism, brought about its own kind of crossfertilization and intervention in the home culture, thus marking the island as a cross-cultural gateway between East and West. The translated texts include both European classical and contemporary literature and Eastern literature (mainly Arabic and Persian). Papaleontiou refers to a lecture given in 1917 by Fasouliotis, a former student at the American University of Beirut, who praises the beauty of the twelfth-century Persian poet Nizami, and speaks favorably of the purity of Nizami's spirituality in contrast to the Byzantine Christian monastics (1997: 275). These communities of the East Mediterranean Cypriot diaspora dissolved in the course of the twentieth century for various reasons, notably the Asia Minor disaster of 1922, the Suez crisis of 1956, and civil strife in Lebanon in the 1970s and 1980s. There is, however, little evidence during the British colonial period of Cypriot literature traveling elsewhere through translation. In the 1940s and 1950s, there were some sporadic translations into English, including some poems translated by Lawrence Durrell in *The London Magazine* in 1954.

Colonial cosmopolitan collusions turned into collisions in the 1950s when the anticolonial movement turned into an armed struggle affecting attitudes toward language, culture, identity, and translatability. The friendship of Durrell and Giorgos Seferis, who both made the island their home in the 1950s, is very telling of the new turn. The two writers became friends and translated some of each other's work. They grew apart as each played different roles in the rival claims and disputes among Britain, Greece, and Turkey over the island. Seferis, an Asia Minor Greek, whose family fled Smyrne in 1922, felt a sense of *nostos* (homecoming) when he came to Cyprus in 1953, and his sojourn on the island led to a series of poems. In the poem "Helen," he suggests an analogy between his poetic persona and Teucer, who settled in Cyprus after the Trojan War, and cites Euripides's *Helen* in which Teucer states that Apollo has decreed that Cyprus should be his home. Seferis's poem alludes (as H.D. did in her poem 'Helen in Egypt') to a version of the story of Helen recounted by some ancient authors, including Euripides in his play *Helen*, that Helen never went to Troy but had stayed in Egypt during the Trojan war. Helen herself declares in Euripides's play that at Troy, there was nothing but a phantom image: "At Troy, nothing: just a phantom image [. . .]. And Paris, Paris lay with a shadow as though it were a solid being" (Seferis 1995). Seferis laments the despair of war and the loss of life over an illusion. The illusion of Helen was just a trick of the gods to destroy humanity. In contrast, Durrell, who lived on the island for four years in the 1950s, witnessed the rise of a fervent anticolonial nationalism, which led him to leave in 1956 in fear of his life. Indeed, it was during the 1950s that English, which was first partially introduced in primary schools in 1935, was taken out because of anti-British feeling during the EOKA struggle in 1955–1959.[1] It was reintroduced as part of the official syllabus in 1965–1966. Durrell's book *Bitter Lemons* (1957) is still an important testimony and was a lightning rod for events on the island at the time, prompting criticism of his colonial Orientalist attitudes. In 1964 the eminent Cypriot Greek poet Costas Montis (1914–2004) wrote a novella-chronicle set in the 1950s entitled *Closed Doors*. It was intended, as the author states, as a response to Durrell's book; however, it was not translated into English until 2004. Durrell's book and Seferis's poems have become touchstones for comprehending the tension between colonial leave-taking and an imagined cultural homecoming, which have often sharply delineated the complicated relationship of language, culture, and national identity in the foundation and subsequent fragmentation of the emerging nation-state of Cyprus.

Between Nationalism and Multiculturalism in Postcolonial Cyprus

The separate nationalisms of the two main ethnic communities defined the direction of the anticolonial movement, and after independence in 1960, the two largest ethnic communities pursued incompatible national trajectories, which led to clashes and the effective division of the island between Greek-Cypriot and Turkish-Cypriot communities. In 1974 the northern part of the island was occupied by the Turkish military, which resulted in the forced dislocation of 40 percent of the island's population. The role of nationalism has since been strong in the conservative reterritorialization of both written and oral cultural practices.

In the majority Greek-speaking part of the island, this process may be observed in the construction of a literary canon through state publications and prizes, translations, and anthologies, as well as efforts by organizations such as Cyprus PEN. One PEN publication, Theoklis Kouyialis's *27 Centuries of Cypriot Poetry*, claims a national history that extends across three millennia and emphasizes a Greek lineage from the Kypria Epics of Stasinos (seventh to eighth century BC) to twentieth-century voices. Like other anthologies that deal with contemporary poets and construct the idea of a tradition of Cypriot Hellenism, *27 Centuries of Cypriot Poetry* attempts to illustrate the tenacity of a Eurocentric narrative of unbroken tradition, which narrowly defines cultural frontiers and remains unaware of its own translatability. Although it includes literary gems from Cypriot literature in Greek, it excludes volatile forms of difference, such as those that emerge in the Ottoman period. The Ottoman period is described in the introduction as one of creative sterility, and nothing originally written in Turkish is included. Cypriot literature in Turkish was also developing separately for the most part with the exceptional literary encounters between writers of the two ethnic groups outside Cyprus. It was impossible in the period 1974–2003 to cross the divide unless for exceptional reasons and with special permission. Remarkably, poet and peace activist Neşe Yaşın has lived in south Nicosia since the 1980s and struggled with the difficulties of crossing. She has been widely translated, and her poem in Turkish, 'My Country Has Been Divided in Two, Which Half Should I Love?,' has been made into a song in Greek by musician Marios Tokkas and has become an anthem for peace and reunification. Nearly two decades after Kouyialis's anthology, Neşe's half brother, the poet Mehmet Yaşın, edited *Step-Mothertongue: From Nationalism to Multiculturalism: Literatures of Cyprus, Greece and Turkey* (2000), which includes essays and poetry written in English and in English translation from Greek and Turkish and includes some remarkable examples of premodern Cypriot poetry selected and translated from different languages. *Step-Mothertongue* combines essays and poetry that challenge the traditional categorizations of Cypriot literature and the delimitations of the literary itself by including, for example, Phoenician tomb inscriptions in its poetry selection.

Though nationalist separatisms have claimed center stage in the Cypriot political and cultural mainstream during the last half of the twentieth century, it is worth remembering that the first president of the postcolonial republic, Archbishop Makarios, played a leading role in the Non-Aligned Movement, and that less than half a century later, the republic is a European Union member state as it continues to be a Commonwealth nation. Indeed, the media prominence of nationalist rhetoric often works to disguise and contain the impact of postcolonial migrations on social and cultural change that became all the more visible by the end of the millennium. Developments of the island's economy have attracted people fleeing from the postcommunist debacle of Eastern Europe and the widespread poverty of South and East Asia. It is now estimated that 27 percent of the population on the south of the island is foreign-born. The north, meanwhile, has been importing thousands of impoverished Turkish settlers in response to the depopulation caused by Cypriot Greeks who fled to the southern part of the island to escape the invading Turkish army in 1974. It is now estimated that Turkish settlers outnumber Cypriot Turks.

New Crossings: 2003 to the Present

These radical demographic changes and the partial opening of the checkpoints on April 23, 2003, which allowed north–south crossings for the first time since 1974, opened translators to new potentials or confrontations. At first the crossings were flooded by Cypriots from both sides in search of lost homes and villages. While the sudden unleashing of energy at the surprise opening of the checkpoints has died down and ten years later there is still no political solution for reunification, the ability to cross easily has enabled the fermentation of new relationships and communities across the divide.

The buzz of excitement after the first border-crossings brought together poets who attempted to destabilize established attitudes toward questions of historical knowledge, national allegiance, and cultural affiliation. In one of the first meetings, I met Jenan Selçuk and heard him read his fine poem 'The Date-Palm' in Turkish. I quote an English translation in full:

I am a tree, a date-palm
in some Mesaoria cemetery.
Civilisations buried in my shade,
their bones
my roots.

Forty curly-haired slaves rowed
the boats
which brought us from Egypt.
My grandfather a Hellene wearing an earring
my circumciser a converted Ottoman barber
a pederast.
I was apprenticed
to Aphrodite in spring
Zenon in winter.
You may not have realized!
I was the model for the Lusignan architects.
Inherited from Venetian merchants

this sweet tongue,
chasing pleasure
Roman Byzantium . . .
A creation of the British
my exhibition
of split personality syndromes.
From time to time
my presumption that I am a human being,
the more I am licked
the more I hold onto lies.
Paranoias
Stitched of flag cloth, a straitjacket
made in Greece
made in Turkey:
I see war when I look in the water!
    (Selçuk; translated from Turkish by Aydın Mehmet Ali with the
    poet 2009)

Date-palms, beautiful and elegant, are scattered around the landscape some-times in groves and sometimes solitary, often recalling those who returned from a *hajj* and planted one in commemoration of their pilgrimage; thus it is the tree of both homecoming and the boon that graced the vision brought home from the pilgrimage. Selçuk's 'Date-Palm' is nurtured in the cemetery, seeking *nostos* in a temporality of haunting, and its line of flight is constrained and threatened by the violence of the referential national cultures of Greece and Turkey and their symbolic order. I loved the poem, but I was not totally convinced by some details in the translation the poet gave me. A few years later, I asked Cypriot Turkish writer Aydın Mehmet Ali (who uses English as her literary language) to retranslate it so I could include it in a special issue of *91st Meridian*, which I had been invited to guest edit. One of the words that troubled me in the earlier translation published in the first issue of *Cadences* was the word 'fold-up' to describe the 'Ottoman barber.' I suspected it was a clumsy translation rather than a daring metaphor and it was revealing to discover, instead of 'fold-up,' the phrase 'a boy kidnapped by the Janissar-ies' as Mehmet Ali's translation for the original Turkish word *devşirme*. The Janissaries were infantry that served as bodyguards to the Ottoman sultan and his household. *Devşirme* refers to the system of recruiting children, usu-ally Balkan Christians, often Greeks, to serve in the Janissaries. The recruits were selected and kidnapped, received military training, and indoctrinated in the religion of Islam. The brightest ones rose to hold distinguished and sometimes powerful positions in the Ottoman Empire. While recruitment was by way of abduction, some families were happy for their children to be recruited as they received a secure future with a salary and a pension when they retired. *Devşirme* has a semantic overlap in its root with the concept of conversion, not only of people, but also of objects, such as chairs, and this is why the word 'fold-up' came up as a misleading dictionary option in the first translation. The translation above was included in *91st Meridian*, but the poet made additional revisions. He used the phrase 'converted Ottoman barber,' and totally omitted the line about the Janissaries. He wanted a minimalist poetic solution and was not happy to have an additional line to explain one word. Regrettably, in my view, because the detail of *devşirme* particularizes the 'conversion' into a local historical context and charges the affective body and the imaginary of the poem. Many conversions, inversions, and reversions take place in a multicultural society as they do in translation, and they are articulated in the tropes and turns that are taken along the path of 'crossing over' in translation. When I read Mehmet Ali's translation with reference to the Janissary, I remembered vividly a story I read many years ago by the nineteenth-century Greek writer Georgios Vizyinos called 'The Only Journey of His Life.' Part of the story tells of a young boy whose family dresses him as a girl to avoid abduction by the Janissaries and he assumes his male identity once again when he reaches puberty and marries.

Movement across languages through the places and spaces of the island is often marked by the kind of intensity that comes from both shared and contested references and histories, and processes of naming and renaming. Niki Marangou maps out the territory in an apparently detached way that allows the tensions and connections to emerge in the disjunctions among layers of names, images, and historical and social details. This is most evident in her poem 'Street Map of Nicosia' (1981: 99):

> Looking at the street map
> of Nicosia and its suburbs
> Fuat Paşa Street ends on Dionysou and Herakleitou
> Defne Yüksel on Hermes Street
> Yenice Şafak on Leontiou Makhaira.
> in the vicinity of Flatro Bastion
> on old maps the river cut through the town
> but Savorniano, the Venetian, changed the flow
> to fill the moat with water.
> There on Sundays the domestic servants
> from Sri Lanka spread out their shawls
> and eat together.
> The palm trees remind them of home.
> (Translated from the Greek by Xenia Andreou and Stephanos Stephanides)

In translating the above lines, one becomes involved in choices of transliteration, so that translation, and walking through the streets of Nicosia with Marangou, becomes a 'nomadism of intensities' (to borrow a term from Lyotard). The negotiation involved for the translator pulled in multiple directions among territorialization, reterritorialization, and de-territorialization becomes very apparent in the transliteration of place-names. Transliterations often involve sites of habitus-governed translational strategies. For example, this also occurred in Turkey, where there were Turkish-speaking Greek communities (*Karamanlides*) who wrote Turkish with Greek letters, and Greek-speaking communities who wrote Greek using the Turkish alphabet. An earlier draft of the translation of Marangou's poems into English transliterated the Turkish street names from the Greek script in which they were written in the original poem. The effect on the ear was that of a speaker of standard Modern Greek pronouncing Turkish names without the sounds of the diacritics and without the palatalization. For example, Yenice Şafak was written Yenidze Safak—if the transliteration wanted to help the English speaker pronounce it, it should read Yenije Shafak. The palatalized fricatives are not found in the phonetic system of standard Greek although they are found in Cypriot Greek vernacular speech. Similarly *paşa* is pronounced 'pasha' by Turks and Cypriots alike (whether Greek or Turkish speakers), but the standard Greek would read the 'sh' as an 's.' Paradoxically, a Cypriot Greek would more closely approximate the Turkish pronunciation by reading the English spelling. I suggested leaving the names in the poem as they are on the actual street signs and allowing them to enter their own process of signification. The reader will confront the names in variable ways each with their own socio-ethnic linguistic and stylistic habitus, their mythic and historical memory. Like the translator, the walker in the city and reader will react differently when confronted with the street signs, depending on where their subjectivity is situated in the interplay of sign, sound, and name. The names themselves function as signifiers that test the boundaries of the mythic past that constructs our cultural memory and the erasures that have taken place. I was familiar with the Greek names taken from classical antiquity, and with the name of the Cypriot medieval chronicler Makhairas. I wondered about the Turkish names. I also wondered about the fact that the Greek names are written only in Roman letters in the poem, whereas on street signs they would be in both Greek and Roman script. I discussed the Turkish street names with two of my Turkish-Cypriot writer friends who did not know the names but assumed the names belonged to the Ottoman past. We also recalled in our discussion that the Roman script for writing Turkish dates back only to Ataturk, so if Fuat Paşa Street, for example, is named after an Ottoman vizier, he would have written his name in Arabic script at the time. The change of script is another kind of erasure or a deliberate turn of direction from past ideology and culture as the Republic of Turkey distinguished itself from its Ottoman past by adopting another set of values and epistemology and another alphabet and language revolution that attempted to exclude words of Arabic and Sufi origin. This complex cultural politics has been scrutinized in the narrative explorations of Orhan Pamuk and Elif Şafak.

Deracination and Relocation

Both poems discussed embodied narratives of deracination and relocation taking sudden and unexpected turns. This is the experience of many people of the island who are internally displaced if not migrants, and whose narratives are translated into the post-memory of their children. It is in this unstable subjectivity that the *poesis* of the island lies. My own deracination from the island of my birth took place at the age of eight when my father suddenly took me to the UK and this marked a sudden rupture with my vernacular Cypriot Greek mother tongue and exile into English, which I was quickly forced to learn. In my twenties, I had traveled and lived in the Mediterranean, hoping to resettle on the island, but the war of 1974 and subsequent partition left me asking, like Seferis in 'Helen': "Where is this island? Who knows it?" (Seferis 1995). In 1978, I ventured on my own second Odyssey, beyond Hesperia, settled in Guyana until the mid-1980s, then moved on to the United States until 1991, when I relocated to Cyprus. It was a meaningful and unexpected coincidence to find in a local bookshop Derek Walcott's (then newly published) *Omeros*, just a few months before he won the Nobel Prize. No doubt it was Homer and Helen that had brought his book to this island in the middle of the Levantine sea, and I was eager to read it and discover what fruit "all that Greek manure under the green bananas" (Walcott 1990: 271) had yielded. What reflexive possibilities of imagined forms of communities would this conjure up for me? I revisited Seferis and read 'Helen,' and found in the lines "Blind voice, you who grope in the darkness of memory/for footsteps and gestures" (Seferis 1995) the radical indeterminacy of the last line of Aimé Césaire's *Cahier d'un retour au pays natal* (originally published in 1939): "c'est là que je veux pêcher maintenant la langue maléfique de la nuit en son immobile verrition!" (Césaire 1983a: 65).[2] In rereading Seferis in the context of these lines, Helen is as elusive as she is ungraspable as is the poet's impossible desire for *nostos* (homecoming) and for cosmopolitanism: "I've lived my life hearing names I've never heard before" (Seferis 1995). It is with this critical collusion of homecoming and cosmopolitanism that I reentered the island, scanning the spectral voices of other Helens/Elenis of my imagination whose name resonated in multiple forms in the archipelago of the Cypriot Greek vernacular: Lella, Lenia, Elli, Ellou, Elenitsa, Elengou. Where did they travel, and what did they bring home? Elengou, my paternal grandmother, told me stories of Saint Helen, or Eleni of Constantinople, mother of Emperor Constantine, who brought cats to the island from Egypt to chase away the snakes and brought Holy Basil from India to keep away evil spirits. Lella, my maternal aunt, came for a short while to Guyana to share in my second Odyssey and stopped to visit the Helen of the Antilles on her return journey. And then there were all the other voices of those who were not Eleni, and who also passed on to me the affective weight of their vernacular tongue calling for translatability.

As a Cypriot writing in English, I find myself always in the tensions and ambivalences on the edges of different languages. For example, the word I hear for a feeling and image may come to me in the vernacular Cypriot Greek as my grandmother would have said the word. In my poem 'Find Peace,' I was caught between using a word like 'epsimo' or 'pekmez' and eventually settled for 'grape molasses' in the lines that follow:

> And then glimpse at your kith
> Far and away now
> Damascene plums on rooftop terraces
> Skins charred shielding their flesh of gold
> Taste their blood
> Thick like grape molasses. (Stephanides 2010: 15)

I became caught between intensifying the meaning by stripping it from the sound of the signifier or allowing the intensity to draw on the vernacular word and territorialize it in the rural grape culture and the sound of my grandmother's tongue speaking of grape must and molasses vibrating within English. When the poem was published, I chose the word 'grape molasses.' In a multilingual translation and poetry workshop, when the poem was translated into Greek, Niki Marangou eventually came up with 'epsimo,' whereas the first thought that came in dialogue with other participants was the standard Greek word to designate the same. I preferred the affective shift toward the territory of the maternal local rural past and wondered if I had made the right choice in the English original and might change it for a future publication. In translation, the pull between deterritorialization and reterritorialization remains, but within a different set of relations and effects.

Conclusion

Translation in Cyprus has multiple entry points and demands negotiation for a way through a labyrinthine path to find a line of flight. The movement of translation inscribes an assemblage of relations in their affective becoming and maps the passage of de-territorialization as seen in the two poems translated from Turkish and Greek previously discussed. This quest for a line of flight is articulated in one of Andriana Ierodiaconou's poems, 'Journey': "Swallows fly to green days directly, without hesitation / we have been walking for years now and the sea has forgotten us and become a word" (Ierodiaconou 1994–1995: 811; translated from the Greek by the poet). The flight in minoritarian literature becomes an experimental literary process, testing limits and boundaries, deviating in different directions, exploring the territory for a way to the sea or the unexpected *nostos* at the end of the above Marangou poem, when after roaming the streets of Nicosia, we find our way to the moat with the Sri Lankan servants eating among the palm trees. The palm tree's signification is opened to another kind of homecoming and a new narrative and journey of migration through its association with palm trees on another faraway island.

A new generation has grown up since partition, and few Cypriot Greeks or Cypriot Turks speak each other's language, so they rely on English as a *lingua franca* and as a language for mediation in translation. Many poets double as translators and translate each other's work mostly through the mediation of English, spawning an experimental literary dialogue and literary transculturation. This collaboration has recently resulted in the publication of two translated anthologies in 2010. One of Cypriot Greek poets in Turkish, selected and translated by poet Gurgenç Korkmazel (and sometimes using older existing translations), and one of Cypriot Turkish poets, selected and translated into Greek by poet Giorgos Moleskis. Some important new initiatives since 2003, such as the journal *Cadences*, have activated the potential of earlier, pre-nationalist forms of cultural cosmopolitanism by bringing together Cypriot writing in English, Greek, and Turkish in the original and/or in the translation, and thus provide an alternative perspective and promise of what Cypriot literature might be by setting off different tongues against each other in cross-cultural poetics. The literature is experimental because we are uncertain of the new intratextual relations it will lead us to as it de-codifies perspectives that are not of the established literary culture. In Cyprus, English as a language of literary translation and cultural mediation is complicit with Cypriot English becoming a 'minor literature,' in Deleuzian terms, because it has to confront disjunctions of content and expression. Minoritarian poems in majoritarian languages do not express an identity of a minority, but open the potential for another perspective, sensibility, and affective attitude by creating new possibilities of speaking, thinking, and writing in the performance of translation.

Notes

1.   EOKA (Εθνική Οραγάνοσης πρίων Αγωνιστών, Ethniki Organosis Kyprion Agoniston, Greek for National Organization of Cypriot Fighters) was a Greek Cypriot organization that fought for the expulsion of British troops from the island, for self-determination, and for union with Greece.
2.   "I will now fish the malevolent tongue of the night in its motionless veerition!" (Césaire 1983b: 85).

References

Benjamin, W. (1968) 'The Storyteller' in *Illuminations*, ed. H. Arendt. Trans. H. Zohn (New York: Schocken Books), pp. 83–109.
Braudel, F. (1973) *The Mediterranean and the Mediterranean World in the Age of Philip II*, Trans. S. Reynolds (New York: Harper and Row).

Braudel, F. (2001) *Memory and the Mediterranean*. Trans. S. Reynolds (New York: Knopf).

Casanova, P. (1999) *La république mondiale des lettres* (Paris: Seuil).

Césaire, A. (1983a) *Cahier d'un retour au pays natal* (Paris: Présence Africaine).

Césaire, A. (1983b) *The Collected Poetry*. Trans. C. Eshleman and A. Smith (Berkeley: University of California Press).

Cobham, C. D. (1908) *Excerpta Cypriana* (Nicosia: The Library).

Dawkins, R. (1932) *Recital Concerning the Sweet Land of Cyprus Entitled 'Chronicle'— The Chronicle of Makhairas* (Oxford: Clarendon Press).

Deleuze, G., and Guattari, F. (1986) *Kafka: Toward a Minor Literature* (Minneapolis: University of Minnesota Press).

Durrell, L. (1957) *Bitter Lemons* (London: Faber and Faber).

Glissant, E. (1989) *Caribbean Discourse. Selected Essays*. Trans. J. Michael Dash (Charlottesville: University Press of Virginia).

————. (1997) *Poetics of Relation*. Trans. B. Wing (Ann Arbor: University of Michigan Press).

Ierodiaconou, A. (1994–1995) 'Journey' in 'Three Cypriot Women Poets,' Selected Poems introduced by S. Stephanides, in *Modern Greek Studies Yearbook, Vol. 10–11* (Minneapolis: University of Minnesota Press), pp. 795–835.

Korkmazel, G. (2010) *Kıbrıslırum Şiir Antolojisi* (Istanbul: Paloma).

Kouyialis, T. (ed) (1983) *27 Centuries of Cypriot Poetry* (Nicosia: PEN).

Marangou, N. (2008) 'Street Map of Nicosia' *Cadences: A Journal of Literature and the Arts in Cyprus* 4: 99.

Μολέσκης [Moleskis], Γ. [G.] (2010) *Σύγχρονοι Τουρκοκύπριοι ποιητές: Απόπειρα επικοινωνίας [Contemporary Turkish Cypriot Poets: Attempted Contacts]* (Αθήνα [Athens]: Εκδόσεις Τόπος [Topos]).

Montis, C. (2004) *Closed Doors: An Answer to Bitter Lemons by Lawrence Durrell*. Trans. D. Roessel and S. G. Stavrou (Minneapolis: University of Minnesota Press).

Παπαλεοντίου [Papaleontiou], Λ. [L.] (1997) *Τα πρώτα βήματα της κυπριακής λογοτεχνικής κριτικής (1880–1930) [The First Steps of Cypriot Literary Criticism]* (Λευκωσία [Nicosia]: Πολιτιστικές Υπηρεσίες Υπουργείου Παιδείας και Πολιτισμού [Cultural Services of the Ministry of Education and Culture]).

Seferis, G. (1995) 'Helen' in *Collected Poems*, trans. E. Keeley and P. Sherrard (Princeton, NJ: Princeton University Press). http://www.poetryfoundation.org/poem/181856 (accessed May 17, 2013).

Selçuk, J. (2009) 'The Date-Palm' in *91st Meridian, Excerpta Cypriana*, ed. S. Stephanides, International Writing Program, University of Iowa, 6.3. http://iwp.uiowa.edu/91st/vol6–num3/two-poems-selcuk (accessed May 17, 2013).

Stephanides, S. (2010) 'Find Peace' *Cadences: A Journal of Literature and the Arts in Cyprus* 6: 15.

Βιζυηνός, [Vizyinos,] Γ. [G.] (1991) «Το Μόνον Της Ζωής Του Ταξείδιον», [The Only Journey of His Life] *Νεοελληνικά διηγήματα, [Modern Greek Short Stories]*, επιμ. Παναγιώτης Μουλλάς [ed. Panayiotis Moullas]. (Αθήνα,[Athens]: Ερμής [Hermes]), σελ.168–201. [pp.168–201.]

Walcott, D. (1986) *Collected Poems. 1948–1984* (New York: Farrar, Strauss, and Giroux).

Walcott, D. (1990) *Omeros* (London: Faber and Faber).

Walcott, D. (1992) 'The Antilles: Fragments of Epic Memory,' Nobel lecture, December 7. http://www.nobel.se/literature/laureates/1992/walcott-lecture.html (accessed May 17, 2013).

Yaşın, M. (ed) (2000) *Step-Mothertongue: From Nationalism to Multiculturalism: Literatures of Cyprus, Greece and Turkey* (London: Middlesex University Press).

8 The Politics of Language Choice in the 'English-Language' Theater of Malaysia

Susan Philip

Malaysia's complex multicultural, multiracial background has left it with a plethora of linguistic choices open to the individual. Currently, many Malaysians are fluent in the national language (*Bahasa Malaysia* or Malay), can function in English, and often speak one other language as well (their 'mother tongue'). However, despite this seemingly unproblematic multilingualism, language choice remains a highly politicized and even emotive point. Language and culture are interlinked in a variety of complex ways that severely complicate issues of national identity, ethnic identity, and the sense of belonging within and ownership of the nation. Individuals who raise questions about the national language policy and language use can be confronted with accusations of intolerance and lack of loyalty; they may even be accused of threatening or undermining the position of the Malay language and thus of the Malays themselves. At the same time that Malay is pushed as the national language, the various languages available to Malaysians are treated as the private reserves of specific ethnic groups. This makes the position of Malay a little ambiguous—it is the national language but, just as Tamil is seen as the language of Malaysian Indians or the Chinese languages are associated with the Malaysian Chinese, it is also the language of the Malays. To whom, then, does this language 'belong'?

While Malaysians do share Bahasa Malaysia (which translates literally as 'the Malaysian language') as a common means of communication, in cultural terms the linguistic terrain is deeply fragmented, as the various ethnic groups generally choose to express themselves in their own languages, and there is also a substantial minority that feels most at home using English.[1] There is a deep and quite widespread desire to insist on the right to hold on to these languages as a kind of defense against encroachment from 'other' languages and cultures. This gives rise to the question of how cohesive the nation is, if languages are still seen as private domains that need to be protected from outside threats. In this chapter, I will be looking at how different theater groups and writers approach the issue of language, examining how they use language and ideas about language to discuss and interrogate Malaysia's identity as a nation.

The general sensitivity about language can be traced back to the formation of Malaysia as a nation. At the time of independence in 1957, Malaya (as it was then known) was inhabited by Malays (seen as being Indigenous), as well as Indians and Chinese who had been brought in, in the nineteenth century, by the British as laborers in rubber plantations and tin mines. There were also Indians and Chinese who had already been in Malaya for several generations, Eurasians of Dutch and Portuguese descent, and a large number of Indigenous people. In this polyglot society, political choices had to be made about the national language as well as the status of other languages, and these choices have had a strong influence on the development of a national identity. In the end, Malay was decided on as the national language, with some schools still allowed to teach in Tamil and Mandarin; privately, there are no strictures against language use, and mother tongues such as the various Indian languages and Chinese dialects flourish.

One can assume that the national language should serve as a kind of uniting element for the nation—that, indeed, is usually the rationale for specifying one official language to serve the whole nation. Has Malaysia's national language managed to unite Malaysia as a nation? I will argue in this chapter that official language policies, as well as political manipulations of the language issue, have worked against the power of the national language to help form a hybrid and inclusive racial, cultural, and national identity. Rather, the nation has seen the growth of an increasingly divided and divisive atmosphere, with increased chauvinism and ethnification at a variety of levels—one has only to look at the emergence of race-specific sociopolitical groups such as Perkasa and Hindraf to be able to support this contention.[2] At the same time, however, mass political and civil movements, such as Bersih,[3] transcend barriers of race, class, age, and gender, indicating that at a broader level, the nation is witnessing an upsurge in unity through political dissatisfaction.

But what is the *language* of unity in Malaysia? It should be, and to some extent is, the national language. However, in cultural terms, the national language is still seen by many, or treated as, the language of the Malays, rather than of Malaysians. English functions as a neutral language of communication for many of those born after 1957 because it is culturally unconnected to any specific ethnic group in Malaysia; furthermore, the current generation is too far removed from the experience of colonization to still connect English with subjugation under the colonial masters. Apart from this, it is also important to note that a distinctly Malaysian variety of English has emerged, and it can, therefore, be claimed by all Malaysians. At the same time, however, despite divisive political policies, younger Malaysians of different races are beginning to claim the national language as their own.

In this chapter, I will discuss how negotiations with the complexities of language take place in the field of what is commonly referred to as English-language theater, and how these negotiations point the way toward a more open and hybrid linguistic and cultural identity that is not narrowly tied to official definitions of race. However, I will then go on to look at an example of the use of the national language in a play that was written and staged within the confines of what is usually thought of as English-language theater; I will argue that the use of Malay in this play points to the potential of the language to function in a much more race-neutral and therefore more uniting way.

Language Policy in Malaysia

Choice of national language was one of the issues discussed in the run-up to independence for Malaya. The colonizers considered the Malays to be the Natives of the land, but there was also a substantial population from (among other places) India and China. This fact caused some problems; as Lee Hock Guan asks, "Given that Malayan society was multilingual, which language(s) should be obligatory to the nation and state?" (Lee 2009: 211). Ultimately, a decision was made in favor of Malay as the national language, but the finer points of the decision caused both disagreement and dissatisfaction:

> the proposed recognition of Malay as the sole national language received support from all ethnic communities. But the Malay and Chinese could not agree on the meaning of Malay as the national language; the crux of their disagreement was whether the language of nation should also be the only language of governance. [. . .] In contrast, the Chinese [. . .] advocated a multilingual official language policy. (Lee 2009: 212)

The Chinese argument in favor of multilingualism at the official level was a response to the fear that their linguistic and cultural identity might well disappear in the face of aggressive language policies. As Milton Esman has noted:

> The recognition of one language as 'national' or 'official' is not a mere matter of convenience or of facilitating communication: it symbolizes respect for the community it represents. The denial of such status and its conferral on another community symbolizes ethnic stratification within the polity. (1992: 381–382)

There were reasons for the seeming paranoia displayed by the Malaysian Chinese with regard to this matter. Prior to independence, a political alliance made up of three communally based political parties was formed,[4] and this alliance has been in power since independence. According to Andaya and Andaya, referring to language policy at the time of independence, "the official Alliance view was clear: an integrated language and educational policy was a key instrument in forging an integrated and united society that would be assimilated to Malay cultural traditions" (2001: 291). This last point was what particularly worried the Indians and Chinese—where did their languages and cultures stand within the new national framework? Did 'assimilation' mean that their languages and cultures would, eventually, disappear? Or did they, their languages, and their cultures have a place within this new national framework?

To some extent, early negotiations about language took this potential problem into consideration, through developments in the education system. In 1951, the Barnes report on education supported a bilingual (that is, Malay and English) education system. The Fenn-Wu report, produced in order to review the position of Chinese education in Malaya, concluded that the proposed bilingual policy would "relegate the Chinese language to an inferior status, with the ultimate result, if not the present purpose, of the extinction of Chinese culture in Malaya" (Lee 2009: 213). Finally, parallel education systems were established that allowed for the setting up of vernacular schools that taught the national syllabus but used either Mandarin or Tamil as the medium of education. This move worked to allay the fears of Malaysians of Chinese and Tamil descent that their cultures would be completely marginalized. Here, the postindependence Malaysian government developed a somewhat pluralistic language policy so that language could function "as an instrument of conflict management, of regulating the competing claims of ethnic groups on the patronage of the state, thereby attempting to achieve workable patterns of peaceful coexistence" (Esman 1992: 382). At the same time, however, this policy had the unfortunate effect of promoting communalism rather than community. Wong Hoy-Kee suggests that "language can also be a barrier against integration, for without a command of the appropriate language, neither an individual nor a group can become members of a community" (1971: 73). In Malaysia, a peculiar situation persists—most individuals and groups have some command of "the appropriate language," but because of the way in which language and culture are treated, some individuals and groups still cannot become full members of the community. There is no doubt that today, Malay functions unproblematically as a language of communication at a variety of social levels within Malaysia. However, culturally it remains very closely linked to the Malays. This is because of the way in which individuals in Malaysia are all classified as belonging to one of four official races (Malay, Chinese, Indian, or 'Other'). Each 'race' is also linked with a specific language and culture so that, for example, people of South Indian extraction are assumed to be Tamil-speaking Hindus, though this is not always the case. Because of this long-standing practice of linking race, language, and culture in this way, Malay does not sit comfortably with many non-Malays as a vehicle for cultural expression. Azly suggests that the notion of language as culture:

runs deeper than merely the need to 'teach language' in schools; it is to preserve and transmit culture for the continuing survival of the essential values of the peoples of the same language. Language, perceived from the social/linguistic anthropological point of view then becomes a political subject and a matter of concern. (2009: 201–202)

Seen from this point of view, Malay as a national language becomes problematic because, although in a broad sense Malaysians can now be seen as being "peoples of the same language," that language does not "preserve and transmit culture" for *all* Malaysians. Is there, in fact, a culture that encompasses all Malaysians? This underlying concern is exacerbated by the National Cultural Policy (NCP, formulated in the 1970s), which states that:

- The national culture must be based on the Indigenous culture of this region.
- The suitable elements from the other cultures can be accepted as part of the national culture.
- Islam is an important component in the molding of the national culture (Lim and Gomes 2009: 234).

The very basis of the NCP, then, is predominantly Malay—it has long been assumed that "Indigenous culture" refers to Malay culture, an assumption strengthened by the focus on Islam as a major component of the culture, and the discursive positioning of non-Indigenous/non-Malay cultures as 'other.' Non-Malays can legitimately question where their cultures feature in Malaysia's official cultural identity. These worries are underscored by some of the comments made from time to time by those in power, as Lim and Gomes point out: "Mohd Adib Aman who was then acting Culture, Youth and Sports Minister in 1982 announced that 'based on these three main principles (of the NCP), the national culture will eliminate racial cultures'" (2009: 234). One way of reading this is to suppose that the NCP will help Malaysians to move away from race-based cultures, toward a culture that transcends the specifics of race. But given the NCP's very particular emphasis on the primacy of Malay culture, it could also mean the loss of non-Malay cultures or their assimilation into Malay culture. Is there, then, a space for non-Malay cultural identities within this framework? Currently, there seems to be no room, at the official level, for the development of a Malaysian cultural identity that transcends these boundaries.

However, as Lim and Gomes also point out, "rarely, if ever, can national culture be decreed or established by policies and regulations" (2009: 233). The same point can be made, to some extent, about national languages. Platt and Weber note that:

although a language may be made officially the national language, this does not of itself make it *de facto* the national language. It is the task of various official, or officially sanctioned, bodies to bring about changes in language use patterns, so that the language does indeed become the national language. (1980: 154)[5]

If we look at national language as something that serves to unite the nation and to give it a particular national identity, it is uncertain whether Malay works this way and whether the 'officially sanctioned' bodies have managed to make the language truly reflective of and embraced by the nation. In the 1970s, Lloyd Fernando welcomed the idea of Malay as the national language; he felt that it "was a move of untold value, not only for restoring the dignity seized from it under the British, but also for fostering cultural solidarity in a multi-ethnic society" (Mandal 2000: 1004). It is important to note that Fernando's focus is on "fostering cultural solidarity," and that he emphasizes the idea of multiculturalism; that is, he feels that it is important that everyone feels that they have cultural ownership of the Malay language.

That this is not yet the case is illustrated by the experience of Malaysian-Malayali writer Uthaya Sankar SB with Dewan Bahasa dan Pustaka (DBP), the national literary body, which can be classified as an 'officially sanctioned' body as mentioned by Platt and Weber. Uthaya writes in Malay, foregrounding his identity as a Malaysian rather than as an Indian or Malayali. He has declared that he feels most comfortable writing about Malaysian issues in the national language, because he is a Malaysian. He has mentioned in his blog, for instance, that "'Bangsa Malaysia' starts with loving 'Bahasa Malaysia'" (2011b), meaning that a Malaysian nation will grow if everyone loves and uses the Malaysian language. But there is still hesitation and reservation about loving the language. That not all non-Malay writers feel the same as Uthaya does is shown by his statement that "there are a few Malaysian Indian writers who believe that since they are writing in 'Bahasa Melayu,' they have to write about 'budaya Melayu' (Malay culture) and 'agama Islam' (Islamic religion)" (2011a). The crux, perhaps, is their identification of the national language as 'Bahasa Melayu' (the language of the Malays) rather than 'Bahasa Malaysia' (the language of Malaysians), a point that brings us back to Uthaya's *contretemps* with DBP.

In 1999, Uthaya compiled an anthology of short stories by Malaysian Indian writers, to be published by DBP. While proofreading the manuscript, he realized that the term 'Bahasa Malaysia,' which he used in the preface, had been systematically changed by the editor to 'Bahasa Melayu.' He was told that DBP "had decided not to allow me to use Bahasa Malaysia," despite official political sanction for the term, because "it's about time we use the term 'Bahasa Melayu' again" (2010). This response suggests a kind of war mentality, implying that the language needs to be rescued, or perhaps reclaimed as the language belonging to the Malays, rather than to Malaysia. How, then, are non-Malays meant to feel in the face of such exclusion? How are they to claim belonging and ownership?

Because culture and language are so intimately linked through official discourse, and because each culture is constructed as being separate from the other cultures, Malay cannot currently be perceived as a language that serves to cross cultural boundaries. Use of Malay as the national language works, in part because of the NCP, to give Malaysian culture a strongly Malay base. It should be noted, however, that construction of cultural identities in Malaysia is such that *none* of the main languages associated with the various racial groups can transcend cultural barriers. I would argue instead that English, as used in Malaysia, currently serves as a language that can cross more easily between and across cultures. However, it does not cross class barriers with the same ease, and, because the medium of education is Bahasa Malaysia, there are many Malaysians who are not fluent in English. Bahasa Malaysia, however, can cross both class and race barriers, and therefore has enormous potential as a culturally uniting language. I would suggest that to some extent, because Bahasa Malaysia has been the language of education for so long, it has been successfully internalized by many younger Malaysians. A kind of schoolyard, colloquial Malay has developed with which Malaysians of all races are comfortable. Uthaya's insistence on using Malay for his writing underlines the idea that it is not necessarily seen by everyone as the language of the Malays. However, these responses are in tension with an institutionalized insistence on yoking language and culture in very narrow and essentializing ways. These are among the issues foregrounded in the texts and performances to be studied here.

English-Language Theater in Malaysia

English has, since independence, to a large extent lost its connotations of colonial dominance, and because it does not 'belong' to any particular racial category, its use is not so culturally and politically loaded. Furthermore, the flexibility and openness of English mean that it can very easily adopt new linguistic and cultural elements, and that it can accommodate the intrusion of other languages. In other words, it has the potential to 'represent' cultures far outside its supposed cultural boundaries. This is not the case with the other languages available in Malaysia; generally, comprehension of these languages (such as Tamil, Punjabi, Cantonese, Hokkien, etc.) is limited to members of that ethnic or racial group, and therefore the cultural concerns expressed tend also to be fairly limited. While Malay cuts across racial lines in terms of comprehensibility, it is linked culturally to the Malay race. English, however, does not belong to any particular racial group, and therefore it has the potential to be more broadly representative.

Although I call it 'English-language theater,' the term is no longer particularly accurate, in that it is in fact a site of multilingual performance. Most of the practitioners in this group would claim English as their main language of communication, but their performances often intentionally stage a multiplicity of languages, dramatizing not only the complexity of Malaysia's linguistic framework, but also the mutual incomprehensibility of these languages. What they end up staging is not some happy picture of a harmoniously multicultural nation, but instead a picture of a linguistically fragmented nation where sensitivity and understanding are called for. This kind of work is, increasingly, beginning to speak to practitioners across the linguistic divides, so that there is now more collaboration between the different language groups.

Thus, we are given productions like *Break ing Ji Poh Ka Si Pe Cah* (staged in 2008), in which three plays are staged, one in English, one in Mandarin, and one in Malay. 'Ji poh' is Mandarin for 'hit (something) until it breaks' and 'kasi pecah' is Malay for 'break it.' The plays are staged one after the other, so there is no linguistic crossover in the performance itself. This reflects the fact that the languages and the people most closely associated with them do still inhabit separate enclaves or domains, although nominally under the uniting umbrella of nationhood. The way in which the play's title is written reflects this idea, with the words forming a single title with a single meaning but still appearing broken and fragmented. In a theatrical framework that has for so long occupied separate spaces, the sharing of stage space and time like this, together with the acknowledgment of common ground implied by the title, is in itself something of a breakthrough. However, fragmentation and separation remain issues that Malaysians must contend with.

The Five Arts Centre, a Malaysian Arts collective, has long been associated with productions that interrogate and express multilingualism and mutual incomprehension. One of their early attempts was the 1999 staging of a devised play called *A Chance Encounter*, which begins in English but then, as Francis Dass notes in his review of the play in the *New Straits Times* on March 27, 1999, "veers towards the sunny side of Bahasa Malaysia for most of its duration." The way in which language is used in this play is instructive. Both characters speak largely in Malay, but this does not mean that communication is unproblematic or that the language is homogenous. One character is a middle-aged Indian-Muslim or *mamak* woman from Penang, who speaks in the 'Mamak Malay' dialect, which differs from standard Malay. The other character is a young Malaysian Chinese cosmetics saleswoman whose dialogue swings from broken English to Cantonese to broken, Cantonese-inflected Malay. Both are, in a way, speaking in Malay, the national language. But it is clear from the different ways in which they speak that Malay is far from being some kind of monolithic, standardized language. While it is possible to see this as a sign of breakdown and fragmentation, it is also possible to see it instead as a sign of the potential for the language to be open and inclusive—there are different varieties of Malay for different people, but fundamentally it is the same language, and the women are able to communicate. Even within the confines of the national language, there is room for difference and for incomprehension, as well as for unity and communication.

Other writers have turned to English as a suitable vehicle for examining and expressing a mixed Malaysian identity. One writer who plays with and manipulates English as he portrays a particular kind of Malaysian identity is K. S. Maniam. A Malaysian of South Indian (Tamil) extraction, Maniam is one of the country's most celebrated writers in the English language, having written numerous novels, short stories, plays, and poems. His main characters are also Malaysian Tamils, and in this discussion I will focus on how Maniam plays with language to create a space of expression for a marginalized and voiceless segment of the population. Plantation workers in Malaysia and their descendants are among the most marginalized groups in the country. In the nineteenth century, the British brought laborers from India to work in the plantations, and for more than a century, labor in the plantation sector was made up predominantly of Indians of Tamil extraction. Most were educated to a minimal level at best, having attended the Tamil-medium schools provided by the plantation management. Poverty demanded that many of them leave school early, in order to help support the family by going out to work. Low levels of education meant that they often had no choice but to work on these same plantations. Poor proficiency in any language other than Tamil, which did not hold great economic value outside the plantation system, meant that it was difficult for them to survive outside that closed world.

Not only were many Malaysian Indians marginalized by social and economic problems; they have also been physically marginalized by the fact that they lived on plantations or in squatter areas, physically distanced from the mainstream Malaysian population, whether urban or rural. There has been uncertainty, therefore, about their sense of belonging within the wider Malaysian framework. Born and brought up within Malaysia, they remain outsiders. Maniam's work serves to bring these marginalized people into a more central position, mainly because he writes in English. His characters would, in reality, speak Tamil. But writing in Tamil would restrict the audience to Tamil-speakers; the concerns Maniam brings up, therefore, would not reach a wider audience. English immediately gives him not just a national, but an international reach. To render his dialogue in Malay, by contrast, would create a strange new dynamic. Because Malay is not just the national language, but also the cultural language of the politically dominant racial group, allowing these marginal characters to speak to each other in Malay would imply a level of participation in the nation that they do not in fact have. It might be argued that English, too, is a 'power' language, given its connections to globalization and international communications. However, Maniam's characters use a kind of English that, in its rhythms, idioms, and nuances, reflects the Tamil they would actually be using in real life. One of the characters, driven to distraction by her poverty and the hunger of her children, shouts out, "I'll put salt on your tails! Your father isn't dead! Why are you all crying? He's probably in some coffeeshop soaking his guts in stout. And I've to borrow salt!" (Maniam 1994: 34). While grammatically correct, there is something about the idiom that is clearly not English. This kind of flexibility to take on other language 'flavors' is not found in Malaysia's other main languages. Thus, while equipping his characters with access to a language that confers a degree of power on them (the power to communicate across linguistic borders), he manages to maintain a kind of linguistic and cultural truth for them.

I noted earlier that in Maniam's plays, which were mainly written in the 1980s and 1990s, Malay was viewed as the cultural language of the dominant group. However, this view of Malay is changing, with newer writers providing more complex responses, both to Malay as the language of the Malays and as the language of Malaysians. Jit Murad, for example, melds both English and Malay in his dialogue, in a way that captures the subtleties and nuances of a particular class in Malay society. Jit Murad's work *Gold Rain and Hailstones* (first staged in 1993 and restaged in 2006) portrays a genuinely hybrid and fluid way of communicating. Jit, who is classified as Malay, writes in this play about privileged Malays who have studied abroad, and who have now come back to Malaysia, only to find that in many ways, they do not belong anymore and must instead carve out their own spaces or find some kind of accommodation with the spaces that are available. Increased Islamization and ethnification have meant that the borders of what it means to be Malay have narrowed over the years. 'Malayness' is defined in Article 160 of the Malaysian constitution: an individual can be considered Malay if he or she professes Islam, habitually speaks Malay, and conforms to Malay customs. Increasingly, responses to this definition have narrowed to the point where stepping outside its boundaries can lay the individual open to disapproval from the community because they are no longer 'being' Malay. The constitutional definition of Malayness is in fact quite remarkably flexible—it implies, for example, that a Chinese convert to Islam can *become* Malay by speaking the language and practicing the customs. But there is no call in this definition to abjure other elements of an individual's culture. Malays "habitually" speak Malay; they do not have to *exclusively* speak Malay. However, increasing narrowness in the understanding of this definition has meant that more and more, the common understanding is that a Malay *only* speaks Malay. As one of the characters in this play discovers, if "you enter a government office, and you're Malay but don't speak it, it had better be because you're mute" (Jit 1993: 17). There is no room for hybridity and a fluid linguistic identity in the current understanding of what it means to be Malay.

Jit, however, challenges these essentializing assumptions by questioning whether his characters are any less Malay, just because they are uncomfortable with the language or are equally comfortable switching between Malay and English. He shows his characters interacting in an almost exclusively Malay social world—but this is a Malay world that is at home with hybridity. Social constructions of Malayness have marginalized and even ignored this group, because it does not adhere to the common understanding of what makes a Malay. Particularly interesting are the conversations he creates between the mothers of the main characters. They speak a language that cannot be classified as either Malay or English, because it slips fluidly and easily between the two (translations are provided in Normal Italics; please note that Sungai Buluh is the location of a leprosarium whose inmates grow and sell plants, while 'Puan Sri' is a term used to refer to women whose husbands have been granted the title 'Tan Sri' by a Malaysian ruler):

Nina's Mother: [. . .] Disturbing ke? *([. . .] Am I disturbing you?)*

Man's Mother: Oh Cik Non. No, no. I was just showing the Filipina girl how to fertilize the new orchids. I baru balik dari Sungai Buluh. Banyak orchid baru—cantik—cantik. Pandai orang leprosy tu. (*Oh Miss Non. No, no. I was just showing the Filipina girl how to fertilize the new orchids. I just got back from Sungai Buluh. Lots of new orchids there—beautiful. So clever, those leprosy people.*)

Nina's Mother: Rajin Puan Sri. Patut your garden cantik. Semua orang kata garden Puan Sri should be in a magazine. (*You're so hardworking, Puan Sri. No wonder your garden is so lovely. Everyone says Puan Sri's garden should be in a magazine.*) (Jit 1993: 2)

This kind of language is often heard among Malaysians (not just Malays) who are fluent in and comfortable with both English and Malay; there is a sense that certain concepts need to be expressed in a particular language, or that using Malay rather than English (or vice versa) will add some kind of force to what is being said. This also happens to some extent with Tamil and the major Chinese dialects, but in Malaysia, the slippage between Malay and English is most common; also, it cuts across race and class barriers. The naturalness of Jit's dialogue, and the ease with which it is spoken onstage by Malaysian performers, indicates that it is quite an ingrained part of the linguistic culture of Malaysia at certain levels of society.

What these examples suggest is that English as it is evolving in Malaysia can provide an inroad into the notion of sharing and translating across cultures, toward the development of a culture that partakes of difference but is not riven by it. However, the fact remains that the national language is Malay, and since it is a language that the majority of Malaysians today do share, then it should also be able to function effectively as a *cultural* language of unity, not just as a practical language of everyday communication. Individuals of all ethnic groups should feel equally comfortable not only communicating in Malay, but also expressing themselves culturally. The fact that we can speak of different language streams in theater, or that the Dewan Bahasa feels it needs to reclaim Malay as the language of the Malays, indicates that this eventuality is still quite a long way off.

An interesting development in this field, however, is the recent staging of the play *Parah* by the Instant Café Theatre Company, in February 2012; the play was written by Singaporean-Malay writer Alfian Sa'at and was directed by Jo Kukathas. While the play was performed entirely in Malay, the involvement of the Instant Café Theatre Company and Kukathas, who have always been perceived as being part of the 'English-language' theater scene, meant that certain cultural boundaries were crossed and linguistic boundaries questioned. This play in fact demonstrates the easy, colloquial, shared language that Malay has become for many Malaysian schoolchildren. The play deals with the interactions among four teenage schoolchildren—a Malay boy and girl (Hafiz and Melur), an Indian boy (Mahesh), and a Chinese boy (Kahoe). Through a series of incidents linked to the use of the controversial novel *Interlok* as part of their Malay literature syllabus, the four teenagers start to rethink their friendships, their allegiances to race, culture, and language, and their positions within the nation.[6] Mahesh and Kahoe demonstrate how difficult it can be for them to have to deal with stereotyped ideas of what they are meant to be. Mahesh, for example, does not speak Tamil (assumed to be the mother tongue of most, if not all, Malaysians of South Indian origin). He declares that his father is Malayali and his mother is Tamil, so they naturally speak to each other in English (Alfian 2012: 2). While the line elicits a laugh, there is a great deal of truth in Mahesh's family's position—theirs is a hybrid family, with mixed allegiances. How are they to decide on just one or the other? The best solution they can find is to compromise and choose a language with which all are comfortable, creating another level in their multilayered cultural identity.

Kahoe recounts a family holiday in China during which he felt like a mute with a frozen tongue, because he could speak neither Mandarin nor good Cantonese. He is immensely relieved when they get back to Malaysia and he finally has a common language with others around him—namely, Malay (Alfian 2012: 31). Both examples indicate an inability on the part of these two Malaysian born and bred youngsters to adhere to simplistic categories that tie them, officially, to particular languages. Their reactions and experiences show them to be undeniably hybrid, and it is the complex explorations of hybridity, similarity, and difference that make this play seem 'not very Malay,' despite being entirely spoken in Malay. The play deals with specifically Malaysian issues, but it cannot be classified as 'Malay' theater because its concerns spread beyond the framework of specifically Malay society (although, as Jit's play indicates, Malay society in itself is fragmented and diverse).

Furthermore, Alfian's use of the language is important—he writes in grammatical and idiomatic Malay, which nonetheless escapes seeming overly formal and therefore unbelievable as a language of communication between the four characters. He also specifically avoids extremely colloquial Malay dialects that might be inaccessible to non-Malays, who would have learned the language in the more formal confines of the school system. He has managed to find a balance between formal and colloquial levels of Malay, which allows almost all Malaysians to understand the dialogue. He to some extent detaches the Malay language from a specific and racially linked cultural context, thus opening up a wider space of ownership and belonging within a cultural milieu that in other instances might be closed to non-Malays. The characters all 'own' the language (Mahesh at one point corrects Hafiz's explanation of the meaning of a word in the novel, indicating that he is at least as fluent as the Malay boy; Kahoe clearly feels that Malay, rather than Cantonese or Mandarin, is 'his' language). Yet, at the same time, the issues brought up in the play through the various reactions to the novel *Interlok*, and the use of derogatory words like 'pariah,' 'keling,' and 'Cina babi,'[7] indicate their individual resentment at being marginalized or (in the case of Hafiz) threatened. They share common ground—the language—but are still kept apart by other issues that stem from authoritative impositions.

Mahesh, for example, is thoroughly at ease with his Malay and Chinese friends. But as they sit together and read the novel, he comes across a paragraph in which the novelist declares that the southern Indians who came to Malaya were mostly from the *pariah* caste (Alfian 2012: 14). The word *pariah* is deeply derogatory, and its use in a novel that is meant to be read by all Malaysians obviously shocks Mahesh, who falls silent and then quickly excuses himself to go home. He has had to confront the fact that within Malaysia's social framework, these kinds of classifications exist and are taken seriously (and indeed are given wide currency and a level of legitimacy through their inclusion in the national syllabus) and that he is therefore unavoidably marked as being 'other' and, in this context, subordinate.

The seeming unity of the small group of mixed-race friends is soon tested. When Mahesh joins other Indian students to protest against the novel, Hafiz asks him when he (Mahesh) joined with 'them' (the other Indian students); he calls the Indian students *keling*, another very derogatory term (Alfian 2012: 16). Despite his close friendship with Mahesh, Hafiz still views Malaysian Indians as an undifferentiated mass, who are labeled with derogatory terms. Mahesh, too, despite being 'different' from the other Tamil-speaking Indians, joins in their protest because, as he points out, there are only four Indians in the whole class—if three of them protest, there is pressure on him to join them simply because they are all 'Indians.' He is defined by broad categories of race, rather than the language he uses or the friends he keeps.

Ironically, even as we watch their friendships breaking down before us, we are aware that they are able to communicate, unproblematically, in Bahasa Malaysia—a language they all share with equal ease and fluency. Thus, Alfian balances the vision of breakdown with the awareness that despite authoritative categorizations, there is still something that binds these characters together—here, it is the shared language. Alfian chooses to end the play with an ambiguously hopeful scene in which the four friends outline their plans for the future, talk about the contributions of all ethnic groups to the development of Kuala Lumpur, and make a pact to meet again every year once they have left school, so that they do not lose touch with each other. We are not sure if this scene is set in the past, before the breakdown of their friendship, or in the present, suggesting that they have overcome their differences. This ambiguity is also reflected in the title, *Parah*, which means 'severe' or 'very grave.' When the letters are reversed, however, it reads *harap*, which means 'hope.'[8]

Conclusion

What is becoming apparent is a certain disconnect between the politicization of the national language and the way in which it is used at the grassroots level. Politically, a kind of siege mentality has been formed in relation to the national language, despite the success with which it has been embedded as the language of education and communication. Because Malay has been so successfully implemented as the medium of education, the general level of English in the country has fallen considerably. Steps were taken to address this issue, with English being reintroduced as the medium of instruction for math and science in primary and secondary schools in 2003. There were protests against this, with some suggesting that to revert to teaching in English would threaten the status of the national language; there were also protests from Chinese educationists, who felt that it was important to maintain the mother tongue. Ultimately, the policy was reversed, and since 2011 those entering their first year of school are once again studying math and science in Malay, or in the mother tongues in vernacular schools. But this sense of threat does not make sense given the extent to which Malay has become a common language among schoolchildren. It arises from a political desire to control through fear and mistrust, without taking into account developments within the community. What the plays under discussion here provide is a view of language that is based more on everyday practice than on political machination.

A Chance Encounter shows the ability of the Malay language to function as a common language of communication, despite very different levels of fluency as well as very different cultural backgrounds. At the same time, it demonstrates difference and fragmentation. K. S. Maniam's plays use English as a common cultural language, reflecting his belief that Malaysians are necessarily hybrid and must embrace that hybridity, rather than trying to remain within narrow, authority-defined cultural enclaves. Jit Murad uses a mixed language to portray mixed, fragmented identities even within a supposedly homogeneous ethnic group, thus questioning authoritative constructions of ethnicity and culture, while also celebrating the fluidity and expressiveness of the hybrid culture. *Parah*, meanwhile, shows an incipient 'Malaysian' culture growing among a multiracial group of school friends, who find that authoritative constructions of who and what they should be seriously disrupt their own burgeoning sense of identity as Malaysians. The theater can, perhaps, function in a performative way to reiterate a broader, more inclusive identity in a public forum.

Notes

1. Officially, the national language is called Bahasa Malaysia, the language of Malaysia. Another term, which is more politically loaded, is 'Bahasa Melayu,' which means 'the language of the Malays.' Issues related to these terms will be brought up later in the chapter.
2. Perkasa, or Pertubuhan Pribumi Perkasa Malaysia, was founded after Malaysia's 2008 general elections, specifically to defend Malay rights, which some quarters see as being slowly eroded. Hindraf, the Hindu Rights Action Force, fights specifically for Hindu rights and heritage—in Malaysia, the term 'Hindu' has become virtually synonymous with 'Indian.'
3. Coalition for Free and Fair Elections—'bersih' means 'clean' in the Malay language.
4. This alliance was made up of United Malays National Organisation, Malaysian Chinese Association, and Malaysian Indian Congress.
5. This is true of Singapore, for example, where Malay is the official national language, but English functions as the de facto national language and Mandarin receives more official support and emphasis than Malay.
6. The novel *Interlok*, by Malaysian literary laureate Abdullah Hussain, is on the syllabus for Malay literature at the secondary level in schools. In 2010, the novel became the center of controversy because of claims that it contained words and ideas that were derogatory to Malaysian Indians. A panel was formed to look into the matter, and a number of amendments were then made to the student edition of the novel.
7. 'Pariah' is a colloquial word referring to the lowest caste in the Hindu system of castes; 'keling' is a derogatory word for Indians in Malaysia, though there is no consensus as to what the term actually means; 'Cina babi' is Malay for 'Chinese pig,' a term that has extra resonance in Malaysia because to Muslims, the pig is unclean or 'haram.'
8. The author himself pointed out this ambiguity in a question and answer session after the performance in Kuala Lumpur on February 6, 2012.

References

Abdullah, H. (1971) *Interlok* (Kuala Lumpur: Dewan Bahasa dan Pustaka).

Alfian, S. (2012) *Parah* (unpublished manuscript).

Andaya, B. W., and Andaya, L. Y. (2001) *A History of Malaysia* (Hampshire: Palgrave).

Azly, R. (2009) 'Introduction: Education, Culture and Identity' in *Multiethnic Malaysia: Past, Present and Future*, ed. L. T. Ghee, A. Gomes, and Azly R. (Petaling Jaya, Malaysia: Strategic Information and Research Development Centre and MiDAS@UCSI University), pp. 201–206.

Dass, F. (1999). 'Penetrating Reflection of Malaysian Life' *New Straits Times* (Malaysia), March 27.

Esman, M. J. (1992) 'The State and Language Policy' *International Political Science Review/Revue internationale de sciences politique* 13: 4: 381–396.

Jit, M. (1993) *Gold Rain and Hailstones* (unpublished manuscript).

Lee, H. G. (2009) 'Language, Education and Ethnic Relations' in *Multiethnic Malaysia: Past, Present and Future*, ed. T. G. Lim, A. Gomes, and Azly R. (Petaling

Jaya, Malaysia: Strategic Information and Research Development Centre and MiDAS@UCSI University), pp. 207–230.

Lim, T. G., and Gomes, A. (2009) 'Culture and Development in Malaysia' in *Multiethnic Malaysia: Past, Present and Future*, ed. T. G. Lim, A. Gomes, and Azly R. (Petaling Jaya, Malaysia: Strategic Information and Research Development Centre and MiDAS@UCSI University), pp. 231–252.

Mandal, S. K. (2000) 'Reconsidering Cultural Globalization: The English Language in Malaysia' *Third World Quarterly* 21: 6: 1001–1012.

Maniam, K. S. (1994) *The Cord* in *Sensuous Horizons* (Kuala Lumpur: Skoob Books), pp. 25–94.

Platt, J., and Weber, H. (1980) *English in Singapore and Malaysia: Status, Features, Functions* (Kuala Lumpur: Oxford University Press).

Uthaya, Sankar SB. (2010) 'My Right to Use Bahasa Malaysia,' January 26. uthayasb. blogspot.com/2010/01/my-right-to-use-bahasa-malaysia.html (accessed July 4, 2012).

Uthaya, Sankar SB. (2011a) 'Speaking in Tongues: Part 1,' October 30. uthayasb. blogspot.com/2011/10/speaking-in-tongues-part-1.html (accessed July 4. 2012).

Uthaya, Sankar SB. (2011b) 'Speaking in Tongues: Part 3,' November 1. uthayasb. blogspot.com/2011/11/speaking-in-tongues-part-3.html (accessed July 4, 2012).

Wong, H-K. (1971) 'The Development of a National Language in Indonesia and Malaysia' *Comparative Education* 7: 2: 73–80.

Part III
Contexts of Translation

9 'Word of Struggle'
The Politics of Translation in Indigenous Pacific Literature

Michelle Keown

The last decade of the twentieth century witnessed the consolidation of translation studies as a discrete discipline, as well as the emergence of more sustained postcolonial readings of the politics and pragmatics of translation (Bassnett and Trivedi 1999; Robinson 1997; Tymoczko 1999). The interface between translation studies and cultural/postcolonial studies during this period (and into the new millennium) brought a new functionalism to translation research, witnessed in studies of the ethical and political consequences of translation as well as in new 'process-oriented' approaches that investigated translators' own reflections on their translation practices and principles (Anderson 2010; Pym 2009; Tymoczko 2007, 2010; Venuti 1998, 2012; Walker-Morrison 2010).

This chapter explores these trends with particular reference to the Pacific region, focusing on translations of Kanak/New Caledonian and Māʻohi/French Polynesian literature by three Aotearoa/New Zealand–based translators—Jean Anderson, Raylene Ramsay, and Deborah Walker-Morrison—who have produced commentaries on their translation practices that take into consideration ethical and political issues surrounding the translation of the work of Indigenous or 'postcolonial' writers. As I will discuss in more detail below, Anderson addresses these ethical issues by adopting a 'resistant' translation method—one that resembles Lawrence Venuti's (1998) concept of 'foreignization'—while Ramsay and Walker-Morrison, who have collaborated on various translation projects, favor what Kwame Anthony Appiah (1993) terms 'thick translation,' making use of paratextual materials to convey to the uninitiated Anglophone reader some sense of the historico-cultural context that surrounds the texts they translate. In what follows I will explore the ways in which these translators position themselves vis-à-vis the source material/writers, as well as discussing formal and stylistic aspects of the source texts and translations that bespeak the translators' varying responses to the pragmatic questions attendant on their work. Before launching into this analysis, however, it is worth dwelling for a moment on the broader context of interlingual literary translation in the Pacific.

Interlingual Literary Translation in the Pacific

The Pacific is marked by extraordinary linguistic diversity, with one quarter of the world's languages (some twelve hundred) concentrated in Melanesia alone (Crocombe 2001). The development of orthographies (largely by European missionaries and linguists during and beyond the nineteenth century) has given rise to a corpus of written material in many of these languages, but colonial incursions into the region frequently resulted in imperial metropolitan languages becoming the main vehicles of communication and publication, with the establishment of separate Anglophone, Francophone, and Hispanophone enclaves. While many Pacific Islanders speak at least one Indigenous Pacific language (and/or contact languages such as Pidgins, Creoles, and Koines[1]), the vast majority of written material in the region has been published in the colonial metropolitan languages (Keown 2007; Keown and Murray, 2013; Lynch 1998).

It has been widely acknowledged that postcolonial studies has for long been focused primarily on Anglophone texts and contexts, and the Pacific is no exception to this general rule, due in large part to the dominance of English as the main language of trade, diplomacy, and intraregional communication (Forsdick and Murphy 2003; Huggan 2008; Keown 2010). Further, Francophone and Hispanophone Pacific Islanders—the former concentrated in French Polynesia, New Caledonia, Wallis and Futuna, and Vanuatu, and the latter in the Chilean colony of Easter Island/Rapa Nui—represent a very small minority of the overall regional population: some 5 percent are Francophone, with even fewer speaking Spanish (Crocombe 2001; Keown 2007; Keown and Murray, 2013).[2]

However, in keeping with recent developments in international postcolonial studies—which have included increasing recognition of non-Anglophone contributions to the field—the late 1990s and beyond have witnessed burgeoning dialogues and collaborations between Francophone and Anglophone Pacific writers,[3] as well as the emergence of a number of English translations of Francophone Pacific texts within Pacific metropolitan centers such as Hawai'i, Australia, and New Zealand (Keown 2010: 242, 244). Texts selected for translation have emerged from the two main 'centers' of Indigenous Francophone Pacific writing: New Caledonia and French Polynesia.[4] While both areas have vibrant, centuries-old oral traditions, Eurocentric educational and publishing policies led to severe underrepresentation of Indigenous peoples within the writing profession, and it wasn't until the late 1960s that local Indigenous creative writing movements began to gather momentum, consolidating in the 1980s and 1990s with the emergence of a new generation of writers galvanized by the Kanak independence movement,[5] as well as protests against French nuclear imperialism in French Polynesia (Nicole 1999: 274; Brown 2004; Keown 2010).[6] Some of this literature has been written in

Tahitian and in the Kanak languages of New Caledonia, but the majority has been published in French.[7]

The English translations that have emerged since the dawning of the new millennium give a good sense of the range and tenor of Indigenous Francophone Pacific writing, manifesting in single-authored works as well as literary anthologies. Of the literature originating from French Polynesia, the first Māʻohi novel, Chantal Spitz's *L'île des rêves écrasés* (1991/2003), was translated into English by Jean Anderson and published as *Island of Shattered Dreams* (2007) by New Zealand publisher Huia. Anderson has also translated another Māʻohi novel, Moetai Brotherson's *Le Roi Absent* (2007), published in English as *The Missing King* (2012) by Little Island Press of New Zealand. *Vārua Tupu*, the first anthology of French Polynesian literature in English translation, was published in 2006 by the University of Hawaiʻi Press, edited by Frank Stewart, Kareva Mateata-Allain, and Alexander Mawyer (with the involvement of a team of translators including, *inter alia*, Stewart and Mateata-Allain). The anthology features the work of first-generation writers and poets (such as Flora Devatine/Vaitiare and Henri Hiro), as well as more recently published authors such as Louise Peltzer, Rai a Mai/Michou Chaze, Titaua Peu, and Célestine Hitiura Vaite (who has written a trilogy of novels in English,[8] which was in turn published in French translation by Au vent des îles of Tahiti[9]).

Indigenous New Caledonian writing is also well represented in English translation. Déwé Gorodé's *L'épave* (2005/2007), the first Kanak novel, was published as *The Wreck* by Little Island Press in 2011, translated by Raylene Ramsay and Deborah Walker-Morrison. Ramsay and Walker-Morrison have also collaborated on two other book-length translation projects. The first, *Sharing as Custom Provides* (Gorodé 2004b),[10] is a translated selection of Gorodé's poetry published by Pandanus Books of Australia (along with a companion volume of Gorodé's prose, *The Kanak Apple Season* (2004a), translated by Peter Brown). Ramsay and Walker-Morrison also worked with a team of co-translators to produce *Nights of Storytelling* (Ramsay 2011), an anthology of New Caledonian writing. The anthology—comprising more than a hundred extracts from literary and historical texts—includes a broad range of material from New Caledonia's Kanak and European traditions, from transcribed Kanak oral narratives and colonial representations of Kanak culture to work by contemporary Kanak writers and performance poets such as Gorodé, Weniko Ihage, Denis Pourawa, and Paul Wamo, and writing by contemporary authors of French settler descent (such as Nicolas Kurtovitch). Excerpts from plays by Kanak dramatists Pierre Gope and Jean-Marie Tjibaou are also included: one is from Tjibaou's 1975 play *Kanaké* (a dramatization of the founding story of the Paicî-speaking Kanak community that has been published in French (1995) and in an English translation (2006)),[11] and the other from *Les dieux sont borgnes* (2002), a play coauthored by Gope and

Kurtovitch that stages a humorous imagined encounter between Captain James Cook and the Kanak people. Another of Gope's plays, *Le dernier crépuscule* (1999)—which explores the impact of commercial nickel mining on Kanak peoples—has been separately published in English translation as *The Last Nightfall* (2001).

The increasing availability of Indigenous Francophone Pacific writing in English translation is viewed by many Francophone writers as a crucial means by which to reunite Pacific Islanders divided by the experience of colonialism. Kareva Mateata-Allain, herself a Mā'ohi literary scholar and translator, as well as a creative writer, links this growing regional consciousness with the theories of Tongan writer Epeli Hau'ofa, who in the 1990s published a series of influential essays advocating a regional 'Oceanic' identity based in the shared marine heritage of Pacific peoples (Mateata-Allain 2008: 40; Hau'ofa 2008). Pacific Islanders developed sophisticated maritime technologies that allowed them to navigate established trade routes throughout the Pacific long before Europeans arrived in the region, but many of these intercultural links were severed as the Pacific was divided into separate French, British, and other colonial spheres of influence, and into Dumont D'Urville's geocultural categories of Polynesia, Melanesia, and Micronesia (Keown 2007: 13). Hau'ofa's 'Oceanic' paradigm is designed to transcend these imposed divisions, uniting and protecting Pacific Islanders against the vicissitudes of global capitalism and climate change, as well as serving as a source of inspiration to contemporary Pacific artists and creative writers (Hau'ofa 2008). This model has been enormously influential throughout the Indigenous Pacific, and Mateata-Allain draws on Hau'ofa's work to posit Mā'ohi writing as a metaphorical *va'a* (voyaging canoe) that can reunite Anglophone and Francophone Pacific peoples through a process of "intellectual cross-fertilization" (Hau'ofa 2008: 41; Keown 2010: 245–246). Images of trans-Oceanic voyaging, and celebrations of putatively common Indigenous Pacific values (such as communalism, spiritual connections to landscape, environmental conservationism, and the centrality of oral traditions to contemporary social practice) also appear in other recent translations of Francophone Pacific writing, such as *Vārua Tupu*, as well as within a wide spectrum of Anglophone Pacific writing and criticism focused around the region's Indigenous peoples (Keown 2007, 2008).

'Translating' Orality in Mā'ohi and Kanak Traditions

These metaphors of intraregional voyaging resonate with the process of 'carrying across' evident in the etymology of the word 'translation' itself, and a particular challenge and focal point for translators such as Anderson, Ramsay, and Walker-Morrison has involved finding viable methods by which to transport the structures and cadences of Pacific oral poetry and narratives—so vital to the intergenerational transmission of values, histories, and ontologies within both pre- and postcolonial Pacific cultures—between media as well as between languages. In both Kanak and Māʻohi cultures, the French term *la Parole* is used to refer not just to the spoken word, but more specifically to the oral traditions that connect all facets of spiritual, material, and social life (Keown 2010; Ramsay 2011: 13).

The creative works of various Māʻohi and Kanak authors engage explicitly with the primacy of oral traditions, and the translators of their work signal the distinction between the written and spoken word in varying ways. Spitz's *L'île des rêves écrasés*, for example, explores the inimical effects of French imperialism across generations of French Polynesians, with a particular focus on the devastating environmental and cultural impact of French nuclear testing. Although the novel is written primarily in French, Spitz decentralizes the authority of the colonizing language by beginning her narrative with a lengthy untranslated Māʻohi creation myth, signaling the primacy of the Māʻohi oral tradition over the French version of the biblical creation myth that immediately follows. This discursive dialectic is maintained throughout the text, with frequent code-switching between French and Māʻohi (for which no glossary, and very little contextual translation, is offered) and consistent use of radically nonstandard French syntax. Jean Anderson, translator of Spitz's novel, is—as mentioned above—an advocate of 'resistant translation,' a practice that resembles Venuti's concept of 'foreignization' in seeking to "respect and reproduce as much as possible" unique stylistic features and other aspects of the source text without making significant allowances for a foreign reader (Anderson 2010: 285–286; Keown 2010). To this end, her translation contains very little contextual or framing matter: a brief glossary of Māʻohi terms (which appear mainly as isolated words and phrases in the source text) is included at the end of the book, and a short translator's note appears in the prefatory matter. In the latter, Anderson outlines some of the ways in which Spitz disrupts "many of the parameters of accepted literary French" by making use, *inter alia*, of marked lexical repetition, capitalization to "stress cultural importance", and widespread code-switching between prose and lyric poetry, as well as between French and Māʻohi (Anderson 2007: 3). Anderson preserves these strategies of aesthetic estrangement through two particular methods. Firstly, she reproduces Spitz's capitalization of culturally significant terms: this is notable, for example, in the widespread capitalization of 'Land' ('Terre' in Spitz's original French), which—as is the case in other Polynesian cultures, such as New Zealand Māori—is accorded spiritual significance as a sacred, life-giving maternal body that must be nurtured and protected. Customarily a child's placenta is buried in the ancestral land on which s/he is born (Spitz 1991/2003: 32–33).

Another important means by which Anderson reproduces the linguistic disruptions of Spitz's text is through the retention of untranslated Māʻohi words (as well as longer passages of untranslated Māʻohi, such as the opening creation myth). Often, untranslated Māʻohi words are used in descriptions of central elements of Māʻohi material culture and ritual. Spitz does not include a glossary, but certain terms are explained through contextual translation or can be partly inferred through the narrative context in which they appear. For example, preparations for a ceremonial feast are described thus: "Les hommes, bien sûr, tuent le cochon, attrapent crabes, poissons et langoustes, déterrent taro, ufi, ùmara, cueillent meià, feî, ùru et enfournent le tout dans le ahimā four traditionnel" (Spitz 1991/2003: 34). In Anderson's translation the sentence appears thus: "Of course the men kill a pig, catch crabs, fish and crayfish, dig up taro, ufi, 'umara, pick mei'a, fē'ī, 'uru and put it all in the traditional oven, the ahima'ā" (Spitz 2007: 25), and, in addition, the Māʻohi words are all translated in the glossary. ('Taro' is glossed as 'root vegetable' and the remaining terms as 'yam,' 'sweet potato,' 'banana,' 'mountain banana,' 'breadfruit,' and 'earth oven.')

However, while able to produce these kinds of stylistic correspondences, Anderson indicates that she was unable to devise a viable method by which to signal the important distinction Spitz makes between 'parole' (associated explicitly with the Māʻohi oral tradition as well as the spoken word more generally) and 'mot' (associated with the colonizing French culture as well as with writing). As I have argued elsewhere, however, this distinction is traceable through the repetition of 'word' (often capitalized) in contexts clearly associated with the vitality of the oral tradition, such as a speech by a Māʻohi patriarch (named Maevarua) that takes the form of a lyric poem reminding his son of his ancestral connections with the land and the rhythms of the natural world (Keown 2010: 251–252). The poem is prefaced with an account of Maevarua's search for the right 'words', and it is clear from the context that these are the *paroles* associated with the Māʻohi oral tradition:

> And then, because since the beginning of time his people have always expressed themselves through the Word, Maevarua searches deep in his soul to find words to offer his son, his flesh and blood. Words, the music of love that he will be able to hear in his memory when he misses his Land too much. Words chosen amongst the multitudes of words in their language to make this world live in him. (Spitz 2007: 29)

Notable in this passage, as in the source text, is the structural repetition used in Māʻohi and other Polynesian oral traditions both for rhetorical emphasis and as an *aide-mémoire* (Keown 2010: 251–252). Where this section of the translation is clearly associated with the vitality of the Māʻohi oral tradition, the association between writing and the formal restrictions of French literary culture is contrastingly evoked in a later passage in which Māʻohi are notified via official letters (in French) of the deaths of their sons fighting in the Second World War: "Twelve letters take the place of twelve children, letters full of leaden words that only the minister can make out, written in that incomprehensible language" (Spitz 2007: 33). It is clear from the context that "leaden words" corresponds with the phrase "des mots inertes" in Spitz's original narrative, establishing a contrast with the dynamism of 'la parole' (Spitz 1991/2003: 44; 2007: 33; Keown 2010: 251–252).

The apprehension of such nuances does require attentive reading, however, and Anderson's decision to include minimal paratextual aids for the monolingual reader does, as she acknowledges, create the risk that at least some of the unique stylistic and cultural specificities of the source text may be obscured (Anderson 2009).[12] Yet this is tempered by the fact that the translation is clearly targeted toward a culturally informed Pacific readership: Huia is a New Zealand publishing company specializing in the production of works by Māori (Indigenous New Zealanders) and "our cousins from the Pacific", and Anderson explicitly refers to Māʻohi as "another Pacific culture" in her translator's note ('The Story of Huia'; Anderson 2007: 3). Significantly, Spitz's anticolonial rhetoric, and her foregrounding of Indigenous oral traditions and environmental conservationism, resonate with the work of Māori writers (such as Patricia Grace, Witi Ihimaera, and Hone Tuwhare), as well as Polynesian authors further afield (such as Haunani-Kay Trask of Hawaiʻi). Similarly, the novel's antinuclear political stance is in keeping with widespread opposition to military imperialism throughout the Indigenous Pacific (Keown and Murray, 2013; Teaiwa 2008).

The translations of Kanak writing produced by Raylene Ramsay and Deborah Walker-Morrison are also targeted at least in part to a Pacific readership: *Nights of Storytelling*, for example, is explicitly aimed at a primarily "Francophile, Anglophone Pacific audience" (Walker-Morrison 2010: 235) and includes a multimedia DVD on which recitations of Kanak oral tales (in French and Paicî) are accompanied by subtitles in New Zealand Māori (as well as English). Anticipating a comparable readership, in *The Wreck*—a controversial narrative focused on the intergenerational sexual abuse of Kanak girls and women—Walker-Morrison and Ramsay translate passages of colloquial French into "Maori-Pasifika inflected" demotic New Zealand English (Walker-Morrison and Ramsay 2011: xxix). The novel exemplifies Bakhtin's notion of polyphony, incorporating multiple registers and discourses, and foregrounding the importance of orality in Kanak culture by including, *inter alia*, oral narratives, foundation myths, rap songs, and poems. It is in the speech of younger characters in particular that Walker-Morrison and Ramsay use 'Maori-Pasifika inflected' English: in a drunken exchange on the street, for example, a compliment paid by one young Kanak to another: "je savais pas que t'avais un vocabulaire, toi!" is translated as "Didn't know you had such a flash vocabulary" (Gorodé 2005/2007: 26; 2011: 21). 'Flash,' an adjective meaning 'impressive,' is commonly used among young New Zealand Māori and Pacific Islanders. Similarly, during the same exchange a young woman, Lila, issues a mock threat: "Mais maintenant, écouter mon historie et arrêter de me couper la parole sinon vous allez tous ramasser mon poing sur la gueule!" which is translated thus: "But anyway, now you listen to my story and shut up interrupting or else all of youse'll get my fist in your faces!" (Gorodé 2005/2007: 26; 2011: 21). 'Youse' is a second-person plural pronoun again commonly used among Māori. Numerous youthful characters in Gorodé's novel use the collocation "cuzzy bro" or "cuzzy babe" ("le/la cous" in *L'épave*), frequently used by Māori as a way of expressing affinity with other Māori who are not necessary close relatives/cousins, and various other Māori/Pacific Islander colloquialisms such as "bit of a feed" ("de quoi se mettre sous la dent" in the original narrative) are widespread (Gorodé 2005/2007: 33, 67; 2011: 30, 63).

There is some overlap between Ramsay's, Walker-Morrison's, and Anderson's translation methods: while expressing reservations about foreignizing translation strategies, Walker-Morrison nevertheless points out that she and Ramsay made "judicious" use of foreignization in *Nights of Storytelling*, for example, by retaining many Indigenous place-names and proper nouns that are printed without italics or gloss, and by using "accepted Kanak spelling" rather than French equivalents (2010: 245–246). In contrast to Anderson, however, Ramsay and Walker-Morrison favor what Appiah terms 'thick translation' strategies, including provision of a significant amount of paratextual material (comprising translators' notes, footnotes, and expository passages) designed to assist a (scholarly) reader in situating the translations within a specifically Kanak literary-cultural context. This is particularly evident in *Nights of Storytelling*, which provides not only a contextualizing introduction, but also expository sections accompanying each translated work, with each text in turn situated within discrete literary periods and genre groupings.

Such an apparatus furnishes the translators with multiple opportunities to convey the centrality of oral traditions to Kanak culture(s). The first part of the book, for example, is entitled 'Kanak Histories' and contains a variety of transcribed and translated oral narratives prefaced by introductory passages emphasizing the primacy of "historico-mythic stories" as vehicles for the "collective memory" of each clan group (Ramsay 2011: 13). These narratives pertain to creation and the origins of (and relationships within and between) clans; relationships between mortals and the spirit world, including its manifestations within the natural environment; morality, taboo, and cultural initiation; and social and physical transformations. The translators emphasize the multiple and mutable layers of translation that underpin this part of the book: many of the translations are based on French-language texts (often produced by French ethnographers, settlers, and missionaries) that are themselves transcriptions of oral tales with multiple variants across different Kanak linguistic communities (Walker-Morrison 2010: 236). Three of these tales—'Teê Kanake' (a Paicî creation story), 'Blind Dancer' (a narrative of marital discord), and 'The Rat and the Octopus' (an animal tale)—are recited (with an accompanying image track and subtitles) on the multimedia DVD that accompanies the volume, produced largely in an attempt to "restage the performative dimension of oral literature and poetry" (Walker-Morrison

2010: 236). As Walker-Morrison observes (in an illuminating essay reflecting on the production of the DVD), Kanak oral narratives frequently "conjure familiar places and shared cultural memories," and the DVD's inclusion of still photographs and contemporary illustrations (by Éric Mouchonnière) of figures and locations featuring in the 'Teê Kanake' narrative—which tells of the creation of the world, the 'evolution' of the first humans, and the settlement of New Caledonia by Teê Kanake and his descendants[13]—functions as a kind of "prosthetic memory, drawing the foreign viewer into closer proximity with this shared space that constitutes the performance condition of traditional oral literature" (2010: 237).

Significantly, the version of 'Teê Kanake' recorded on the DVD is recited, first in Paicî and then in French, by Déwé Gorodé, whose grandfather Philippe Gorodé first transcribed the story (as recounted by Pierre PwêRêpwea) for ethnologist Jean Guiart (Guiart 1963; Walker-Morrison 2010: 241–242). Gorodé is just one of a number of Kanak consultants involved in the production of the DVD, a process that bespeaks Ramsay and Walker-Morrison's acute sense of responsibility as translators of works by Indigenous writers hitherto marginalized by the metropolitan Francophone literary establishment and largely unknown within the Anglophone Pacific. As Ramsay puts it in the introduction to *Nights of Storytelling*, the anthology opens up to Anglophone readers "an important location of decolonization

Figure 9.1   A contemporary sculpture of Teâ Kanaké superimposed against a line of hills (in the Tjamba Valley) that bears his name.

Credit line: Image courtesy of Deborah Walker-Morrison and Neil Morrison © 2011.

in the French Pacific," and she and her co-translators "have aimed to speak *with* rather than stand for the original voices of our texts, seeking to [. . .] provide our readers with an experience of the texts and their contexts that puts them into the shoes of the original audience while also signaling essential elements of cultural difference" (2011: 1, 9). Such a statement resonates with Ramsay's and Walker-Morrison's professed desire to achieve 'dynamic equivalence,' which, in Eugene Nida's terms, aims to ensure that "the message of the original text has been so transported into the receptor language that the *response* of the *receptor* is essentially like that of the original receptors" (Nida and Taber 1969: 200; Ramsay and Walker-Morrison 2009). Significantly, Walker-Morrison has New Zealand Māori ancestry, and in her 2010 book chapter reflecting on the production of *Nights of Storytelling* and the accompanying DVD, she switches into Māori to thank the various Kanak people who offered advice on the project: "Ngā mihi nui ki a rātou katoa!" ("Many thanks to all of them!") (2010: 243; my translation). Later, in asserting that for her, the primary significance of the project "lies in a capacity to bring indigenous audiences and artists from different regions and continents into closer contact through translation," she closes the chapter with another Māori sentence: "Na reira, tēnā ra tātou katoa!" ("Therefore, that's all of us!"), thereby incorporating all those involved in the project within the salutatory parameters of Māori ceremonial speech exchanges (Walker-Morrison 2010: 250; my translation). Both Ramsay and Walker-Morrison have spent extended periods living and working in New Caledonia and view this experience as crucial to a responsible translation strategy (Ramsay and Walker-Morrison 2009).

Gorodé's participation in the rendition of 'Teê Kanaké' is, therefore, the result of a careful process of collaboration between the translators and the local Kanak community, and helps ameliorate the risk that the recording of a single version of the creation story ends up "solidifying the dynamic, fluid nature of oral literature, reducing its multiplicity into a single interpretation which implicitly claims authority over others," given that Gorodé's Paicî-medium recitation of the narrative signals her status as a representative of the community from which this version of the story originates (Walker-Morrison 2010: 241). Gorodé's involvement also lends a political edge to the rendition, given that she has herself played a key role not only in the Kanak independence movement[14] (which has sought, *inter alia*, to reclaim ancestral lands alienated by French colonizers), but also in collecting and transcribing Melanesian stories and mythological narratives for use in schools, in order to counter the prevailing Eurocentrism of the New Caledonian education system (Brown 2004: xi–xii; Keown 2010). As Walker-Morrison points out, the inclusion of Gorodé's recitation in Paicî (which was performed from memory rather than from a script) not only brings the audience closer to the conditions of a live storytelling performance, but also "constitutes a powerful, appropriate and readily available means of [. . .] assisting indigenous language regeneration and survival" (2010: 238). Significantly, Gorodé has herself taught Paicî at a number of New Caledonian schools since the 1970s, and was involved in the establishment (in the 1980s) of experimental Indigenous schools (Ecoles populaire kanak) that educated Kanak children about their cultures and in their ancestral languages (Walker-Morrison and Ramsay 2011: vii).

In reflecting further on the process of producing the DVD, Walker-Morrison points out that the process of audiovisual translation—specifically, subtitling—also poses challenges for a culturally sensitive translator, in that the necessary process of condensing and rewriting (resulting from the technical constraints of the medium) potentially undermines "the initial project of restoring the 'orality' of the texts" (Walker-Morrison 2010: 236). A further risk is that the "domesticating, audience-centered norms" of the medium potentially conflict "irreconcilably" with "calls for translations of postcolonial and/or indigenous literature to be situated firmly within a resistant, source-text centered, foreignizing paradigm" (Walker-Morrison 2010: 236). However, one could argue that these potential problems are circumvented in various ways in the *Nights of Storytelling* DVD.

Firstly, the translators themselves point out that "inevitable translation losses" are mitigated "by the multi-sensory nature of the medium, since the audience receives the auditory stimulus in the source language simultaneously with the visual input from the image track and subtitles," thus conveying some sense of the dynamism and immediacy of the oral storytelling experience (Ramsay and Walker-Morrison, forthcoming). Further, the provision of subtitles in Māori, the language of another Indigenous Pacific culture, counterbalances the predominantly Anglo/Eurocentric bias of the international subtitling industry, allowing Māori viewers to experience what Hawai'ian translation theorist Pua'ala'okalani Aiu terms "a deeply felt metaphorical gestalt" by substituting culturally resonant Māori words for similarly freighted terms from Kanak culture (Días Cintas and Anderman 2009: 8; Aiu 2010: 94).

In 'Teê Kanake,' for example, where the word 'earth' is used in the English translation and subtitles—in the opening sentence "The elders say that the Earth, curled up in a spiral, used to touch the moon" (Ramsay 2011: 22)—the Māori subtitles use 'Papatūānuku,' which is the Māori name for the goddess of the earth, as well as the land itself. This lexical choice conveys to Māori readers the corresponding sacred significance of the land to Kanak peoples: in both cultures, clan or iwi (tribal) groups are linked through genealogy to specific geographical locations (Keown 2007; Ramsay 2011: 14). Similarly, where the English translation and subtitles use the French word 'tertre'—a term that denotes a mound or place of origin associated with a particular clan group, whose identity "is inscribed in the landscape by way of the names of places passed through and inhabited by the founding fathers" (Ramsay 2011: 14)—the Māori subtitles use the term 'papakāinga' (literally, 'home earth'), which has a comparable cultural resonance. Such approximations are also evident in other translated oral tales on the DVD: in 'The Rat and the Octopus,' for example, where the English translation uses the word 'Kiak' (glossed as 'swamp hen' in the English subtitles), the Māori subtitles use 'Pūkeko,' the Indigenous term for a type of swamp hen found in Aotearoa/New Zealand. This process of cultural (as well as linguistic) translation is significant given that this particular animal tale (which details the animosity between the rat and the octopus that putatively developed after the rat, rescued from drowning by the octopus, defecated on his benefactor's head) has local variants in Tonga and many other parts of the Pacific (Benson 1993: 104).

Another example of the way in which the DVD approximates Pacific oral storytelling conditions is in its presentation of the work of contemporary Kanak spoken word poet Paul Wamo. Here, the DVD includes filmed footage of Wamo reciting two of his poems, 'Belle au bois dormant' and 'Amnésie Traditionelle' (both of which explore the alienation of urbanized Kanak youth). Wamo is a highly charismatic performer, and the DVD recordings of his poems allow the viewer to apprehend voice modulations, rhythms, gestures, and facial expressions that are crucial to a full appreciation of his work. Much of his work exists only in oral form: 'Belle au bois dormant,' for example, has only appeared in print in *Nights of Storytelling* (in an English translation entitled 'Sleeping Beauty') and (in French and English versions) in Walker-Morrison's essay reflecting on the translation project (2010: 253).

When preparing the subtitles for 'Belle au bois dormant' on the DVD, Walker-Morrison made the decision to slightly speed up the subtitles to allow the translation of the poem to be presented in full, thereby avoiding having to "compromise" the poem's rhetorical richness and technical precision (2010: 247).[15] The poem is composed in Alexandrine rhyming couplets (a form favored in classical French poetry), but with a slight variation: where the classical form uses twelve syllable lines with a caesura after the sixth syllable, Wamo introduces his caesura after the word 'culture' that appears at the beginning of each verse. This deliberate metrical irregularity is matched by radical stylistic shifts in the lexis of the poem, which, as Walker-Morrison notes, juxtaposes "very traditional, formal, almost dated, literary language" (such as the line "J'arpenterai les coulisses de mon histoire," translated as "Behind scenes of the past I search the night") and references to European fairy tales and Classical mythology (including an analogy drawn between the 'Sleeping Beauty' fairy tale and the latent 'culture' the speaker seeks to re(dis)cover, as well as a reference to Chronos, the Greek god of time), with "inventive poetic collocations" and terms drawn from contemporary "global youth culture" (such as the line "Pilleurs fantômes de ma cause desperados," translated as "Phantom tomb raiders of my Paradise Lost") (Walker-Morrison 2010: 247, 253). Such formal and stylistic shifts underscore the poem's theme, which juxtaposes the urban environment (permeated with

Figure 9.2   Paul Wamo reciting 'Belle au bois dormant' in the grounds of the Centre Tjibaou, Nouméa.

Credit line: Image courtesy of Deborah Walker-Morrison and Neil Morrison © 2011.

metropolitan French and global cultural influences) with the young urban speaker's sense of estrangement from (and yearning toward) traditional cultural values and social practices associated with life in the tribu (a French term that refers both to a clan group and the customary land or village in which it is situated). The filmed rendition of the poem reinforces these juxtapositions, not only in the modulations of Wamo's delivery, but also through visual cues: Wamo wears a T-shirt and beanie hat redolent of the urban youth culture he describes, but he is filmed against the backdrop of a taro garden in the verdant grounds of the Centre Tjibaou (a Kanak cultural center named after pro-independence activist Jean-Marie Tjibaou, who was assassinated in 1989 by a disaffected Kanak militant).

Even for a foreign viewer, the leafy backdrop to Wamo's recitation of 'Belle au bois dormant' signals the potential for cultural regeneration, and for those locals who recognize the precise location of the filming, there is arguably an added resonance in the Centre's associations with an efflorescence of Kanak political consciousness in protest against the expropriation of Kanak lands and the denigration of Kanak culture under French colonialism. Indeed, other Wamo poems, such as 'Je Suis Noir' (from his 2008 CD book *J'aime les mots*), are explicitly anticolonial, bespeaking Wamo's place within a wider community of young Indigenous Pacific performance poets who combine notions of "community representation and responsibility" central to Pacific

oral traditions with the political imperatives and aesthetic innovations associated with Black American and Caribbean performance poetry and music
(Marsh 2010: 211). Wamo's poem is reminiscent of the *négritude* movement in
its appeal to an international Black community of oppressed peoples: he situates Kanak nationalism alongside the struggles of peoples of African descent
and enumerates various racial slurs and forms of exploitation suffered by
these communities ("On me nomme souvent: / Non civilisé—Non eduqué /
NOIR SAUVAGE! [. . .] On m'a exploité / Parce que j'étais Noir [. . .] On
m'a pris pour le Diable / Car je n'étais pas Blanc" (2008: n.p.).

I want to end this chapter by reflecting on a final example of Ramsay's and
Walker-Morrison's poetry translation strategies, this time with reference to
Sharing as Custom Provides, their edition of Gorodé's poetry. This volume has
the added benefit of appearing as a bilingual edition, allowing the translators' decisions to be evaluated with less reliance on paratextual commentary.
In fact, Ramsay and Walker-Morrison had intended to include translators'
notes with the edition, but this option was vetoed by the publisher, so they
had to resort to footnotes as a means by which to explain particular cultural
references or to offer definitions of Paicî words (which are used sparingly
but regularly throughout the collection, but remain untranslated within the
poems themselves). This strategy of preserving Paicî words in the translated
poems is significant given that, as Samia Mehrez points out, texts written by
"postcolonial bilingual subjects" problematize the assumption (within traditional translation theory) of a transaction between discrete, clearly defined
source and target languages, instead creating a hybrid 'in-between' linguistic
milieu that demands a mode of evaluation beyond "conventional notions of
linguistic equivalence or ideas of loss and gain" (Mehrez 1992: 121; Keown
2010: 253). In *Sharing as Custom Provides*, Gorodé's native language remains
the only constant between source text and translation, acquiring a transcendental quality that poses a challenge to the dominance of the two 'metropolitan' languages (see also Keown 2010: 255).

This dynamic is reinforced by the fact that various poems in *Sharing as
Custom Provides*, like the work of other Kanak and Māʻohi writers discussed
in this chapter, place heavy emphasis on the centrality of oral traditions to
Kanak culture. Several of Gorodé's works juxtapose speech and writing in
terms that relegate the latter to a subordinate status, in keeping with the
dual significance of 'parole' as a term that refers both to speech and to the
Kanak oral tradition. The poem 'Word of Struggle,' ('Parole de Lutte' for
example—written in 1974, while Gorodé was imprisoned for her involvement
in the Kanak independence movement—emphasizes the significance of the
spoken word (linked with ancient Kanak cultural practices and the ritualized
relationship to place) as a means by which to express "the misery" of Kanak
peoples under French colonialism (6). The spoken word—*parole* in the source
text (7)—is also identified as a medium through which to develop a language
of praxis and political resistance, a "radical poetics" expressing "a politics

of struggle" (6). In their translation, Ramsay and Walker-Morrison draw explicit attention to this link between the oral tradition and political activism by including with the translation a footnote explaining the dual significance of 'parole.' This provides the Anglophone reader with a clear context in which to interpret later poems such as 'speaking truth' ('dire le vrai'), which again emphasizes verbal expression as a means by which to, in this case, counter the epistemic violence of colonial or dominant discourses, the "chorus" of the "on behalf ofs" ("le refrain des au nom de") that effaces the voices of Kanak peoples (108, 110). Similarly, another poem, 'écouter,' ('listen'), accentuates the primacy of the spoken word, not just through the lexis of speech, but also through assonance and alliteration, in order to underscore the poem's aural theme: "Écouter/ une note / un mot [. . .] un cri [. . .] une rime / un rhythme" (102). In their translation, Ramsay and Walker-Morrison are able to preserve the repeated vowels *graphically* ("a note / a word [. . .] a cry [. . .] a rhyme / a rhythm" (100)), even if the aural patterning is lost to some degree because of the wide variety of vowel phonemes in English. Indeed, this and other poems in the volume depend at least in part on the graphic aspects of their composition for their particular linguistic effects (resonating with Jacques Derrida's notion of 'différance'[16]), and in poems such as 'writing' ('écrire'), the written and spoken word are accorded equal status in the process of reclaiming Kanaky through iteration: "writing" creates a space in which Kanak peoples "may speak" their "oneness of thought" (48). Similarly, 'creation' ('création') details the process of "sorting words"–the "sound" of a "consonant" as well as the "quaver" of a "comma" or the "closure" of a "bracket"–in order to "[carve] out" a space in which to "[write] the self" (94–96). Here, Gorodé muses on the difficulty of achieving full expression in a "language / that is not mine" (French), but concludes that it is possible to "[seize] sense" in order to secure linguistic and ontological freedom (95).

Conclusion

The various source texts and translations I have discussed in this chapter have 'carried across' the oral traditions of Kanak and Mā'ohi peoples into print and audiovisual formats, as well as between languages, and the work of Gorodé and Spitz in particular conveys an acute sense of the ways in which writing can enhance, rather than erode, the centrality of oral traditions to contemporary Indigenous Pacific cultures. Similarly, in carrying across untranslated Mā'ohi and Paicî from source text to translation, Anderson, Ramsay, and Walker-Morrison accord these languages a transcendental status that–in keeping with Samia Mehrez's arguments on plurilingualism–underscores rather than dilutes the counterdiscursive aspects of both Gorodé's and Spitz's work (see also Keown 2010). All three translators have indicated their keen awareness of the ethical challenges involved in the translation of the work of Indigenous or 'postcolonial' writers and have approached the task with sensitivity and cultural awareness, making productive use of para-textual materials that serve both to bridge gaps between cultures but also to emphasize that which is untranslatable and unassimilable, respecting those "essential elements of cultural difference" (Ramsay 2011: 9) that are crucial to the singularity and survival of Indigenous Francophone Pacific cultures, and the literatures in which they receive such compelling expression.

Notes

I would like to thank the Carnegie Trust for the Universities of Scotland for funding that allowed me to undertake research for the chapter in New Zealand, and Jean Anderson, Raylene Ramsay and Deborah Walker-Morrison for allowing me to conduct interviews with them.

1. These contact languages developed in commercial plantations in the Pacific during (and beyond) the colonial period. During the late nineteenth century, when the British Empire was at its height, various Pidgin languages (which used English vocabulary but whose grammatical and semantic systems were based on local languages) were spoken throughout most of the Pacific Basin. During the early decades of the twentieth century, many of these Pacific Pidgins died out, but Melanesian Pidgin survived, and when a new generation of Melanesians grew up speaking Pidgin as their first language, it was thus transformed from a Pidgin (used only as a second or contact language) into a Creole (spoken as a first language). Fiji's plantation history gave rise to Fiji Hindi, a koine (dialect mix) deriving from a variety of North Indian dialects spoken by the original indentured laborers who came to Fiji in the late nineteenth century (see Lynch 1998; Keown 2007).

2. The countries listed here are ones in which French or Spanish are official languages.

3. For example, Māʻohi writer Chantal Spitz, whose work is discussed below, has published a series of articles in the Māʻohi literary journal *Littérama'ohi* (established in 2002 by Spitz and several other Māʻohi writers) in which she argues for the importance of fostering relationships with other Pacific writers that transcend the Francophone–Anglophone linguistic divide. The fifth issue of *Littérama'ohi* (entitled 'Rencontres Océanienne') answered this call, featuring the work of a range of New Caledonian writers (of both European and Kanak descent), as well as translations into French of material by Anglophone Indigenous Pacific writers such as Russell Soaba (Papua New Guinea), Teresia Teaiwa (of I-Kiribati and African American descent), Anita Heiss (Australia), and Sia Figiel (Samoa). Within New Caledonia, since 2003 biannual Salons du livre have included both Anglophone and Francophone Pacific writers, and Kanak author Déwé Gorodé (discussed later in this chapter) has translated into French a selection of poetry by Grace Mera Molisa (1997), an Anglophone writer from Vanuatu with whom she has expressed a particular affinity. See Keown (2010) for a fuller account of these interlingual dialogues.

4. There is a considerable corpus of Francophone Pacific literature produced by writers of European descent (particularly in New Caledonia), but this chapter focuses primarily on Indigenous writing. I use the term 'Indigenous' (where appropriate) rather than 'postcolonial' to reflect the fact that with the exception of Vanuatu (a former Anglo-French condominium that achieved independence in 1980), the 'French' Pacific is neither 'postcolonial' nor strictly 'colonial' in political status. Until relatively recently, French Polynesia, Wallis and Futuna,

and New Caledonia were designated French 'Territoires d'outre-mer,' enjoying greater local autonomy than 'Départements d'outre-mer,' such as French Guyana and Guadeloupe. As of 2003, however, French Polynesia and Wallis and Futuna became known as 'Collectivités d'outre-mer,' while New Caledonia, following the Nouméa Accord of 1998 (which has led to improved socioeconomic conditions for Kanak peoples and raised the possibility of independence by majority vote in a series of referenda planned from 2018), was uniquely designated 'Pays d'outre-mer' and granted even greater political decentralization (Brown 2004: xxxii; Keown 2010: 242; Walker-Morrison and Ramsay 2011: v).

5. New Caledonia's colonial history has been marked by vigorous Kanak opposition to French rule, with violent uprisings taking place in 1878 and 1917, but a new phase of political protest began in the 1970s and 1980s, following revelations that as a result of an influx of new French settlers arriving during the nickel 'boom' years of the 1960s, Melanesians had become a minority ethnic group for the first time. These protests—which culminated in a deadly standoff between Kanak militants and the French authorities in 1988—helped bring about the signing (that same year) of the Matignon Accords, which restored relative peace by establishing a constitutional framework within which to debate the territory's future and to improve socio-economic conditions for Kanak peoples. Further advances were made in the 1998 Nouméa Accord (Brown 2004: x–xii; Keown 2010).

6. French nuclear testing in French Polynesia took place across a thirty-year period (from 1966), with atmospheric tests in the Tuamotu island group until 1975, followed by testing under the coral atoll and the lagoon, primarily in Moruroa. These tests caused immense environmental damage and precipitated riots and demonstrations from French Polynesians throughout the testing period, as well as drawing protest from a broad spectrum of other nations within and beyond the Pacific (see Keown 2007: 96–99).

7. There are twenty-eight extant Kanak languages in New Caledonia. The label 'Kanak' derives from 'canaque,' the pejorative French colonial term for Indigenous New Caledonians, but the ultimate source is in Polynesian terms for 'man/person' or 'people' ('kanaka' in Hawai'ian and 'tangata' in New Zealand Māori, for example), and Indigenous Caledonians have recently reclaimed the label and (re)indigenized its spelling.

8. These include *Breadfruit* (2000), *Frangipani* (2004), and *Tiare* (2006), all focused on the family/social life of a Tahitian mother, Materena Mahi.

9. Au vent des îles has also published French translations of novels and short stories by a variety of other Anglophone Indigenous Pacific writers, including Albert Wendt (of Samoa), Rowan Metcalfe (of Tahitian/Pitcairn Islander descent), and Māori authors Patricia Grace, Witi Ihimaera, Alice Tawhai, and Isabel Waiti-Mulholland (see http://www.auventdesiles.pf/notre-catalogue/39–litteratures-du-pacifique.html, accessed September 26, 2012).

10. A number of the poems in this volume were first published in *dire le vrai/to tell the truth* (1999), a bilingual collection of poetry, coauthored by Gorodé and Nicolas Kurtovitch (a New Caledonian poet of French settler descent), with English translations by Raylene Ramsay (Gorodé) and Brian McKay (Kurtovitch).

11. The Paicî linguistic community, located on the central east coast of the grande terre (large/main island of New Caledonia), is the second largest (after the Drehu-speaking community) (see Lynch 1998: 33).

12. Anderson's translation strategy is broadly equivalent in *The Missing King*, aiming for 'a minimum of adaptation or other interference' (viii), though the brief translator's note at the beginning of the text is in this case supplemented by some brief notes on the Tahitian language, Tahitian geography and the French education system that appear (along with a more extensive glossary) in the end matter. The novel—an autobiographical narrative by a Marquesan man that is subsequently appropriated by a French psychologist—is less stylistically experimental than Spitz's, but does include unusually long paragraphs and irregular uses of tense characteristic of Tahitian oral narrative that Anderson preserves in the translation.

13. There are variations in the spelling of Teê Kanake's name: it appears as Teâ Kanaké on the DVD.

14. Gorodé is one of the founders of the independence organizations Groupe 1878 (formed in 1974 and named after the 1878 Kanak uprising discussed in note 5) and PALIKA (Parti de Libération Kanak, formed in 1976), and was jailed twice in the 1970s for her involvement in anticolonial protest activity.

15. Where most subtitles on the DVD allow a minimum 1.5 seconds per one line subtitle, the Wamo subtitles at times allow less than two seconds' screen time per two-line subtitle (Walker-Morrison 2010: 247).

16. I refer here to Derrida's (1976) argument (in *Of Grammatology*) for the importance of written text in differentiating homophonous terms, for example, as well as his contestation of the privileging of speech over writing in Western philosophy.

References

Aiu, P. D. (2010) 'Ne'e Papa I Ke Ō Mau: Language as an Indicator of Hawaiian Resistance and Power' in *Translation, Resistance, Activism*, ed. M. Tymoczko (Amherst: University of Massachusetts Press), pp. 89–107.

Anderson, J. (2007) 'Translator's Note' in *Island of Shattered Dreams*, by C. Spitz, trans. J. Anderson (Wellington: Huia), pp. 1–3.

Anderson, J. (2009) Unpublished interview with Michelle Keown, February 24.

Anderson, J. (2010) 'La Traduction résistante. Some Principles of Resistant Translation of Francophone and Anglophone Pacific Literature' in *Cultural Crossings: Negotiating Identities in Francophone and Anglophone Pacific Literatures*, ed. R. Ramsay (Brussels: Peter Lang), pp. 285–301.

Appiah, K. A. (1993) 'Thick Translation' *Callaloo* 16: 808–819.

Bassnett, S., and Trivedi, H. (eds) (1999) *Post-Colonial Translation: Theory and Practice* (London: Routledge).

Benson, C. (1993) *Pacific Folk Tales* (Suva: Institute of Education, University of the South Pacific).

Brotherson, M. (2007) *Le Roi Absent* (Papeete: Au vent des îles).

Brotherson, M. (2012) *The Missing King*. Trans. J. Anderson (Auckland: Little Island Press).

Brown, P. (2004) 'Introduction' in *The Kanak Apple Season*, by D. Gorodé, trans. Peter Brown (Canberra: Pandanus), pp. ix–xxxix.

Crocombe, R. (2001) *The South Pacific* (Suva: Institute of Pacific Studies).

Días Cintas, J., and Anderman, G. (2009) 'Introduction' in *Audiovisual Translation: Language Transfer on Screen*, ed. J. Días Cintas and G. Anderman (London: Palgrave), pp. 1–17.

Derrida, J. (1976) *Of Grammatology*. Trans. Gayatri Spivak (Baltimore, MD: Johns Hopkins University Press).

Forsdick, C., and Murphy, D. (eds) (2003) *Francophone Postcolonial Studies* (London: Arnold).

Gope, P. (1999) *Le dernier crépuscule* (Nouméa: Grain de Sable).

Gope, P. (2001) *The Last Nightfall*. Trans. Baineo-Boenengkih and P. S. Keable (Nouméa: Grain de Sable/Suva: Institute of Pacific Studies).

Gope, P., and Kurtovitch, N. (2002) *Les dieux sont borgnes* (Nouméa: Grain de Sable).

Gorodé, D. (2004a) *The Kanak Apple Season: Selected Short Fiction of Déwé Gorodé*. Trans. P. Brown (Canberra: Pandanus).

Gorodé, D. (2004b) *Sharing as Custom Provides: Selected Poems of Déwé Gorodé*. Trans. R. Ramsay and D. Walker (Canberra: Pandanus).

Gorodé, D. (2005/2007) *L'épave* (Nouméa: Madrépores).

Gorodé, D. (2011) *The Wreck*. Trans. R. Ramsay and D. Walker-Morrison (Auckland: Little Island Press).

Gorodé, D., and Kurtovitch, N. (1999) *dire le vrai/to tell the truth* (Nouméa: Grain de Sable).

Guiart, J. (1963) *Structure de la chefferie en Mélanésie du Sud* (Paris: Institut d'ethnologie).

Hau'ofa, E. (2008). *We Are the Ocean: Selected Works* (Honolulu: University of Hawai'i Press).

Huggan, G. (2008) *Interdisciplinary Measures: Literature and the Future of Postcolonial Studies* (Liverpool: Liverpool University Press).

Keown, M. (2007) *Pacific Islands Writing: The Postcolonial Literatures of Aotearoa/New Zealand and Oceania* (Oxford: Oxford University Press).

Keown, M. (2008) '"Our Sea of Islands": Migration and *Métissage* in Contemporary Polynesian Writing' *International Journal of Francophone Studies* 11: 2: 503–522.

Keown, M. (2010) '*Littérature-monde* or *Littérature Océanienne?*: Internationalism versus Regionalism in Francophone Pacific Writing' in *Transnational French Studies: Postcolonialism and Littérature-monde*, ed. C. Forsdick, D. Murphy, and A. Hargreaves (Liverpool: Liverpool University Press), pp. 240–257.

Keown, M., and Murray, S. (2013) '"A Sea of Islands?": Globalization, Regionalism and Nationalism in the Pacific' in *The Oxford Handbook of Postcolonial Studies*, ed. G. Huggan (Oxford: Oxford University Press), pp. 607–627.

Lynch, J. (1998) *Pacific Languages* (Honolulu: University of Hawai'i Press).

Marsh, S. T. (2010) 'Pasifika Poetry on the Move: Staging Polynation' in *Cultural Crossings: Negotiating Identities in Francophone and Anglophone Pacific Literatures*, ed. R. Ramsay (Brussels: Peter Lang), pp. 197–216.

Mateata-Allain, K. (2008) *Bridging Our Sea of Islands: French Polynesian Literature within an Oceanic Context* (Saarbrücken: Verlag Dr. Müller).

Mehrez, S. (1992) 'Translation and the Postcolonial Experience: The Francophone North African Text,' in *Rethinking Translation*, ed. Lawrence Venuti (London: Routledge), pp. 120–138.

Molisa, G. M. (1997) *Pierre Noire*. Trans. Déwé Gorodé (Nouméa: Grain de Sable).

Nicole, R. (1999) 'Resisting Orientalism: Pacific Literature in French' in *Inside Out: Literature, Cultural Politics, and Identity in the New Pacific*, ed. V. Hereniko and R. Wilson (Lanham: Rowman and Littlefield), pp. 265–290.

Nida, E. A., and Taber, C. R. (1969) *The Theory and Practice of Translation, with Special Reference to Bible Translating* (Leiden: Brill).

Pym, A. (2009) 'Humanising Translation History' *Hermes* 42: 23–48.

Ramsay, R. (ed) (2011) *Nights of Storytelling: A Cultural History of Kanaky-New Caledonia* (Honolulu: University of Hawai'i Press).

Ramsay, R. and Walker-Morrison, D. (Forthcoming) '"Mon Whare, ton Fare": Writing towards each other through the Translation of Pacific Literatures' in *Littératures du Pacifique*, ed. S. André and J. Bessière (Paris: Champion).

Ramsay, R., and Walker-Morrison, D. (2009) Unpublished interview with Michelle Keown, March 13.

Robinson, D. (1997) *Translation and Empire: Postcolonial Theories Explained* (Manchester: St. Jerome).

Spitz, C. (1991/2003) *L'île des rêves écrasés* (Tahiti: Au vent des îles).

Spitz, C. (2007) *Island of Shattered Dreams*. Trans. Jean Anderson (Wellington: Huia).

Stewart, F., Mateata-Allain, K., and Dale Mawyer, A. (eds) (2006) *Vārua Tupu: New Writing from French Polynesia* (Honolulu: University of Hawai'i Press).

Teaiwa, T. (2008) 'Globalizing and Gendered Forces: The Contemporary Militarization of the Pacific/Oceania' in *Gender and Globalization in Asia and the Pacific*, ed. K. E. Ferguson and M. Mironescu (Honolulu: University of Hawai'i Press), pp. 318–332.

'The Story of Huia.' Huia Publishers. http://www.huia.co.nz/?sn=8&st=1&pg=404 (accessed September 26, 2012).

Tjibaou, J.-M., and Dobbelaere, G. (1995) 'Kanaké' *Jeu scénique Mwa Vée, Revue Culturelle Kanak*, September 10, 9–19.

Tjibaou, J.-M., and Dobbelaere, G. (2006) *Kanaké, A Three-Act Play*. Trans. Roy Benyon (Suva: University of the South Pacific).

Tymoczko, M. (1999) *Translation in a Postcolonial Context: Early Irish Literature in English Translation* (Manchester: St. Jerome).

Tymoczko, M. (2007) *Enlarging Translation, Empowering Translators* (Manchester: St. Jerome).

Tymoczko, M. (2010) 'Translation, Resistance, Activism: An Overview' in *Translation, Resistance, Activism*, ed. Maria Tymoczko (Amherst: University of Massachusetts Press), pp. 1–22.

Vaite, C. (2000) Breadfruit (Auckland: Random House).

Vaite, C. (2004) Frangipani (Melbourne: Text Publishing).

Vaite, C. (2006) Tiare (Melbourne: Text Publishing).

Venuti, L. (1998) The Scandals of Translation: Towards an Ethics of Difference (London: Routledge).

Venuti, L. (2012) '1990s' in *The Translation Studies Reader*, 3rd ed., ed. Lawrence Venuti (London: Routledge), pp. 271–280.

Walker-Morrison, D. (2010) 'Voice, Image, Text. Tensions, Interactions and Translation Choices in a Multi-Language, Multi-Media Presentation of Kanak Literature' in *Cultural Crossings: Negotiating Identities in Francophone and Anglophone Pacific Literatures*, ed. R. Ramsay (Brussels: Peter Lang), pp. 235–253.

Walker-Morrison, D., and R. Ramsay (2011) 'Introduction' in *The Wreck*, by D. Gorodé, trans. R. Ramsay and D. Walker-Morrison (Auckland: Little Island Press), pp. v–xxxi.

Wamo, P. (2008) *J'aime les mots* (Nouméa: L/Herbier de Feu/Grain de Sable).

10 Translation and Creation in a Postcolonial Context

Franca Cavagnoli

The Language of Postcolonial Literature

Referring to the work of his fellow countryman, Seamus Heaney wrote that James Joyce managed to turn English from "an imperial humiliation" into "a native weapon" (1978: 40). This definition can also apply to several postcolonial authors. Minor literatures—that is, the literatures written by cultural minorities in the languages of the majority—and postcolonial literatures share many features (Albertazzi 2001: 26–28); and as in the case of many postcolonial authors, Joyce's is a clear example of the dominant language being used creatively, as we can already see in his early works. Indeed, while nobody questions the daring prose experimentations carried out by Joyce in his later works, one is not always aware of the fact that right from the beginning of his literary activity, Joyce strove to give exposure to the language of a minority. The incipit of one of his earliest and most famous short stories, *Eveline* (1904), reads: "She sat at the window watching the evening invade the avenue" (Joyce 1977: 32). A discerning ear will easily grasp the alliteration in *window/watching*, and the assonances in *sat/at* and in *evening/invade/avenue*. Even in his first collection of short stories, *Dubliners* (1904), a collection that is still traditional in structure and narrative modes, Joyce cannot be removed from the Irish context that gives so much meaning to his work—a meaning that transcends the themes dealt with in the stories. Here, too, Joyce pours into his prose the sounds of the Irish language, putting great care into the text's sound and not just its semantics. Hence, as we will see in the second part of this chapter, when translating Joyce's works one ought to follow in Joyce's steps and try to mold the language one is translating into on the Irish language, in order to offset the mistake made by many translators working from Irish, who "kept turning Irish into English, rather than remodel English as Irish" (Kiberd 1996: 628). Translating Joyce does not mean to simply translate from English into another language. It means translating from *an English molded on Irish* into another language.

Much postcolonial fiction contains stories of pain, of tormented detachment from one's native soil, of displacement and outright transportation. We read stories of exile, dislocation, and alienation from one's past due to colonization and to the imposition of another language and another culture. Even when the stories tell us about migration or indentured labor, the choice of leaving one's country—while voluntary in appearance—in fact forces on those who leave a painful separation from their childhood places and from their families of origin. Postcolonial fiction is written in a language that bears the mark of the torments and tribulations of history. The violence of history and the tensions it has generated are contained ideally in the prefix *post-*, which should be intended not so much in a chronological sense—what comes after the colonial experience—as in the sense of *anti*, as a "sign of reaction" by the former colonies against colonial power (Albertazzi 2001: 115). The margins of the world rebelled against the imposition of a language that was not theirs and mixed it instead with their own native language as well as with other languages, some of them local and others that came with colonization. As it originates from the presence of two or more cultures in a given geographical area, postcolonial writing is contaminated: the different *englishes* spoken in the former colonies of the British Empire are the hybrid fruits stemming from the encounter between the motherland's English and the languages used in a given area. Hence, the language of postcolonial fiction is often the outcome of the suffering inflicted by history, but it is also the outcome of the tension originating from the wish to cancel out the center's English, as a normative code, and the will of the local populations to appropriate that very same English (Ashcroft, Griffiths, and Tiffin 1989: 8, 10).

The most interesting aspect of postcolonial writing is how it marks the difference from Received Standard English. It takes over the language of the center and replaces it with an impure language, thus adapting it to the area that suffered colonization (Ashcroft, Griffiths, and Tiffin 1989: 38). The same language is used, but it is taken further and further from the center and from the rules imposed by the center; and these marks of a progressive detachment from the standard—these sudden swerves—are what brings out the uniqueness of postcolonial writing. This uniqueness is achieved by using language variance; these distinctive marks are precisely what gave rise to the varieties of English spoken around the world. The difference is visible on a number of levels—spelling, vocabulary, morphology, and syntax—and these discordances are what express the cultural difference of postcolonial writers, a difference suggestive of their desire to belong and their will to have their own identity in a world upset by the intrusion of colonization. This process is quite clear in the works of Amos Tutuola and Ken Saro-Wiwa; in their literary creations, they search for the "creative popular spirit" as Gramsci intended it, and they use this "raw material" to build an identity that treasures the cultural richness of those in a subaltern position (Gramsci 1975: 1385). Both Tutuola and Saro-Wiwa know that the assertion of African identity passes through a confrontation with the language imposed by the colonizer. Hence, there is a very close bond between the definition of African identity and the political and cultural battle in their native Nigeria.

In his 1952 Yoruba-folktale based *The Palm-Wine Drinkard*, Amos Tutuola gives life to a brave literary experiment. In his work, the presence of another culture is apparent, and the title itself shows the traits of the experimental workshop Tutuola has given life to in his novel. *Drinkard* refers on the one hand to *drinker* and on the other to *drunkard*. The novel begins like this: "I was a palm-wine drinkard since I was a boy of ten years of age. I had no other work more than to drink palm-wine in my life. In those days we did not know other money except COWRIES, so that everything was very cheap, and my father was the richest man in town" (Tutuola 1952: 3). Tutuola creates a language with a wealth of expressive inventions, sourcing from the creative popular spirit of his people and working on lexical and syntactical calques, as we can see in the first sentence: "I was a palm-wine drunkard since I was a boy of ten years of age." The language of the subaltern rises from below to undermine the order, the cleanliness, and the propriety of the dominant language. The interferences of one language with another—the Yoruba that Tutuola spoke as his native tongue and the English he learned at the mission school—give rise to new and unexpected usages of the English language, where the creative popular spirit of the subordinates contaminates the dominant language. The outcome is a linguistic blend that on the surface reads like English, but in depth preserves the structures of Yoruba, one of Nigeria's main languages (Vivan 1983: 251–252). As we can see from the previous example, Tutuola denies the supremacy of English and then appropriates it in order to twist the English language so as to tell his story/history, through a "process of capturing and remoulding the language to new usages, (in order to mark) a separation from the site of colonial privilege" (Ashcroft, Griffiths, and Tiffin 1989: 38).

In *Shame* (1983) and in one of his landmark essays, *Imaginary Homelands* (1991), Salman Rushdie makes a statement destined to leave its firebrand on postcolonial writing and on the history of postcolonial translation: "I, too, am a translated man" (Rushdie 1991: 17). This migrant condition is something writers share with many people that move today from one part of the world to another. Migrants are homeless; for them, the adjective *transnational* is almost synonymous with *translational* (Bhabha 1994: 5, 172): without a fixed abode, always in search of an elsewhere, the migrant crosses the national borders and often lives in many countries, in perpetual *translation*. This permanent in-betweenness—with the pain it entails but also with the extraordinary creative possibilities offered by liminal space—is the real place inhabited by postcolonial authors. The postcolonial writer is a translated subject because he willingly chose to *translate himself* from one geographical area to another, or because he was *translated* by his own life. Along with him, his words were also translated from one cultural territory to another (Rushdie 1991: 17). This implies that postcolonial novels and short stories are already translated to begin with. In Rushdie's case, it was he who chose which aspects of his native culture to include in *Midnight's Children* (1981) and how to do it. It was Rushdie who chose which culturally specific elements and which everyday objects should be translated into English and which, instead, should be left in Hindi or Urdu (Prasad 1999: 41). For instance, in one of the crucial metaphors of his most famous novel he chose to talk about "pickles of history" and not "chutney of history" or "kasaundie of history." He chose to translate, to take himself to the reader, to domesticate an aspect of his country's material life. *Pickle* is the word he chooses to translate into English *chutney* or *kasaundie*, and he occasionally enjoys catching the reader off guard with "mango pickles, lime chutneys and cucumber kasaundies" (1981: 139), when we might expect *cucumber pickles* and *mango kasaundies* (I'm thinking of Ganesh mango kasundi, whose label does bear the translation "pickle in oil"). This is Rushdie—or rather, Saleem Sinai—at his best: his cheeky chuckle at our urge for order resounds in our ears.

Postcolonial authors are the first interpreters and translators of their own texts. When they set out to write a novel or a short story, they must decide how to transpose their culture into English. Here, translating means choosing what to transpose of the social system, of the legal system, of their history and religion, and, concretely, which elements of material life to translate and how to translate them. Postcolonial authors give body to what Gramsci writes concerning the extent to which a philosophy may fully manifest itself in a legal corpus, as he observes in regard to Greek philosophy reinterpreted by the Roman legal code (1975: 1492). This observation carries an embryonic idea of intercultural translation, where a given cultural reality is analyzed and compared with another cultural reality in order to assess which elements one can "transport" (*transferre*) from one context to another. The selection of culturally specific elements and their translation can be more or less aggressive; in other words, authors must decide whether they want to highlight the differences and thus have an alienating effect on the reader; or cancel them out by taking the text to the reader; or act as mediators between their own culture of origin and the reader's culture (Schleiermacher 1992: 42; Tymoczko 1999: 20–21). In the case of interlinguistic translation, carefully assessing whether one should translate or not translate the culturally specific elements makes it possible to escape "cultural imperialism," that is, the "systematic penetration and domination of the cultural life of the popular classes by the ruling classes of the West in order to *reorder* the values, behavior, institutions, and identity" of the subaltern groups so that they conform to the interests of the mainstream (Petras 1993: 140).

In-betweenness is a fertile soil for postcolonial translation. We should not forget that "it is the 'inter'—the cutting edge of translation and renegotiation, the *in-between* space—that carries the burden of the meaning of culture" (Bhabha 1994: 38–39). That is why it is important to investigate the area where two or more languages and two or more cultures come together, where their distinctive traits are blurred by the process of superimposition. This *interstitial* zone is "the zone in which source and target cultures melt and generate a culture under way which resembles, yet is also markedly different from them" (Bartoloni 2003: 468). The culture of many postcolonial authors is a composite fabric, resulting from the juxtaposition of diverse elements that often reveal ambiguity and effectively disorient the reader.

In *The Location of Culture*, Bhabha introduces the concept of a *Third Space*, based not "on the exoticism of multiculturalism or the *diversity* of cultures, but on the inscription and articulation of cultural *hybridity*" (Bhabha 1994: 38). One of the fields in which the creative potential of liminal space and the 'inter' described by Bhabha can be innovatively explored by those concerned with postcolonial translation is the area represented by contact languages. Pidgins and Creoles fluidly inhabit this interstitial area. They developed precisely in a contact zone, that is "the space of colonial encounters, the space in which people geographically and historically separated come into contact with each other and establish ongoing relations, usually involving conditions of coercion, radical inequality, and intractable conflict" (Pratt 1992: 6). Pidgin has long been labeled as 'broken English,' 'coolie language,' or 'cookhouse lingo,' but in fact it is a new language. If a *lingua franca* is a language formed by a mixed vocabulary and a very simplified grammar, used as a common tongue among peoples of diverse speech, then Pidgin is a *lingua franca* born for commercial reasons in areas where different linguistic groups came into contact, such as ports and forts in Africa during the slave trade. It is spoken as a second language and is characterized by morphological and syntactical simplification and by a limited vocabulary. When a community gives up its own language and takes up Pidgin as a mother tongue, Pidgin turns into Creole (Holm 1988: 8–9).

In *Sozaboy* (originally published in 1985), the novel on the civil war that ravaged Nigeria in the late 1960s, Ken Saro-Wiwa works on three linguistic levels: Nigerian Pidgin English, corrupted English, and "occasional flashes of good, even idiomatic English" (Saro-Wiwa 2005: vii). The book's renowned incipit reads: "Although, everybody in Dukana was happy at first" (Saro-Wiwa 2005:1). What strikes us immediately is the use of *although*: we expect the sentence to carry on, rather than find a comma. We are surprised by the absence of a follow-up—an absence that triggers many conjectures in the reader. Or we might suppose that the comma ended up there by mistake—a misprint—and the sentence should be read as if the comma were not there: "Although everybody in Dukana was happy at first . . ." like a secondary clause introducing a main one. We get the impression that the narrator wishes to tell many things but is not used to doing it, or is so emotional that his utterance is flurried, or that his linguistic skills are lacking. If, after *although*, there were suspension points instead of a comma, we might read *although* as the introduction to a concessive clause—a sort of *and yet*, which would catapult the reader in *medias res*. That *although* with a comma right after it carries a great semantic wealth and makes Saro-Wiwa's text very open. The presence of this contradictory element is as surprising as the incipit of *The Adventures of Huckleberry Finn*: "You don't know about me, without you have read a book by the name of *The Adventures of Tom Sawyer*, but that ain't no matter" (Twain 1988: 49). Here, too, *without* instead of *unless* catches the reader off guard and marks from the very outset a feature of Huck's speech, as we find out by reading on: this is not a novel written in the literary language we were taught at school.

In fact, the reader of *Sozaboy* need only be patient, because things become clear a few pages later: "So, although everyone was happy at first, after some time, everything begin to spoil small by small and they were saying that trouble have started" (Saro-Wiwa 2005: 3). The comma finds its proper place in the sentence and the mystery is solved. The questions remain concerning the reason of that first sentence—and one could write pages about it—but what we are interested in here is the anomaly of that first sentence, an anomaly on which the translator should dwell, just like the reader and the critic. The protagonist and narrator of Saro-Wiwa's novel is Mene, a very young and barely literate Nigerian army soldier—a sort of African Huck Finn for whom the author creates an original linguistic pastiche. The rot of a society in disarray, at the mercy of corrupt politicians and torn asunder by a brutal civil war, is reflected in the young soldier's rotten language. Ken Saro-Wiwa twists the English language to tell other stories, stories that are a direct consequence of the British Empire's violence. In the foreword to the novel, the author states that *Sozaboy*'s "language is disordered and disorderly. [. . .] It thrives on lawlessness, and is part of the dislocated and discordant society in which Sozaboy must live" (2005: vii). The English language is twisted under the weight of another history. The language of *Sozaboy* is located along the contact line between two thoroughly different cultures: the protagonist speaks a language that is no longer his native language and at the same time is not quite English. It is something in between. In other words, Mene tells us his story in a language that preserves the memory of its origin—a culture fallen under the blows of colonization—and expresses all the wonder and mystery of the arrival in an alienating elsewhere. The language of *Sozaboy* is located precisely in the *inter* described by Bhabha: it lives in the interstice.

Translation and Literary Creation

The liminal space postcolonial authors move in is an area left mostly unexplored by the Italian publishing industry, which seems to turn a deaf ear to the appeals coming from translation studies, that urgently call for "a new politics of in-betweeness, for a reassessment of the creative potentialities of liminal space" (Bassnett and Trivedi 1999: 6). In fact, language is only one of the aspects that must be taken into consideration during the translating act: translations have always been set in history, culture, and ideology. Translation as a place in which to preserve cultural and historical difference is a concept that, in Italy, has always been—and often still is—difficult to accept.

Hence, it is arduous to encourage a more open-minded approach to translation that takes into account all the implications—linguistic, literary, cultural, historical, semiotic, philosophical, ideological, and political—of the translating act. Referring to the features of the American publishing industry, Lawrence Venuti observes that a "translated text [. . .] is judged acceptable by most publishers, reviewers and readers when it reads fluently, when the absence of any linguistic or stylistic peculiarities makes it seem transparent [. . .] The illusion of transparency is an effect of a translation strategy, of the translator's effort to ensure easy readability by adhering to current usage, maintaining continuous syntax, fixing a precise meaning" (1995: 1). In Italy, too, the main concern is often that the prose be void of lexical ambiguity, and that morphology and syntax be orderly and proper. When translating the text of the Other into one's own language, instead of receiving the foreign elements of the other culture and the possible deviations from the standard language, the text's distinctive marks, the stylistic peculiarities, one tends to manipulate the text, repressing innovation (Lefevere 1992: 7) and making the Other similar to the self.

This happens especially at the expense of the novels and short stories by postcolonial authors. Often, the Italian publishing industry finds it hard to comprehend the concepts of contamination and hybridism that are, in fact, the lifeblood of postcolonial fiction; this is because nothing more radical than these concepts can be juxtaposed to the notions of syntactical and lexical cleanliness, order and propriety. Another risk is the homogenization of texts; hence, texts translated into Italian face the same fate of those translated into English, even though Italian is in no way 'the language of the strongest': "In the act of wholesale translation into English there can be a betrayal of the democratic ideal into the law of the strongest. This happens when all the literature of the Third World gets translated into a sort of with-it translatese, so that the literature by a woman in Palestine begins to resemble, in the feel of its prose, something by a man in Taiwan" (Spivak 2004: 372). Translators, revisers, and editors should take the responsibility of not wasting the savory, hybrid fruits born of the encounter of multiple languages and cultures; but the adjective that best describes this type of culture—*hybrid*—is eyed suspiciously by the greater part of the Italian publishing industry and is, indeed, considered to be ambiguous. Any Italian dictionary will attach a negative connotation to the definition of the adjective *hybrid*. The nouns *giustapposizione* (juxtaposition) and *accostamento* (match) are, for the most part, collocated with the adjectives *arbitrario* (arbitrary) and *incongruo* (incongruous). Emphasis is placed on the presence of diverse elements that fail to mix well, as if they were mismatched; there is no unbiased highlighting of the diversity and plurality of the composition of what is hybrid, and hence its sheer wealth. Hybridity strikes fear into the hearts of many editorial staffs; the peaceful sanctuary of homologation, order, propriety, and purity is far more inviting. One way not to waste the hybrid fruits of liminal space is not to give in to the brutality of the ethnocentric drives that tend to assimilate what is different (Berman 1999: 29–31). These considerations are valid for every type of literary translation and especially for the works of postcolonial authors, because the core of their discourse is otherness, the fragmentation of a precarious identity, the recovery of what was traditionally considered to be subaltern. Translators, revisers, and publishers of postcolonial authors should set themselves the ethical aim of the translating act, that is, to receive the Foreign as Foreign (Berman 2004: 277). For this to happen, translation strategies must be chosen where the receiving culture and language are twisted so as to reflect the deviations from the dominant language, just as postcolonial writers have twisted the centrality of English in order to tell their stories from the margins of the world. In order to translate the hybrid writing of postcolonial authors, one should find language variation strategies that lead the language further and further away from the norms of the written language. The interesting aspect of the 'inter' comes from the "'foreign' element that reveals the interstitial" (Bhabha 1994: 227) and hence from its ability to create something new. These two elements—the foreign and the new—are what enable the translator to explore the creative potential of liminal space while challenging the cultural values of the publishing establishment. But these very elements—receiving the foreign in all its manifestations and the enactment of innovative translation strategies—instill the most fear in those who work on a book's translation.

Let us now try and translate the passages discussed in the first part of this chapter. Taking into account the aspects considered so far, we will observe the active role that interlinguistic translation can play in a postcolonial context. If the incipit of *Eveline* were translated as "Sedeva alla finestra e guardava la sera invadere il viale," we would definitely lose the alliteration in *wi*ndow/*wa*tching but we would at least preserve the sound *ua* in 'guardava' (which would be lost if, instead, we used *osservava*). The assonances given by the three *v* sounds in *eve*ning/in*va*de/a*ve*nue would also remain in the translated text: sede*va*/guarda*va*/inva*de*re/*via*le. In fact, the *v* sounds would become four, hence one more than in the English text, and this would partly make up for the loss of the alliteration in *wi*ndow/*wa*tching; the assonance in *sat/at* is preserved in "sede*va* . . . guarda*va*." Compensation is one of the most widespread translation strategies: if something is lost because the semantic fields do not match and the syntax is not equivalent, or because the cultural heritages are different and it is therefore difficult to preserve the implicit connotations of a given phrase, there is nothing to do but to accept it. Paul Ricoeur wisely suggests that we abandon the dream of the perfect translation and accept the insurmountable difference between the self and the Other. It is not a question of denying that something gets lost in translation, but of accepting that this loss is inevitable. It is this lossless gain we must learn to give up (Ricoeur 2008: 56). Moreover, something is often gained in translation (Rushdie 1991: 17). Care for the text's overall sound, which to me is clearly what Joyce aims for and is therefore the text's dominant feature (Jakobson 1987: 41) in the translation I have proposed, is the reason why I translated with "Sede*va* . . . e guarda*v*" instead of "Seduta . . . guardava" or "Sedeva . . . guardando." All of these are, of course, legitimate translations; however, the translator must be willing to bet on the text's intention, to interpret and make conjectures on "what the text says or suggests in relation to the language in which it is expressed and to the cultural context in which it was born" (Eco 2002: 123). If we believe that the better part of the semantic content of Joyce's prose is conveyed to the reader through his style's expressiveness and evocativeness and through his great care for the overall sound, our choices will come as a consequence. These choices may come as a surprise to the Italian reader, who is not accustomed to prose with poetic features such as assonances and alliterations; I firmly believe that when translating, one must take into account the different cultural and rhetorical traditions. The hiatus between prose and poetry is a feature of Italian literature but not of the culture of other countries. Similarly, the issue of *variatio* and *repetitio* reflects a centuries-long dialectics and goes back to two equally noble rhetorical traditions. English and German are arguably more prone to repetition, whereas Italian and French prefer variation. Still, if we translate by using variation where the author uses repetition, we are making an ethnocentric tendency prevail and we are leading the text back to the cultural models of the receiving language.

As for Tutuola's incipit, in order to avoid erasing his literary creation and reducing it to mere information to the detriment of his innovative aesthetic conception, the translator must perform an act of courage. On the one hand, the translator must reject the requests of most of the publishing industry, which tend to level out the more radical literary experiments; on the other hand, the translator must resist the temptation of stressing the deviation from the morphosyntactic standard in order not to commit the deforming tendency of ridiculing the Foreign (Berman 2004: 285–286). Here is a possible translation that respects Tutuola's paragraph: "Sono stato un ubriacatore di vino di palma fin da quando ero un bambino di dieci anni d'età. Nella mia vita non ho avuto altro lavoro se non bere vino di palma. A quei tempi non conoscevamo altri soldi tranne le conchiglie di CIPREA, e così tutto era a buon mercato e mio pade era l'uomo più ricco della città." The neologism *ubriacatore* comes from the fusion of *bevitore* and *ubriacone*, in the same fashion that led Tutuola to create *drinkard*. On the morphological level, too, one must stick to the destabilizing use of verbal tenses, because the syntactic turbulence that rattles Tutuola's prose and subverts the reading experience of the source novel must somehow also reverse the Italian reader's expectations. The formal expression "dieci anni d'età" matches the author's syntactical structure; he decided to write "since I was a boy of ten years of age" rather than the more common "since I was a ten-year-old boy." Another possibility is to shift the sentence to the lowest step of the sociolinguistic *continuum* (Berruto 1987: 29–42) and source from the resources of popular Italian: "fin da quando che ero un bambino di dieci anni d'età." This would honor the creative popular spirit that runs through Tutuola's narration. It is equally important to preserve the parataxis of the text and the juxtaposition of very short sentences. Finally, since Tutuola uses different typographical fonts in his text, such as 'COWRIES,' this formal choice should also be respected in translation. I also believe it would be better to write "conchiglie di ciprea" rather than to opt for the more general "conchiglie," since the Italian word *ciprea* indicates the mollusk and not the pretty, colorful china-like shell that encloses it. The creative popular spirit that, in Tutuola's prose, irreverently upsets the order and propriety of the dominant language cannot be bridled with rationalizations or ennoblements. Doing so would be tantamount to relegating once again into a subaltern state a language that is trying to make itself heard and to mark a clear separation "from the site of colonial privilege" (Ashcroft, Griffiths, and Tiffin 1989: 38).

As for Pidgins and Creoles, traditionally in Italy they have been ignored in translation, the dialogues in these languages having been translated into standard Italian as if they had been written in Standard English. Or they have been considered as "wrong versions of other languages" (Holm 1988: 8–9), as second-class versions of noble European languages. As a result of considering Pidgins and Creoles just as representations of bad grammar use, Italian translations are often full of mistakes and awkward sentences. The result of such an attitude is the ridiculing of the character speaking Pidgin or Creole.

Translating the incipit of *Sozaboy*, it is important to preserve the anomaly deriving from the comma after 'although'; this would make it possible to re-create in the Italian reader the same effect of surprise and wonder the original sentence has on the English-speaking reader: "Malgrado, all'inizio tutti erano contenti a Dukana." After 'malgrado' one would expect the sentence to carry on, as one would after other common translations for 'although' such as 'benché' or 'sebbene.' And in the next sentence one might attain the same clarification of the source text by going back to—and completing—the opening sentence: "Così, malgrado che all'inizio tutti erano contenti, dopo un po' le cose poco alla volta prendono ad andare a male e tutti dicevano che erano cominciati i casini." In this case, too, the target language makes an effort to receive the creative popular spirit that subverts the reading experience and upsets the morphosyntactic system. The alternation between present and past that characterizes Mene's story can also be found in the translated text, where *imperfetto, presente,* and *trapassato prossimo* alternate ("tutti erano contenti" / "prendono ad andare a male" / "tutti dicevano che erano cominciati"). Furthermore, translating 'although' with 'malgrado' makes it possible to build the concessive conjunction 'malgrado che,' a link that in Italian requires the subjunctive. Since one of the most radical deviations in the Italian morphosyntactic system is the use of the indicative mood instead of the subjunctive, we should seize the opportunity and immediately violate the literary norm using a nice indicative where the reader would expect a subjunctive. Finally, translating 'troubles' with 'casini' seems legitimate given the narrator's young age; this justifies recourse to youth language (Beccaria 2006: 73). What should guide us in the translation of Mene's language should be not so much a "normative grammar" but rather a "spontaneous grammar," that is, how language is used, particularly the spoken language (Gramsci 1975: 2341, 2362). Recourse to the diamesic, diaphasic, and diastratic variations makes it possible to express the composite diatopic variety of the language Saro-Wiwa creates just for Mene, without ridiculing the character (Berman 2004: 285–286). Indeed, recourse to local usages of the Italian language would be an extreme attempt of naturalizing the Foreigner: Mene would sound Italian—so Italian, indeed, that he would pass off as coming from Naples, Rome, or Venice. The effect would be unduly farcical and smack of commedia dell'arte. Understanding Mene's language and rendering it in translation requires cultural openness on the part of the translator as well as on the part of the reviser and editor: Mene's rotten English creates consciousness, a consciousness rooted in concrete and contingent circumstances.

As for Rushdie's pickles, it is interesting to retrace their adventurous journey in the Italian edition of *Midnight's Children*. The word first appears in "pickle-jar" (Rushdie 1981: 19), where it is translated with "vasetto di sottaceti" (Rushdie 2008: 24), whereas "pickle-factory" (Rushdie 1981: 38) is translated first with "fabbrica di pickle" (2008: 52) and then with "fabbrica di salse" (132). Aside from the inconsistency of using two different translations within the space of a few pages, the word 'fabbrica' in Italian recalls a place where iron and steel are processed, rather than food ('stabilimento alimentare'). Then we find "pickle di mango" (2008: 199) for "mango pickles" (1981: 139) and, finally, the famous "pickles of history" (1981: 461) turned into "pickle della storia" (2008: 650). Why can't they make their minds up, one might say! Of course, the question here is more complex: Rushdie himself makes an assimilating choice by using the word 'pickle' for a metaphor crucial to his novel (Tymoczko 1999: 25). Although leaving the word 'pickle' in the Italian text is quite legitimate, the Italian reader in fact faces a foreignizing translation while the English-speaking reader faces a domesticating one. If we wanted to adhere to Rushdie's assimilation, we might translate 'pickles' with 'conserve.' The verb 'conservare' recalls food preservation ('conservare i peperoni sott'olio') as well as preserving something from oblivion, in the sense of guarding it, enshrining it, keeping it unaltered through time. The 'conserve della storia' would make it possible to 'conservare' also in the Italian the deep metaphorical meaning of Rushdie's 'pickles of history.'

Authorial Authoritativeness and Authoritarianism

The state of living between two languages and two cultures, or even several languages and several cultures, is a state of living in an uncomfortable but necessary place. For the postcolonial writer, it is the natural state in which to live and work, but it is also the natural state of the translator. The most interesting aspect of this *framezzo* (Bartoloni 2003: 468) comes from the foreign element that encourages translators to question their knowledge; translators are all too often imprisoned within their familiar vocabulary and a complacent mental grammar. Only in this way can translators test their ability to create something new—new for themselves and for their own language. This does not mean forcing their native language in an unnatural way, but rather broadening their own linguistic and cultural horizons and, hence, those of the future readers of the book they are working on. It is in this place that one must test oneself and proceed through trial and error throughout the entire translation: just like being aware of the inevitability of translation loss makes it possible to translate, being aware of having to err—in the sense of making mistakes as well as of straying—in an uncomfortable place makes it possible to find something that partly makes up for what gets lost. If we reflect on the role played by translated works in a given country and on the relationships between translated literature and basic translation choices, we can make some useful discoveries. If the subsystem of translated literature occupies a place of prominence within a given country's literary polysystem, then the translation activity takes part in the creation of new models. In this kind of situation, the translator's main concern is not to seek out conventional models and hence to stick to the rules set out by the publishing industry; in fact, the translator can be more daring and violate the system's conventions. "Under such conditions the chances that the translation will be close to the original in terms of adequacy (in other words, a reproduction of the dominant textual relations of the original) are greater than otherwise" (Even-Zohar 2004: 203). It is the translator's duty, as it is that of the intellectual, "not (to) respond to the logic of the conventional but to the audacity of daring" (Said 1994: 47). Violating the system's conventions does not, however, mean running wild. In Italian—and this is a peculiar usage—the word *traduzione* is used in everyday language only by the police, to indicate when a prisoner is transferred from one prison to another. Similarly, the word *tradotta* indicates the railway convoy used exclusively to transport military units. In both cases, the word *tradurre* goes back to its etymological meaning of 'to transport' (*transferre*). The fact that the use is limited to these two fields makes one wonder if the bonds are not already implicitly there, in the usage—as if there were a lack of total freedom, or as if there were only a limited freedom within the groove of a path traced by others.

As a writer and translator, there is a translation-related problem I am particularly sensitive to. When one translates, there is more that comes into play than just natural languages and cultural systems of reference. There are also the personal and imaginary worlds of the author and of the translator-writer. I believe the translator-writer's narrative language must not superimpose the translated author's: translator-writers must hand over their pen, so to speak. One must be discreet, because translating is an activity where "in order to objectify cultural meaning, there always has to be a process of alienation and of secondariness *in relation to itself*" (Bhabha 1990: 210). In other words, translator-writers must move, within themselves, in the cramped space between their own imagination and that of the author they are translating. This *framezzo* is an uncomfortable place in which to work, a place to receive a conception of writing different from one's own, to face up to interpretants— one's own and those of others—that can differ and conflict (Peirce 1982). Mistranslations can be due to poor knowledge of the foreign language, of one's own language, or of the cultural context; more often than one would expect, though, they are due to a noncorrespondence between the author's interpretant and the translator's. This psychological interference is responsible for a part of what does not get conveyed in translation. Contemporary psychology postulates the existence of an inner language we are unaware of (Osimo 2002: 623). As in every reading process, the translator's mind plays an active part in interpreting the text; this often occurs unconsciously. It is therefore inevitable that, during the interpretation process, translators bring into play their own personal story made of feelings, affections, traumas, slips, memories related to a given situation described in the novel they are working on, or to a given word. It is therefore virtually inevitable that the text will be unconsciously manipulated. What should not happen, however, is that translator-writers assimilate the Other, project on the Other their own idiosyncrasies, making their own writing dominant and the Other's subaltern. By shifting their attention from themselves to the object of their work—because this is the *subject* of their work—translator-writers can intervene authoritatively in the translation process and place their own authorial skills at the service of the Other's authorship. To translate is not to overinterpret, to adapt, or to appropriate what belongs to the Other. If, as in the case of many postcolonial authors, "for a man who no longer has a homeland, writing becomes a place to live" (Adorno 1951: 87), it would mean appropriating their home. The language of postcolonial authors is a receptacle of their history and of the violence inflicted by history on language. It is a language that, when translated into another language, must not be shoved back into a state of subalternity; instead, it must be listened to and respected in its otherness, accepting that the truth of the elsewhere opposes itself to our truth (Glissant 1998: 35). The gesture of the translator-author must be authoritative, not authoritarian.

References

Adorno, T. W. (1951) *Minima Moralia: Reflections from Damaged Life* (London: New Left Books).

Albertazzi, S. (2001) *Abbecedario postcoloniale* (Macerata: Quodlibet).

Ashcroft, B., Griffiths, G., and Tiffin, H. (1989) *The Empire Writes Back: Theory and Practice in Post-Colonial Literatures* (London: Routledge).

Bartoloni, P. (2003) 'Translating from the Interstices' in *Translation Translation*, ed. S. Petrilli (Amsterdam: Rodopi), pp. 465–474.

Bassnett, S., and Trivedi, H. (eds) (1999) *Post-Colonial Translation: Theory and Practice* (London: Routledge).

Beccaria, G. L. (2006) *Per difesa e per amore. La lingua italiana oggi* (Milan: Garzanti).

Berman, A. (1999) *La traduction et la lettre ou l'auberge du lointain* (Paris: Seuil).

Berman A. (2004) 'Translation and the Trials of the Foreign' in *The Translation Studies Reader*, ed. L. Venuti (London: Routledge), pp. 276–289.

Berruto, G. (1987) *Sociolinguistica dell'italiano contemporaneo* (Rome: NIS).

Bhabha, H. (1990) 'The Third Space. Interview with Homi Bhabha' in *Identity, Community, Culture, Difference*, ed. John Rutherford (London: Lawrence and Wishart), pp. 207–221.

Bhabha, H. (1994) *The Location of Culture* (London: Routledge).

Eco, U. (2002) 'Riflessioni teorico-pratiche sulla traduzione' in *Teorie contemporanee della traduzione*, ed. S. Nergaard (Milan: Bompiani), pp. 121–146.

Even-Zohar, I. (2004) 'The Position of Translated Literature within the Literary Polysystem' in *The Translation Studies Reader*, ed. L. Venuti (London: Routledge), pp. 199–204.

Glissant, É. (1998) *Poetica del diverso* (Rome: Meltemi).

Gramsci, A. (1975) *Quaderni del carcere*. Ed. V. Gerratana (Turin: Einaudi).

Heaney, S. (1978) 'The Interesting Case of John Alphonsus Mulrennan' *Planet: The Welsh Internationalist* 41: 34–40.

Holm J. (1988) *Pidgins and Creoles* (Cambridge: Cambridge University Press).

Jakobson, R. (1987) 'The Dominant' in *Language in Literature*, ed. K. Pomorska and S. Rudy (London: Belknap Press of Harvard University Press), pp. 41–46.

Joyce, J. (1977) *Dubliners* (London: Panter Books).

Kiberd, D. (1996) *Inventing Ireland* (London: Vintage).

Lefevere, A. (1992) *Translating, Rewriting and the Manipulation of Literary Fame* (London: Routledge).

Osimo, B. (2002) 'On Psychological Aspects of Translation' *Sign System Studies* 30: 2: 607–627.

Peirce, C.S. (1982) *Writings of Charles S. Peirce: A Chronological Edition*, ed. M. Fisch, E. Moore and C. Kloesel *et al* (Bloomington: Indiana University Press).

Petras, J. (1993) 'Cultural Imperialism in the Late 20th Century' *Journal of Contemporary Asia* 23: 1: 139–148.

Prasad, G. J. V. (1999) 'Writing Translation. The Strange Case of the Indian English Novel' in *Post-Colonial Translation. Theory and Practice*, ed. S. Bassnett and H. Trivedi (London: Routledge), pp. 41–57.

Pratt, M. L. (1992) *Imperial Eyes: Studies in Travel Writing and Transculturation* (London: Routledge).

Ricoeur, P. (2008) *Tradurre l'intraducibile*. Ed. M. Oliva (Vatican City: Urbaniana University Press).

Rushdie, S. (1981) *Midnight's Children* (London: Picador).

Rushdie, S. (1983) *Shame* (London: Jonathan Cape).

Rushdie, S. (1991) *Imaginary Homelands. Essays and Criticism 1981–1991* (London: Granta Books).

Rushdie, S. (2008) *I figli della mezzanotte*. Trans. Vincenzo Mantovani (Milan: Mondadori).

Said, E. W. (1994) *Representations of the Intellectual. The 1993 Reith Lecture* (London: Vintage).

Saro-Wiwa, K. (2005) *Sozaboy* (London: Longman).

Schleiermacher, F. (1992) 'On the Different Methods of Translating' in *Theories of Translation*, ed. R. Schulte and J. Biguenet (Chicago: University of Chicago Press), pp. 36–54.

Spivak, G. C. (2004) 'The Politics of Translation' in *The Translation Studies Reader*, ed. L. Venuti (London: Routledge), pp. 369–388.

Tutuola, A. (1952) *The Palm-Wine Drinkard and His Dead Palm-Wine Tapster in the Dead's Town* (London: Faber and Faber).

Tymoczko, M. (1999) 'Post-Colonial Writing and Literary Translation' in *Post-Colonial Translation. Theory and Practice*, ed. S. Bassnett and H. Trivedi (London: Routledge), pp. 19–40.

Twain, M. (1988) *The Adventures of Huckleberry Finn* (London: Penguin).

Venuti, L. (1995) *The Translator's Invisibility. A History of Translation* (London: Routledge).

Vivan, I. (1983) 'Nota' in *La mia vita nel bosco degli spiriti*, by A. Tutuola, trans. A. Motti (Milan: Adelphi), pp. 241–253.

11 Opening Up to Complexity in the Global Era
Translating Postcolonial Literatures

Biancamaria Rizzardi

If religion is an answer, if political ideology is an answer, then literature is an inquiry.

—Salman Rushdie, *Imaginary Homelands* (1991)

Introduction

It is a well-known fact that when a system of words, ideas, or principles reveals itself as inadequate as a means for making sense of the state of things, of what we usually call ordinary reality, even in its own particular complexity, everything becomes unreal, absurd, and even the small-scale problems of our day-to-day routine can be thrown off-kilter. English literary culture is a case in point: we have always known that English literature does not coincide with its own name, that Scotland or Wales, not to say anything of Ireland, have produced writers who, before being defined as Scottish, Welsh, or Irish, have been considered as part of a literary tradition that clutches everything in a sort of 'motherly embrace.'

Until recent times we were not fully aware of the difference between literatures stemming from English literature, or at least it was not a relevant feature—if we exclude some biographical information on the author—when presenting each writer. Eliot's America, Yeats's Ireland, Katherine Mansfield's New Zealand, for example, were only details of a biography, not a cultural context in which one might rightly place their works, in order to interpret fully the literary world of the author. Even the literature of the United States, which broke away from its homeland by means of a violent revolution, a war of independence, was considered, as a sort of appendix to the great tradition of English literature. This problematic issue is not limited to English literature. Consider, for instance, the case of French literature or that of Iberia: they find themselves in a similar situation, although perhaps their playing field has not been made as level as that of the English-speaking world.

For the purpose of this chapter, I am going to circumscribe my observations to the domain of Anglophone culture; there will be observations providing a brief, methodological introduction to approach the complexity of contemporary English literature through the act of translating. Too often the dominant attitude, in the field of both postcolonial studies and translation studies, has been focused on a desire to penetrate and possess these new cultural territories with a view to collocating them within a familiar universe, outside of which there is *nulla salus* and whose interpretative key is now more well-oiled and in demand than ever.

Even today, immersed as we are in ever-changing political-economic and cultural scenarios, we may not be fully aware of the manner we relate to 'our' way (by 'our,' I mean in our contemporary world) in order to cope with the Other, be it cultural, linguistic, or textual Other. It is for this reason that I should like to take this opportunity, for which I am very grateful to Simona Bertacco, to bring to your attention a few observations and a proposal, originated by my direct experience as a reader and scholar of English-speaking postcolonial authors. My intention is to try to overcome some dichotomic concepts and discourses (defense, acceptance, refusal, integration), so as to bring about a real, authentic relationship with the Other and also to let the Other act effectively in our contemporary world, as happens in every honest translating act. Indeed, translation has in itself a great creative potential that should be used properly and with expertise; from being a means of negation or distortion of the Other (as a certain part of the publishing business would have it), it can become a place where what is different from ourselves may be unconditionally accepted. In this way the ethical objective of the act of translating is achieved, which, in the words of Antoine Berman (1992), consists in accepting the Foreigner as a Foreigner, accepting the Other precisely as Other.

Accepting the Other, the Foreigner, instead of rejecting him (or neutralizing him, which is in any case the same thing) by subjecting language to an ethnocentric translation, ought not to be an imperative, nor should we feel constrained to do so. But once we decide to follow that path, it is the equivalent of making an ethical choice, a choice not only translators, but also journalists, spokespeople, and more generally those who work with other people's words should remain faithful to.

It is a widely accepted opinion, shared by both the believer and the unbeliever that the Bible is an extremely realistic text that deals with concrete problems and situations. A text that does not claim to have found solutions to everything, but that tries to stimulate the readers, the listeners, to spur them toward change, in order to open up new horizons. For the importance given to the presence of the Other, of the Foreigner, the Bible provides us with significant food for thought. Among the vast range of examples one could draw on, the famous episode taken from the Old Testament where Abraham gives hospitality to three men in his tent (Genesis 18:1–16) is the first one that comes to mind: Abraham acknowledges in his guest, in the Foreigner, a gift, an opportunity, not a danger to protect himself against. Abraham keeps silent before his guests and listens to them. He listens to them for what they are, without judging them or 'labeling' them according to his own set of values. There is also the episode of the two disciples at Emmaus (Luke 24:23–35), which shows additional steps being added to the staircase of hospitality as seen in Abraham's tale: here indeed we see the capacity to share another's path, to listen to what they have to say, and catch the difference therein, by allowing ourselves to be cross-examined and put on the spot, because the Foreigner is a critical figure, capable of questioning our cultural assumptions. This will not happen through an unfocused, generically benevolent sense of tolerance or charity on our part, but only because a foreigner is capable of revealing to us our real identity.

In our globalized era, one of the main tasks facing teachers, of which I am deeply aware precisely because of my role as a cultural mediator, is that of opening up to complexity.

Language, Identity, Religion, and Literature

To reflect on our contemporary world, on the problems connected to the translation of postcolonial English literatures and educational issues, I will use language as a *leitmotiv*. It is no mere accident that language—the imposition of one's language, culture, and religion on other people—went hand in hand with colonialism. And it is no mere accident that a lot of intellectuals from the ex-colonies have long been questioning the relationship between language, culture, and identity.

The Martinique psychiatrist, writer, and philosopher Frantz Fanon claimed that language is the first tool by which an emigrant tries to integrate into White society. Furthermore, language is the first tool by which White society judges the emigrant. Often it is precisely the way an emigrant masters the new language that determines his personal integration. His attempt to be "more French than the French" (we could say also more English than the English or more Italian than the Italian) is partly caused by their desire to show they have attained a high level of civilization. Fanon also claims that a Black person from the Antilles will be proportionally whiter, more manly, according to his own ability to speak good French.[1]

The young man leaving home to study in France knows very well that he will have to abandon his Creole language because, once he arrives in France, it will be the label by which he will be judged and possibly separated from the others. He will try to express himself as best as he can, he will try to be whiter than White people (Fanon 1961/1963) to show his own culture no matter what. A Black person knows he will be accepted only if he succeeds in assimilating the new culture. When he gets back home, he will certainly adopt a critical attitude toward his fellow countrymen. His refusal to use his mother tongue—Creole—will highlight the final displacement he has undergone.

The migratory flows following decolonizing processes have made their contributions to the reshaping of the physiognomy of our contemporary world in quite a contradictory way: on the one hand, in many societies we have witnessed the rebirth of nationalisms, fundamentalisms, attempts to preserve one's cultural and linguistic identity. On the other, much interest is focused on globalization, on the indiscriminate flow of personal and collective histories, language and cultural heritage, thus running the risk of a general cultural leveling. Many contemporary writers have tried to identify a more effective and less superficial way to think about these issues, about the way, for example, contemporary literature from the English-speaking world reflects on the relationship between identity, language, culture, and religion.

In the texts written by Salman Rushdie, religion plays an important role. He often tries to disclose the spiritual needs of contemporary subjects, to give voice to their wonder, their astonishment, and their excitement faced with the world, to highlight "how profoundly we all feel the needs that religion, down the ages, has satisfied" (Rushdie 1990: 421). But he also wonders whether, through his own writing, some precious aspects of religion and the religious mentality might not be able to survive if stripped of dogma.

The search for 'technical solutions' that might allow for the presence, side by side within the text, of both religious and political thought—two ways of creating images of the world and interpreting it—has led in his work to an attempt to develop a new narrative form. For Rushdie, it is essential to create a new fictional form that "allows the *miraculous* and the *mundane* to co-exist at the same level—as the same order of event" (1991: 421), and explains that "one reason for my attempt to develop a form of fiction in which the miraculous might co-exist with the mundane was precisely my acceptance that notions of the sacred and the profane both needed to be *explored*, as far as possible without pre-judgment, in any honest literary portrait of the way we are" (417). This intellectual stance leads him to conceive of art as sacred as well as mundane, as "the third principle that mediates between the material and spiritual worlds" (417). The writer asks himself: "Might it by 'swallowing' both worlds, offer us something new—something that might even be called a secular definition of transcendence? I believe it can. I believe it must. And I believe that, at its best, it does" (420).

For Rushdie, literary language—despite being intrinsically influenced by sociological ideologies and conditions—has its own specific function: its dialogic, flexible, and inclusive dimension, its ability "to hold a conversation with the world" (Rushdie 1991: 415–429) and assimilate different cultures and ideas, letting them be shaped into unexpected and unhierarchical combinations, is what differentiates literature from other discursive, monolithic systems. Literature (particularly the novel) is to Rushdie "the stage upon which the great debates of society can be conducted" (420). The only privilege literature has—a privilege essential for its own existence—is to be "the arena of discourse, the place where the struggle of languages can be acted out" (427). While meeting our need for wonder and understanding of the world, literary texts activate, refine, and improve the critical ability of the readers by providing them with no ultimate truths but rather alternative perspectives on reality and by acting as a stage on which different visions clash polyphonically: "It hands down no commandments. We have to make up our own rules as best as we can [. . .] and it tells us there are no answers; or, rather, that answers are easier to come by, but less reliable than questions" (423).

"Great literature, by asking extraordinary questions, opens new doors in our minds" (Rushdie 1991: 423). For Rushdie this is a point of vital importance. What is forged in the sacredness of the reading act, the production of meaning generated from the encounter between the literary text and the pragmatic context of reading (Segre 1979: 35), brings "the 'privileged arena' of conflicting discourses *right inside our heads*" (Rushdie 1991: 426). By the plurality of its communicative attitudes, literature opposes "the partisan simplifications beamed down to us from satellites" and, despite the hasty cliché-ridden times we live in (Rushdie 2002: 169), spurs readers to cultivate an intellectual preference for complexity, for the capacity to assimilate 'many-sided truths.'

The Language of Postcolonial Texts

All the works written by authors from the former colonies of the British Empire draw on, mix, and condense not only many languages, codes, and traditions, but also a series of apparently oxymoronic processes. From the second half of the twentieth century we have witnessed, in the literary field, an attempt to 'save' the literary traditions and identities that were damaged during colonialism, to shape national literatures with distinct and specific features, to give dignity to one's language (consider all the variants of English spoken in the Caribbean). Diasporas and large-scale migrations, along with the processes of globalization, have all triggered original and unusual hybridizations.

As far as the linguistic expression is concerned, many authors have decided to write in the European language introduced by the colonizer and that subsequently became the official language of the new postcolonial nation, or its *lingua franca*. In the case of the English-speaking world, for instance, the English language has, over the course of this process, undergone a profound metamorphosis and given rise to numerous variants, dialects, Pidgins, and Creoles. In appropriating the language of the empire, postcolonial authors renew its lexicon, modify its syntax, and create new forms, myths, and images. The texts of the postcolonial world are, for this reason, always linguistically contaminated, displaying a great deal of plurilingualism, bilingualism, and diglossia. The new languages emerging from these extraordinary hybridization processes become, on the page, both the means and the message of the narration: "what is being transmitted in the language chosen is another culture, a whole world of references which post-colonial literatures invite us to discover."[2]

We are dealing here with a truly expressive kaleidoscope enriched with unusual and international hybridizations, which give their contribution to the reshaping of the English language. In this way, the English literary language turns into the polyphony of our contemporary world, a contemporary world that is essentially fluid, thus widening its interpretative horizon. Now more than ever plurilingualism manifests itself as a means, a technique, and a narrative strategy, while simultaneously encapsulating a content message (Tchernichova 2009: 195–215).[3] This intrinsic plurality of the text, the different linguistic realities it contains, leads us to recognize the importance of translation, the importance of becoming perpetual translators so that we can read this plurilingual world and, in parallel, lead even the most Eurocentric reader to give up an old-fashioned imperialistic vision of dominant cultures and more or less prestigious languages. Raja Rao, one of the most important Anglo-Indian writers, writes in the introduction to his famous novel *Kanthapura*:

> The telling has not been easy. One has to convey in a language not one's own the spirit that is one's own. One has to convey the various shades and omissions of a certain thought-movement that looks maltreated in an alien language. I use the word "alien," yet English is not really an alien language to us. [. . .] We are all instinctively bilingual, many of us writing in our own language and in English. We cannot write like the English. We should not. We cannot write only as Indians. [. . .] Our method of expression therefore has to be a dialect which will someday prove to be as distinctive and colourful as the Irish or the American. (1967: vii)

A similar concept is expressed by Salman Rushdie in one of the essays in his collection *Imaginary Homelands*:

> I hope all of us share the view that we can't simply use the language the way British did; that it needs remaking for our own purposes. [. . .] But the British Indian writer simply does not have the option of rejecting English, anyway. [. . .] The world 'translation' comes, etymologically, from the Latin for 'bearing across.' Having been borne across the world, we are translated men. It is normally supposed that something always gets lost in translation; I cling, obstinately, to the notion that something can also be gained. (1991: 17)

It follows that, depending on the sensitivity and the personal perspective, the authors display a series of strategies to valorize and localize their work through the language, which often becomes the real protagonist of the narration. One could point, just to cite a few examples, to the linguistic strategies used by Rao to maintain in his novels the rhythms of Kannada; to Anand's mastery in letting the reader perceive the 'flavor' of Punjabi; to how Narayan keeps the presence of Tamil; the English contaminated by Bengali, by Hindi, by Urdu, and sometimes by Bhojpuri, also by Lascar, in Amitav Ghosh's *Sea of Poppies* (2008); the Yoruba poetic sensitivity of Tutuola; the Nigerian Pidgin and the idioms of the Ibo culture in Achebe's works; and the Creole of Trinidad (or, rather, Port of Spain) often used by Naipaul. In postcolonial texts, the 'watersheds of outsiderness'—that is, those passages that at first reading pose a translation problem because of the great distance separating the source language from the target language—may be indicated, for example, by the insertion of untranslated words or transliterated lemmas, the use of strategies such as marginal notes, code-mixing or code-switching, the adoption of rhetorical devices (metaphors, comparisons, epithets) belonging to a cultural repertoire that is not British or European, or in the alteration of syntactical structures. Syntactical strategies are often an attempt to recuperate the sounds of an oral tradition and maintain the rhythms of orality in the written word.

In this way, for instance, the eccentric articulation of Tutuola's sentences—linked to the rhythm of performance—allows the deeper structures of the Yoruba language to come to the surface through the English syntax. In the works by many novelists from the Indian subcontinent, from Raja Rao to Salman Rushdie to Amitav Ghosh, the expressive organization is intrinsically connected to the oral tradition of storytellers. The long sentences, the repetitions, the parallelisms, and the cross-references convey in prose the typical rhythms of this peculiar genre. Another example is the use of the spoken language of the Black and *métis* world, with its short sentences, or the syncopated rhythms of some of Abraham's texts, which mirror the Afro-American everyday experience and the influence of jazz.

The strategies of linguistic and cultural localization used by postcolonial writers to mark their difference are one of the most problematic aspects in the translation of their texts. The translator of postcolonial texts, once s/he acquires the specific cultural preparation, must succeed in communicating in the target language the relation of "tension and integration in the original text between the vernacular and the *koiné*, between the underlying language and the surface language" (Berman 1992: 55; my translation), between the codes of international communication and the idiomatic forms of the vernacular, between the danger of an exotic reading and a too great information surplus, "too great for comfortable assimilation by the receiving audience" (Tymoczko 1999: 22).

When dealing with the issue of linguistic and cultural localization, the problem of equivalence has to be put necessarily in second place. In the target culture and language, equivalent words for terms connected to everyday activities (such as food, tools, clothes, habits, and laws) or to the natural world (plants, animals, weather conditions) often do not exist, if not in rare or technical forms. However, if translation is conceived as a moment of interpenetration between the outsider's and one's own linguistic space, as a process in which the potential of the target language can and must be extended and exploited to the fullest, the attention will not be focused mainly on the search for equivalent terms. In a passage devoted to the comparison between translation studies and the linguistic approach to translation, between the concept of translatability and the question of 'losses' and 'gains,' Berman claims that "when facing a variety of terms with no equivalent in one's own language, the translator will have at his disposal more choices" (1992: 242), ranging from the use of neologisms, strategies ranging from 'compensation,' 'deformation,' and 'homologous substitution' to the insertion of an untranslated word.

How Can This Complexity Be Transferred to a Translation?

When translating we usually tend to normalize the text as much as possible in order for the text to be smoother, a domesticating process that tries to 'shrink' diversity to a recognizable sameness. But to purge a text of its estranging elements in order to facilitate the reading is like mutilating its physiognomy, and in so doing we deceive the readers instead of facilitating their task. As early as 1813 Schleiermacher indicated two completely different paths a translator could follow: "Either the translator leaves the writer alone as much as possible and moves the reader towards the writer, or he leaves the reader alone as much as possible and moves the writer towards the reader."[4] The translator who decides to follow the second path destroys the features of the source language and culture and normalizes them. What this kind of translator has in mind is a lazy reader who is not willing to make a small effort, not even an imaginative one. The reader who wants to undertake a journey to widen the horizons of his mother tongue and culture needs another kind of translator and another translation. This kind of reader needs a translator who, thanks to the encounter with the Other, has made the discovery of his own mother language and its potentialities and latent resources. As Hölderlin remembered in a letter to Böhlendorff dating back to April 12, 1801: "What belongs to us, what is proper to us, must also be learnt in exactly the same way as we learn about what is alien. That is why the Greeks are so indispensable for us. It is only that we will not follow them in our own, national [spirit] since, as I said, the *free* use of *what is one's own* is the most difficult" (Hölderlin 1988: 43).

Translation is in fact synonymous with transfer, transfer of the self to another level and to another language, according to Rushdie, and with transculturation. The aim of the translating act, often conceived of as a 'medium' of individualities, is nowadays that of inventing "a language connecting a language to the other, a common language, but in a certain way an unpredictable one with respect to each of them." When this happens, as Édouard Glissant observes, translation does indeed become "an art of hybrid crossings which aspire to world-totality, art of vertigo and healthy wanderings" (1995: 166). Besides, the great creative potential of the English language can, through the act of translation (which is not only a 'bearing across' but also a 'fertile coming together'), contribute to the renewal and modernization of the target language (Glissant 1995).

In some of the scholarship on the topic, there emerges a debate on the inability, or at least the difficulty, of the Western reader to comprehend 'correctly' (and therefore interpret and translate) texts coming from other latitudes without domesticating them through the superimposition of Western values, thus falling into the trap of cultural imperialism and its "universalizing master narratives" (Lyotard 1979/1984). Even if it is true, as Lefevere suggests in his unsettlingly titled essay 'Composing the Other,' that "[a] huge investment in re-education is needed if we are to arrive at the goal of understanding other cultures on their own terms" (1999: 65), it is also true that no reader can prescind from his own hermeneutical context, which is necessarily specific and contingent. However, according to Gadamer (1989: xxviii), the interpretative act is based on the idea that the hermeneutical and experiential horizons of the author and the reader can overlap to a certain extent and produce meanings. Instead of trying to aim at a neutral or objective reading (which is impossible), or impoverish the debate with a polemical attitude, it is to be hoped that we approach the reading of postcolonial texts by adopting an authentically dialogical perspective, even though partly centered on Western ethics and philosophy. In a comparative perspective on literature, seen as the 'colloquial' coming together of world literatures, the translation of postcolonial texts, which is the encounter with the Other, must necessarily be reconceived of as a form of exchange and relation. As Mona Baker reminds us, "Towards the texts, authors, society and dominant ideologies with and in which he works, every translator adopts a shifting stance that is ever-changing and continually negotiable" (2009: 390).

It is true that a reader cannot prescind from his own particular hermeneutical and contingent context, and he will approach the reading with his own set of social, historical, and cultural values, as this is the necessary background to the reading act. And it is true that when a text is transferred from one historical-cultural context to another, it is enriched with new meanings, which cannot be predicted either by the author or by its first readers. But it is equally true that each text is historically and culturally situated and bears the traces of its own horizon. Any interpretative act, therefore, will involve— according to Gadamer's theories—a fusion of the horizons of the reader and the text, an intersection of the reader's repertoire and that of the text. This fusion and intersection must not implicate an imperialistic appropriation of the text and a distortion of its contents; too often we have ignored that the experience of reading, the encounter/clash between the author and the reader, can bring forth new languages—what Lotman (1984) called "Creole languages"—and modify the norms and the values of the reader who will be changed forever by the act itself of reading.

A translation that is particularly attentive to the text, to its rhythms, features, and internal symmetries, to its polysemy, to its syntactic, phonic, and lexical structure, is no doubt a good antidote to the deforming tendencies that in the past have characterized the Western attitude to translation. Tendencies such as rationalization, clarification, ennoblement, and exoticization of the vernacular, the destruction of the underlying network of repetitions and signification, are just a few of the textual tendencies that deform the original and present the readers with normalized texts purged of their strangeness. The textual competence of the translator must be connected to a detailed critical reading that tries to individuate (and communicate in the translating act) not only the network of the fundamental terms and associations, but the *system* of the text itself: "as a matter of fact, the coherence of a translation is valued on the basis of its systematicity" (Cavagnoli 2012: 63).

The 'Outsider Test' and the Apprehension of [What Is] One's Own

There is still a topic to reflect on now, and that is the ethical responsibility of the translator as one who has the power to construct the image of a literature and a culture, which will then be consumed by readers from another culture, and the difficult task of mediating between the author, the text and the reader. Many pages have been devoted to this kind of mediation, and to the confluence and underlying network of the translating process. I firmly believe that, in the case of the reading and translation of postcolonial texts, the effort the translator has to make (and the reader as well) must necessarily be guided by a sort of bipolar simultaneity. On the one hand, the translator must strive to decentralize his own self, thus forcing the reader "to go out of himself, [. . .] to perceive the foreign author as foreign" (Berman 1999: 62). On the other, the translator must listen carefully and accurately, demonstrating a particular "listening attitude" toward his linguistic space so as to explore the nonnormalized zones of the language that allow for the exploitation of etymology to the fullest, to the coining of neologisms, to the stretching of the meaning of words, and an effortless increase in the elasticity of the language.

I would like now to go back to an issue I touched on at the beginning of my chapter and reflect on the possible implications of the Other's 'critical gaze'; in this case, the possibility that, through the translation of English literatures, their polylinguistic substratum, and the immense creative potential of the English language we can make our contribution to the renewal and modernization of the target language. What I wish to highlight here, in

firm opposition to any translation discourse based on deconstructionist techniques of resistance and 'disruption,' is that this process has nothing to do
with any strategy aimed at enriching the Italian language and culture—as the
translational context I speak from—by merely adding a touch of exoticism or
a hint of New Age.

Instead we should conceive of the translating act as a critical confronta-
tion with the foreign language by looking at the critical, poetic, and transla-
tion tradition of the period following World War II—the so-called "translation
decade," in the words of Cesare Pavese—which marked a turning point in
Italian culture, thanks to intellectuals and scholars such as Emilio Cecchi,
Cesare Pavese, Elio Vittorini, Leo Ferrero, Leone Traverso, and Eugenio
Montale. During that decade, and the following ones, the translation of North
American literature contributed to undermining the literary autarchy of the
Fascist regime by drawing on ideas and cultural models from abroad. The
poetic translation of authors like Joyce, Eliot, Pound, Auden, Stevens, Wil-
liams, Thomas, Tate, and many others (in anthologies or in monographic
volumes) had a tremendous impact on the Italian reading public. New collections of translated poetry were published and were brought to the attention
of the reader; magazines like *Poesia* (published by Mondadori) or *Botteghe
Oscure* devoted many of their pages to this kind of publication. Following the
example of modern authors, poets from the past were rediscovered: poets like
John Donne, Gerard Manley Hopkins, Emily Dickinson, Herman Melville,
and even William Blake and William Shakespeare, who, translated again in
this cultural climate, appeared as new and fresh (Rizzardi 2006).

The cultural renewal made possible by this generation of poets and translators (Claudio Gorlier, Agostino Lombardo, Sergio Perosa, and Alfredo
Rizzardi to name just but a few) left an indelible mark by means of the
literary language they contributed to graft on the sclerotic structures of the
common language, enriching it with new meanings, new connotations, and
a different metaphorical potential. This was possible because the translating
act itself was based on the idea of discovery, the introduction of a new experience that would have an impact, even violent, on the Italian language—of
course not with the use of Anglicisms, but through a new perspective focused
on the spoken language, the language of everyday truth, the "language of
the confessional," as Baudelaire had said years before, thus paving the way
for modern poetry. In other words, the Italian language was intensified and
enhanced by the impact with a new tradition.

Reflection on the mechanisms that triggered this extraordinary cultural
phase is a good starting point in order to open up to, and become aware
of, complexity in the global era, leading to the kind of education that must
necessarily be characterized by a refusal of the logic of sameness, of mono-
mania, or of any totalitarian tendency. On the contrary, any honest translating act should be characterized by real interpenetration and dialogue
between different voices (despite a certain assimilationist aim that has often

characterized translation in the Western world) and by the idea that "the essence of translation is to be an opening, a dialogue, a cross-breeding, a decentering. Translation is 'a putting in touch with,' or it is *nothing*; it opposes the dominance of one side over another; it is relation without sublation" (Berman 1992: 4). Opening up to complexity, leading the reader through the act of translating toward a syncretic and multicultural knowledge, means instilling a sense of respect toward cultural and individual specificities, not only of the individual writer, but also of the individual text in a global context.

Toward the end of his introductory essay to *Imaginary Homelands*, Salman Rushdie quotes from a novel by Saul Bellow, *The Dean's December*. At the end of that novel, Professor Corde is walking along the road and hears a dog barking incessantly. Bellow wonderfully has his character imagine that what the dog is doing is protesting about the limits of dog experience; he imagines that the dog is saying, "For God's sake, open the universe a little more" (Rushdie 1991: 21). With Rushdie, I strongly hope this will become our motto, the *motto* of us literati, "Please, let us open our universe a little more!"

Notes

1. See Fanon (1952); see above all Chapter 1, 'The Black Man and Language.'
2. See Salvador (2006); see also Prasad (1999: 42).
3. On this topic, see also Meherez (2009).
4. Friedrich Schleiermacher's lecture 'Ueber die Verschiedenen Methoden des Uebersezens' ('On the Different Methods of Translating') was delivered to the Royal Academy of Science in Berlin on June 24, 1813. Schleiermacher (1963: 38–70).

References

Baker, M. (2009) 'Guerre di parole: strategie di *reframing* nella traduzione dei conflitti' in *Oltre l'OccidenteTraduzione e alterità cultural*, ed. R. M. Bollettieri Bosinelli and E. Di Giovanni (Milan: Bompiani), pp. 387–423.

Berman, A. (1992) *L'Épreuve de l'étranger: culture et traduction dans l'Allemagne romantique* (Paris: Gallimard).

Berman, A. (1999) *La traduction et la lettre, ou L'auberge du lointain* (Paris: Seuil).

Cavagnoli, F. (2012) *La voce del testo. L'arte e il mestiere di tradurre* (Milan: Feltrinelli).

Fanon, F. (1952) *Peau noire, masques blancs* (Paris: Seuil).

Fanon, F. (1961/1963) *The Wretched of the Earth*. Trans. C. Farrington (New York: Grove Weidenfeld).

Gadamer, H. G. (1989) *Truth and Method*, 2nd ed. (London: Sheed and Ward).

Glissant, E. (1995) *Introduction à une poétique du divers* (Paris: Gallimard).

Ghosh, A. (2008) *Sea of Poppies* (New Delhi: Viking-Penguin).

Hölderlin, F. (1988) *Friedrich Hölderlin: Essays and Letters on Theory*. Trans. T. Pfau (Albany: State University of New York).

Lefevere, A. (1999) 'Composing the Other' in *Post-Colonial Translation: Theory and Practice*, ed. S. Bassnett and H. Trivedi (London: Routledge), pp. 75–94.

Lotman, Y. (1984) 'On the Semiosphere' *Sign Systems Studies* 17: 5–23.

Lyotard, J.-F. (1979/1984) *The Postmodern Condition* (Manchester: Manchester University Press).

Meherez, S. (2009) 'Traduzione ed esperienza postcoloniale: il testo nordafricano francofono' in *Oltre l'Occidente: Traduzione e alterità culturale*, ed. R. M. Bollettieri Bosinelli and E. Di Giovanni (Milan: Bompiani), pp. 115–145.

Prasad, G. J. V. (1999) 'Writing Translation: The Strange Case of the Indian English Novel' in *Post-Colonial Translation: Theory and Practice*, ed. S. Bassnett and H. Trivedi (London: Routledge), pp. 41–57.

Rao, R. (1938/1967) *Kanthapura* (New York: New Directions).

Rizzardi, B. (2006) 'Il testo ricreato: lezioni di arte della traduzione' *Anglistica Pisana* 3: 1, 50–61.

Salman Rushdie. (1990) *Is nothing Sacred?*, (London: Granta Books).

Rushdie, S. (1991) *Imaginary Homelands: Essays and Criticism 1981–1991* (London: Granta Books).

Rushdie, S. (2002) *Step across This Line: Collected Non-Fiction 1992–2002* (London: Jonathan Cape).

Salvador, D. S. (2006) 'Documentation as Ethics in Postcolonial Translation' *Translation Journal* 10: 1. http://accurapid.com/journal/35documentation.htm (accessed May 12, 2013).

Schleiermacher, F. (1963) *Das Problem des Übersetzens*. Ed. H. J. Störig (Darmstadt: Wissenschaftliche Buchgesellschaft).

Segre, S. (1979) *Semiotica filologica* (Turin: Einaudi).

Spivak, G. C. (1993) 'The Politics of Translation' in her *Outside in the Teaching Machine* (London: Routledge), pp. 179–200.

Tchernichova, V. (2009) 'Tradursi all'altra riva' in *Gli studi postcoloniali*, ed. S. Bassi and A. Sirotti (Florence: Le Lettere), pp. 195–215.

Tymoczko, M. (1999) 'Post-Colonial Writing and Literary Translation' in *Post-Colonial Translation: Theory and Practice*, ed. S. Bassnett and H. Trivedi (London: Routledge), pp. 19–40.

Part IV

Colonial Past, Digital Future

12 Civilized, Globalized, or Nationalized?

Peter Greenaway's *Pillowbook* and Postcolonial Calligraphy

Evelyn Nien-Ming Ch'ien

When colonized by another culture, the postcolonial subject's linguistic identity is drastically interrupted by the imposition of a new language. But does the subject lose a nation-state or a form of life? Even in traditional forms of colonialism, the substitution of one language for another can be a more profound loss than territorial rights, as it reaches beyond borders into the very heart of a civilization, a civilization that existed before definitive borders or nation-states emerged. Such an enduring loss has always made postcolonial loss a vital, living one even if borders have ceased to indicate national identities. In the virtual world, loss at the hands of cyber colonization also begins with language.

In the internet age, colonization has particular resonance. Computers programmed in English are colonizing populations, and local cultures are experiencing cultural colonization in the twenty-first century. While other some forms of colonization are becoming less imposing, technology's dominance over populations is proliferating. Such dominance, and its attendant globalization, illuminate the difference between the loss of territorial boundaries and losses of culture and civilization. While borders may be crossed and territorial entitlement erased in the virtual world, cultural differences and assertions of civilizations continue. Thus cultural colonization is a distinct phenomenon, to be distinguished from geographic colonization, and in the age of the Internet it has become as aggravating as geographic colonization.

Theories of postcolonialism are particularly relevant now as technological imperialism ushers us into an era of borg-like cyber-colonialism; technology is the culture that colonizes with more reach than other cultures possess. Technology is an instrument of power over populations, and its command over territory is fantastic and real. While the actual mass of virtual territory is quantified in bodies (users) rather than measures of distance (kilometers, miles), its psychic force on the individual is analogous to physical colonialism: individuals are inhabited by a new culture that imposes itself on them and demands a fidelity of sorts in exchange for transactional rights (both social and economic). On a global level, technological pervasiveness within countries demonstrates that country's potential to colonize.

A map of the Internet presence and social media in countries is an indicator of developed countries; thus, Internet presence also creates the possibility for Internet armies, forces for colonizing minds in other countries.[1]

While technology may seem like the central force, it is really only one medium; language and writing remain the colonizers' tools that change the physical landscape. The virtual self may be free to roam, but it is also teth-ered by the local, physical self. A borderless world does not alter the fact that much culture is local and physical—and exists despite and sometimes in defi-ance of borders and borderlessness. Furthermore, in order to inhabit global linguistic space, populations often need to know English—English dominates much programming and sites that are used internationally. Moreover, the voice of the subject must be filtered through new technological mediums. Such transitioning catalyzes the development of a new self, instigating pathos in the transformation; the interruption of linguistic identity arrests the cycle of linguistic birth, growth, decay, and death. Both the postcolonial experi-ence and that of globalization thus disrupt the natural human flow and devel-opment of language. The trauma to the self at the hands of globalization manifests itself in a similar manner as traditional colonialism. Globalization, like colonialism, separates generations and makes them alien to each other; technologically enabled youth culture exhibits a form of life inaccessible to older generations. Globalization through the Internet and social media dominates the rhythms of life, separating the high-speed existence of glo-balized subjects from the local-speed existence of those who are not wired. Communicative devices force language to develop at their speed, thus the mode of linguistic transmission is altered. The body habitus of the globalized generation contrasts sharply with the unwired populations who have not yet been digitally colonized. Because of this separation, the cultural continu-ity formerly created and kept intact through linguistic exchange—memories, cultural habits, exchanges between preceding and succeeding generations—experiences a halt in its cultural flow, a disruption of its coherent societal practices, when adjusting to colonial intrusion.

Postcolonial Calligraphy

While the voyage toward a more technologized world highlights a brand of colonialism, this world also creates linguistic colonialism with its associated linguistic confusion, hybridity, and mixing. Peter Greenaway's (1996) film *Pillowbook* explores the impact of changing historical circumstances on the practices of calligraphers and aspiring calligraphers, as well as the impact on the medium of writing, which is essentially the film's principal character as well as subject material. All the characters in the film interact through writing, because the protagonist insists that she find a writer-lover and has many encounters with writer-calligraphers before deciding on one. Through this theme, the film also examines how adopting new writing systems and language can generate new selves as Nagiko Kiohara, the main character, inhabits new roles with new uses of language and systems of writing. Also the film demonstrates how the recovery of handwriting—a stark break from technological imperialism—can return a subject (in this case, Nagiko) to her humanity, though with the caveat of making her almost unfit for survival in a technological context. The dilemmas of the postcolonial and postglobalized subject are simultaneously elided and resolved in the narrative of the protagonist. While the protagonist becomes an adult during the age of the Internet, she also feels loyal to her local customs. Her affinity for writing is inherited from her father, who early on affirms writing as a way of creating an identity; thus writing begins for her as a form of calligraphy separate from the mediation of other technology. However, as the culture of calligraphy becomes anachronistic, she is forced to assert her identity in an increasingly technologized and globalized world, one that is both colonized physically (by the British in Hong Kong) and virtually (through technology), and the narrative of her identity and struggle to maintain linguistic coherence provides a metaphor for the phenomenon of linguistic disruption that is occurring around her on a larger scale.

Born in Japan in 1974, Nagiko subsequently spends much of the movie in colonial and postcolonial Hong Kong (her mother declares that when Sei Shōnagon's book of observations has its one thousandth anniversary she will be twenty-eight, and the book was written in 1002). Though his film *Pillowbook* (1996) was produced a few years after the advent of the Internet, the film thematically explores the notion of virality and writing but in a non-internet context. Still the concepts of uncontrolled dissemination and imposterhood resonate with internet culture, despite the fact that Nagiko's context is calligraphic, not digital. The film illuminates the subversions of writing when disconnected from the writer, and its capacity to escape from the writer and take on a life—and even a body—of its own (writing is offered a life unmediated by computers). Rather than getting lost in the ether, writing is transferred from body to body, organically rather than digitally.

Because writing's distributions happen on bodies than screens, it exerts a strong emotional influence on relationships and life choices. Greenaway's *Pillowbook* is a movie in which the protagonist and her lover literally give up their bodies, their material lives, for writing. Writing is a ubiquitous character in the film, appearing often as a calligraphic *objet d'art*. As if to make the point that writing is absolutely necessary to drive a human life (in a parallel role, writing appears in subtitles and as design for the film frames, thus narrating the film), in one of the telling opening scenes we see a small girl's face being painted on by her father, who signs his name on the back of her neck when he is done as the film narrates his work: "he painted in the eyes, the nose and the lips; he brought the clay model into life by signing his own name." While the scene is filmed in black-and-white, the writing is accomplished in a bright red ink, implying—among a variety of associations—a fall from grace: with writing comes knowledge and the exit from paradise. The idea that humans are composites of stories is materialized very literally in this film; repeatedly the characters are writing small histories, poems, or other material suggesting their origins. Writing spawns the creation of an identity, through a signature, in this case, that of Nagiko.

In the film, writing and creation are intertwined and later fused, but is it writing or a sense of identity that comes first? The direction of the movie pushes for their entwinement from the very beginning, and the fundamentally operative nature of writing in the formation of identity. Writing is the beginning of the manifestation of consciousness, and thus one's first words designate a kind of identity and must therefore be valued (and even, as the film shows, ceremonialized). Yet if writing is imposed on an individual, this can create a fractured sense of self. Before Nagiko can write, her relationship to writing has been imprinted on her by her father; from the very beginning, writing is established as intertwined with human error, exacting an intimacy that is at first innocent but later becomes doused with iniquity. The film then shows how Nagiko-as-child grows up into a writing fanatic who sells her body in order to obtain calligraphy. The subversive content of writing is symbolized by the bloodred color of the ink and paint that appears in the parts of the film that are shot in black-and-white. Writing opens the door for the entry of original sin through the mask of vanity. When introduced to writing before one is ready, writing can be dangerous. Nagiko's self-knowledge mixes with knowledge of her father—thus her consciousness of self leads to carnal knowledge. Her identity is, at the origins, written by her father, thus it is fateful that Nagiko follows her father as someone who combines sex and writing. Her father, in order to publish his works, enters—in all appearances extremely reluctantly—into a sexual relationship with his publisher. Nagiko, however, chooses another to engage in the sexual relations with the same publisher—her own lover, Jerome. Her choice to prostitute another in order to publicize her own work allows the iniquity of her birthright to surface and eventually destroy Jerome. As Greenaway asserts in interviews, Jerome alludes to an ancient Latin Christian priest who undertook revisions of the Latin Bible and produced a prodigious collection of polemics, scriptures, and translations.[2] Controversial because he favored extreme asceticism, Jerome is known for his extreme commitment to writing. Thus he is appropriate for a film in which writing drives the relationships between the characters, while their personal relationship to writing is deeply self-inflected.

Whether Nagiko could have controlled her sexuality and writing remains an unnswered question in the film, but the inevitable relationship between writing and sexuality dominates the preoccupations of many of the film's characters. Writing and the writing self are so entwined in this film as to suggest one could not exist without the presence of the other. But the mode of their relationship is organic. Concretely, events lead to a standoff between Nagiko, whose greatest idea of love is the worship of body writing in her own exalted sense, and the publisher, who makes writers and books into sexual objects, writing and writing instruments with pure lust and sensuality. However, Nagiko and the publisher share what appears to be an obsession for writing that borders on mental disorder, so that their behaviors elide and overlap; the publisher commits atrocities that Nagiko intimately understands but punishes him for. She is able to understand his highly sensual relationship with writing and in order to catch his attention sends him books written on bodies—the fusion between body and book is roundly explicated in the first of thirteen she sends him. Just as valid as the content is where it is placed. For example:

Throat:
I want to describe the Body as a Book
A Book as a Body
And this Body and this Book
Will be the first Volume
Of Thirteen Volumes.

Ribcage:
The first bulk of the book is in the torso,
Seat of the lungs
That fan the wind that dries the ink.
Seat of the heart
That pumps the inks
That is always red
Before it is black.
The heart and two lungs are held upright,
Close, but not touching neighbors,
Sheltered by the covers of the ribcage,
Watermarked with dark twin punch-hole paper titles.
The breath of inspiration runs amongst them
Drawn down from the air by their shared influence.

Nape to Coccyx
No function of book or body is singular
If a multiple service can be performed.
So the inspirational air
Shares the same passageway
With salts, words,
Sentences, Sweeteners, Paragraphs.
They all come tumbling down to flutter onto the ruminating page,
To lie in serried rows like rice-stalks
In a field, or stitches in a tatami,
Patiently awaiting irrigation
By water or by vision,
Even if a reader does not appear for a thousand years.
(film, *Pillowbook*)

The voice continues, "And so on for the belly, penis, and scrotum."

This film restores sensuality to writing and in relation to that, knowledge. The side effects in linking writing and sex are emotional and psychological. Knowledge as depicted in the biblical scene creates rage and shame—and the film plunders those emotions in its restaging of writing's sensual powers and its capacity to evoke anger. Nagiko's first husband becomes extremely jealous of her pillowbook and finally turns violent—toward the book, ironically, but not her. He rips up her book, shoots its pages with arrows in an archery game with his friends, and expresses his jealousy that the book is written in a foreign language that he cannot understand (she uses both Chinese and English in her writings). Finally her husband burns her pillowbook.

This film makes writing a sensual process that affects the audience of the film, too, and the way in which the film is absorbed. The sensuality throughout is palpable; Nagiko asserts that she possesses a strong sense of smell and that the smell of paper reminds her of the smell of skin. There are scenes of her smelling paper. "The smell of paper is like the smell of skin of a new lover who has just paid a visit out of a rainy garden," she says. She continues, "And the black ink is like lacquered hair. And the quill? Well the quill is like that instrument of pleasure, whose purpose is never in doubt, but whose surprising efficiency one always, always forgets." While imbuing writing with vitality, the film suggests that it can be just as sensual as the oral. But also just as liable to disintegration. Though words can endure, on certain surfaces, with a quasi-immortality, they are ultimately disposable.[3] This film documents indulgence: like the real pillowbook, it relates sensual lists of everything, positive and negative, and writing as a kind of visual art is ubiquitous. The Asian characters and writing tell the story much more so than anything said. Nagiko searches for her calligrapher no matter what language he uses; she transacts in multiples gestures and cultural modes. Again, this movie does not attempt to acoustically render all the languages, no doubt leading to a cumbersome and clumsy result. The writing in this film is an illustration of how beautifully these languages can be incorporated as design, especially written in calligraphy and on the body; there is no pressure to understand them as communicative, simply to appreciate them as artistry.

At times this aestheticization of writing does breed resentment and spawn pathologies. It is a running question as to whether Nagiko's obsession with writing is a decadent habit or a higher calling. But for her, only beautiful writing that emanates from human gestural practice—handwriting—is worthy. Writing and the body are in almost every frame of the film, be it Nagiko's body or the men she employs later in the film to communicate to the publisher. Nagiko's need to be a writer's surface, to be in fact, a book, to somehow integrate all of these things in her inheritance, results in very strange desires. Her father's own pathologies regarding the combination of books, writing, and sex are Nagiko's questionable inheritances.

Though there is little judgment passed in the film, as viewers we are suspended in this world of intimacy with writing until it becomes entwined with violence. Such feeling is inspired, as Sei Shōnagon writes:

> Letters are commonplace enough, yet what splendid things they are!
> When someone is in a distant province and one is worried about him,
> and then a letter suddenly arrives, one feels as though one were seeing
> him face to face. Again, it is a great comfort to have expressed one's
> feelings in a letter even though one knows it cannot yet have arrived. If
> letters did not exist, what dark depressions would come over one! When
> one has been worrying about something and wants to tell a certain person about it, what a relief it is to put it all down in a letter! Still greater is
> one's joy when a reply arrives. At that moment a letter really seems like
> an elixir of life. (1991: 207)

Nagiko's search for a lover-calligrapher is playful until she encounters Jerome—and though their relationship has its aspects of playfulness, it soon becomes darker when Jerome negotiates his sexual relations between Nagiko and the publisher who had sexually exploited her father. Through Jerome, Nagiko becomes a writer instead of a body to be written on, instead of an empty book. Jerome insists that she write on him; he becomes her writing surface, a book, an ultimate sacrifice to writing. Scenes of Nagiko writing on Jerome imply the theme of sacrifice as she writes the Lord's Prayer on his body and he is often in crucifix-like positions. Jerome's presence summons a song called 'Le Dernier Ange' (which alludes to the book that chronicles the life of a decadent Parisian bohemian who falls into the supernatural world of another and ultimately gives up his life for that world). He is barely a personality, a metaphor for an empty blank book. Nagiko and Jerome take separate paths in indulging their writing pathologies. He becomes the ultimate martyr to writing. Jerome accepts pills from a photographer who deceptively provides him with real poison masquerading as sleeping pills. Jerome, who wants Nagiko to come back to him and thus stages a death scene in order to attract her, remakes himself into a writing tool; he drinks ink that spills from his mouth when Nagiko attempts to revive him.

Though up until now we have considered the process of making the book as involving manual labor, we have not associated that labor with violation. But this film frames each act of writing, binding, and bookmaking as violations when practiced on the human body. On some level humans are all palettes, composites of stories; this is materialized very literally in this film. From the moment the brush is thrust like a sword on Nagiko's face in the beginning to the climax when Jerome's body is exhumed and mutilated as it is carved, dried, and made into a scroll, writing and bookmaking are a sinister practice. Nagiko sleeps on her pillowbook in the film, after finishing her regular entries. Her intimacy with the pillowbook—the least ferocious, perhaps, of these other encounters between book and body—still raises the question of whether there is a level of appropriateness or inappropriateness of intimacy with books. In fact the question has been raised again and again with respect to books/people/things/technology. What is an acceptable level of intimacy in dialectic relationships? Where do we determine the particular juncture at which relationships with people or things become pathological? There is certainly a difference between pathology and obscenity, although the film flirts with these intersections; while Nagiko's obsession with finding a calligrapher-lover manifests itself in pathology, such pathology is presented as relatively benign in comparison to the publisher's behavior. The publisher's relationship to writing and his sexualization of it are, in contrast, presented as psychotic and obscene. The publisher's inappropriate displays of sexual behavior toward books are captured in scenes where he licks and smells books with a visceral perversity—*as if they are alive*. The ultimate perversity—an act that Nagiko finds unforgivable and so criminal as to demand the publisher's execution—is the exhumation of Jerome's body, and it subsequent re-creation into a book, which the publisher receives and sexually engages with in a grotesquely sensual reception of the book. The dead body-as-book is yet another level of violation—if writing is the presence of absence of the living, then interacting with a body-as-book is necrotism, a form of zombie love.

Writing and Pathology

As shown earlier, writing can incite pathology.[4] Perhaps it is the origin of human pathology. Nagiko is forever marked by the significance of her birthday salutation—she searches throughout her life for someone who can fulfill her father's birthday inscription (the drawing of the features on her face and signature on her neck) and engages many lovers who fail the mission. This birthday salutation is a central trope in the movie: she attempts to paste the greeting on herself after typing it (this fails, and she throws the typewriter in the toilet); her first husband is unwilling to paint the greeting on her, and this is symbolic for the failure of their marriage, but also their fallen status.

Like the publisher, Nagiko is promiscuous in her pursuit of a calligrapher-lover, her pursuit is flecked with high standards about calligraphers (she initially scorns Jerome, her eventual lover-calligrapher, for being a "scribbler" not a "writer") and a connection to organic human-produced writing (again, the typewriter she buys during a stay in Hong Kong ends up in the toilet); she is seeking, in her idealistic way, the lover-writer. The publisher is also promiscuous but, on the other hand, profits and takes advantage of idealistic writer-types by exchanging books or promises of publication (with Jerome it is books, with her father promise of publication) for a sexual relationship, thus reducing his sexual partners to prostitution.

The narrative voice-over says: "She was determined to take lovers who would remind her of the pleasures of calligraphy like Sei Shōnagon." The film delivers the flavor of this sensuality; writing is its real sensual protagonist. Such sensuality—the constant displays of calligraphy on Nagiko's nude body created by each of her lovers—demands aesthetic appreciation and interpretation. Greenaway had clear intentions: "The basic driving force is that every time you see flesh you see text, and every time you see text you see flesh. That's the main theme, the main self-indulgence, the main excitement."[5]

However, writing sometimes outcompetes the compelling attraction of the body; even the body cannot compete with the sensuality of writing. In one scene we are witness to a calligrapher who paints her body with gold and black; we view a close-up of her body covered in print. She stands in the frame in full frontal nudity and her nipples are painted gold, but the moment is immune from raciness as she is covered in print. She walks into the rain and, as the print washes away, we are awakened to the presence of the body underneath and realize that, much like the exhibit of Xu Bing's print-covered pigs, the print is a cultural filter that distracts from the body. Nudity is as empty as a blank book. As Paula Willoquet-Maricondi (1999) writes, "the living body is literally, not simply metaphorically, sacrificed in the name of the written word. [. . .] If an analogy is drawn between the human body and the body of the world, and between text-making and map-making, Greenaway's film can be taken as an allegory of the process through which the map comes to replace the territory—through which, in the film, Jerome's skin is literally fashioned into a book. Jerome's flesh is removed, separated from the skin, and discarded as garbage."

This film has the feel of an artifact; there is not a single computer in the movie. The only sign of technology's influence is the abandoned typewriter and an occasional telephone. It is crowded with scenes at old temples, in the middle of Hong Kong, but always with the shadow of the pillowbook, whose evocative phrases and lists—for example, using the words of Shōnagon:

> Elegant Things
> A white coat worn over a violet waistcoat by a lover on his second
>   night-time visit.
> Duck eggs.
> Shaved ice mixed with liana syrup and put in a new silver bowl.
> A rosary of rock crystal.
> Wistaria blossoms.
> Plum blossoms covered with snow.
> A pretty child eating strawberries. (Greenaway 1996: 92)

In one scene the poetic fallout that is sprinkled throughout the film in a voice-over is like an abstraction of poetry or haiku. One of Nagiko's calligrapher-lovers in the film says to her:

The word for rain should fall like rain
The word for smoke should drift like smoke
Never be afraid of making a mistake
Remember the brush may be made of wood
But the writer is only human.

He adds later that his brother, a member of the forestry commission, writes in green "to remind his bosses of their green responsibilities" and then ponders with amusement about the color an employee of a whaling company would use since whales are color-blind. Whimsical moments such as this encounter between Nagiko and her lover occur throughout the film, and all of her lovers come from diverse professions and backgrounds. The movie repeats the message that Nagiko continued to be determined to take lovers who would remind her of the pleasures of calligraphy like Sei Shōnagon.

Greenaway uses several techniques, along with narrative shaping, to reinforce that writing is the emotional figure of the film. The whole film is focused on the visual and on writing, both in the story and on the surface, as it is subtitled; different frames are simultaneously cast for the audience to juggle.[6] The dialogue is very sparse, almost nonexistent. Writing—in several languages and formats—is dispersed throughout, sometimes as design.[7] Even the acoustic noise of the film is orchestrated to be monotonous and sonorous, at the beginning of the film, for instance, it is simply Buddhist hymns. On top of Japanese, Chinese, and English (Nagiko), the other languages featured include Jerome's linguistic palette, which includes Yiddish, Italian, Arabic, French, English, German, and Latin. Subjectivity, then, is provided visually, not acoustically. On the other hand, the film also speaks to the rawness of language when creativity is applied to it; Shōnagon's use of language was not refined in some aspects but later provides a vivid record of court life:

> we use just one Yiddish word in the film, when Jerome writes the word "breasts" on the appropriate anatomical part on our heroine. It's interesting also that Yiddish was a 19th century vernacular language, which in the latter part of the century began to develop a written form. That has certain parallels with the creation of the Japanese language. There's something about Sei Shōnagon's use of the diary form with its continual fragmentation of narrative ideas which is so completely different from her exact contemporary Murasaki who wrote the famous The Tale of Genii, which in some senses precedes the notion of the English, French or Russian grand saga novel. So I suppose if we were to regard The Tale of Genji being more associated with Tolstoy or Zola, we could think of Sei Shōnagon as much more related to Baudelaire. We tried very hard in the film to represent this fragmentation in the different ways we used

black and white, high color, low color. We borrowed not just the notions of the creation of a new language as she was doing in the year 995, but also made correspondences to what the creation of a new language would be about.[8]

The small frames inserted in the larger frames suggest a simultaneous narrative. In this film, even bustling, emerging cultures seem secondary to the influence of writing. Throughout are scenes of busy Hong Kong streets, but the film's frames always feature an insert of an elaborately coiffed and dressed Sei Shōnagon. We are treated with scenes at old temples, in the middle of Hong Kong, but always with the shadow of the *Pillowbook*, which is associated with evocative phrases and lists, including "children eating strawberries," "shaved ice in a silver bowl."[9] All of these images are meant to appeal to the senses. The film is a strong reminder that in contemporary twenty-first-century Western contexts, writing is often not presented as an art as much as it was in earlier centuries—both in content and form.

Writing can be deviant and decadent; it can substitute for human presence but its immortality is often a half-presence and half-aliveness rather than being truly substitutive of human presence—therein lies its perversity. The essence of the perversity of writing is not located in the fact that the characters in the movies write on forbidden spaces—intimate and nonintimate areas of the body; such acts can be intimate and gentle. The film starts with a father kindly writing on his daughter's face; it is unusual but not cruel or perverse. Nagiko is quirky but not perverse in her love of body writing. However, when bodies are conscripted for utility—remade into books, for example—perversity is undeniably present. Redesigning the body with the consent of its owner in a permanent way—tattoos, horns, piercings that cannot be removed without surgery—is often narrativized as existing on the spectrum of body pathology, depending on the extent of the changes and the context of these changes. Too much alteration and mutation—such as the Mona Lisa plastic surgeries or those who reconstruct the shapes of their faces and bodies, morphing themselves into animals or mythological creatures—often appears as newsworthy subject matter in supermarket and pop publications because of their grotesque affect. At times these tendencies are considered a general disrespect of the human. Again, this is a borderline judgment call. In contrast, clear acts of disrespect are actions on the dead. To maul a dead body in a violent and disfiguring way or to leave it unburied is considered profoundly disrespectful. The creepiest part of the film is when the publisher unrolls his new scroll, formerly Jerome's body, and inhales its aroma as if it were still living. The publisher goes beyond strangeness with his erotic attraction to books as he licks the pages of the scroll made out of Jerome's body and is constantly seen inhaling the odor of his book. But his sense of the book as still retaining attraction as a sexual object is one of the strongest pathologies (among the countless others associated with this kind of mentality). When the body is metaphorized as a book, when writing is cutting and ink is blood—when in fact the kinds of metaphorizing are applied to the book—pathologies are born. The publisher loves books so much that his desire has become sexual for them, even if they are inanimate. Furthermore, loving books should not be confused with loving people just as loving the dead should not be enacted in the same way as loving the living, though sometimes reading seems like such an intimate practice and the dead often seem spiritually proximate. Nagiko and her husband also battle over the intimacy of the book and the past; the husband sees her indulgence in harboring feelings for both as a disease, as odd, as deviant. But Nagiko's affliction is mild, while his own violent tendencies toward her and the pillowbook are radically disproportionate to her eccentricities; still both of them are guilty of overindulgence and the film's script literally incinerates their histories, though the pillowbook lives on.

The details of remaking a body into a book are undeniably gruesome no matter how compelling the the conceptual framework for such an act can be, however. Jerome's skin is surgically flayed, dried, and cleaned so that it can be remade into paper for a long scroll. In these scenes of surgery, organ dumping, and fabrication, the red ink and blood become almost indistinguishable, as does skin and paper—another example of the death of the dead. The result of the work is a grotesque two-dimensional referencing of Jerome's body, a body flattened and dried and still appealing sexually to the publisher, a desecration of the human. The dark side of Seijo Ozawa's comparison of pages to skin has been spawned; the publisher is the evil *doppelgänger* to the idea of literati, one whose desire for writing has twisted into a sexual disorder.

Still, while this is occurring, another part of the film features a courtesan sniffing a scroll, the narrator comments how "the pages of a book smell like skin" (see above), citing this as one in a list of small pleasures in life. Finally, when Nagiko creates her own book using live bodies—sending emissaries to the publisher who each represent a book (for example, one young man arrives nude with words written on his eyelids, his groin, and other "secret" places in order to communicate the "Book of Secrets," while another appears with characters on his tongue to represent the "Book of Silences"[10]), we see that she plays with the pathology of the publisher. But in some ways her work is therapeutic, as the publisher then begins to read the books instead of desire them sexually. Nagiko accomplishes her mission; she is able—by sending the publisher *bodies* (literally) of writing—to get him to see the characters printed on bodies instead of have sex with them. He has his minions transcribe the writing on the bodies so that he does not miss a word. The realization that he has desecrated himself, that he has dishonored a body (Jerome) and the entire practice of bookmaking, shames him into *seppuku*. Bizarrely, the book that was Jerome ends up at the bottom of a bonsai plant, where Nagiko waters it along with the plant. The book returns to the earth—the base of this potted bonsai—where both are watered together like disposable, though precious, organic material. Writing is only human—and recyclable; we invent and reinvent following the predestined rhythms of human existence.

The narrative of Nagiko is compelling as a metaphor that describes how writing can become a fundamental part of identity and accrue an organic presence within a culture. But it also makes apparent the violence of linguistic disruption for the postcolonial subject for whom writing is a corporeal act. To violate one language's existence by substituting it with another is as invasive as forcing new bodies onto populations. The anachronistic system of calligraphy is an apt metaphor for the native language of the colonized; their old systems that have controlled their body habitus and orientation to the world become anachronistic phenomena. An entire form of life—its rhythms and values—are wrapped up into the world of calligraphy. In the epoque of the internet, the form of this writing actually isolates Nagiko despite the fact she uses many of the same characters as the locals (Japanese contains many of the complex Chinese characters used in Hong Kong). Her repeated feelings of isolation and irrelevance accrete and manifest themselves as pathology, as a desire for comprehension remains unsatisfied. The subsequent tragedy of Jerome's death makes Nagiko realize that she must return to her native Japan: Jerome, who understood her need for linguistic confirmation, was himself colonized (by the publisher) and confused linguistically. Nagiko's calligraphic zone could not be in a colonized, technologized, and globalized space, so she returned to the linguistically coherent context of her birthplace, opting out of the postcolonial space that spawned her pathology. She ultimately rescued her writing at the price of leaving the postcolonial territory in which she lived, showing postcolonial calligraphy to be a contradiction in terms.

Notes

1. See http://www.labnol.org/internet/favorites/world-atlas-internet-map-social-media/1489/ accessed January 12, 2013.

2. See Pascoe (1997: 166): "Jerome presented a problem to painters, since his career offered few opportunities for creating a sympathetic figure: his record as a scourge of heretics and a champion of virginity was notorious; he performed no famous miracles or works of charity; nor did he suffer any spectacular martyrdom. Nevertheless, in him Greenaway sees a figure who habitually places book before body."

3. In a similar tone, the calligrapher ponders on color, saying (my paraphrase): "My brother is in forestry commission so he writes in green 'to remind his bosses of their green responsibilities.' Then he says he asked him what color he would use if he worked for a whaling company as "whales are color-blind."

4. Still, writing characters and the tradition of Chinese and Japanese calligraphy require a physicality. Asians spend a lot of time writing—gesturing, rather—on their hands to show others what character they are referring to. Characters are recognizable. This is standard practice.

5.   See http://www.salon.com/june97/greenaway2970606.html (accessed January 2, 2011).
6.   In 'Play, Create and Untie: Cognitive Participation as Interaction in Films,' Pelin Aytemiz (2011) writes that with "a type of interactivity in *Pillow Book* by using multiple images and allowing the spectator to participate actively by selecting which image to focus and which event to follow, Greenaway challenges the passivity of cinema that he criticizes. Greenaway in an interview, considering *Pillow Book*, says that 'there are several images to choose from and it's up to you or the audience in which order you choose them or how you utilize them.'" He redefines the spectator's relation with the film by allowing them to reconstruct the meaning of the work by themselves, which includes mental participation and interactivity (page 60).
7.   "The cinema of the future is going to look much more like the pages of an encyclopedia. It's going to be much more concerned with interactions, rather like sophisticated forms of vernacular advertising which are now extremely adroit at putting image and text together. The cinema of the future is going to embrace these notions and continually develop that sophistication of the comic strip which already influences the Internet page. All the films we've seen so far that have been influenced by the comics are in some senses remarkably naive. They haven't taken what the comic book can really offer us, which are ideas of changing aspect ratio, of interaction of text and image in very sophisticated ways. This vocabulary has been developed all over the world in terms of the American, French, and the Japanese comic books, but they have not been embraced in cinema. So there is maybe another example of a local vernacular developing itself slowly to become a major language. All these pursuits are very much alive for me. I planned *The Pillow Book* with lots of diagrams—I was always going to fragment the screen in various ways— but as soon as we transferred the original super 35mm film onto tape and edited the whole movie on an Avid computer system, I was immediately struck by what the software could offer me. The diagrams for the original script became remarkably redundant because the complexities of the new languages were offering me so many other potentials. Since the information was undifferentiated, 'objective' and infinitely maneuverable backwards, forwards, together, apart, segmented, chronology became irrelevant. Does the past have to come before the present? Does the future have to be ahead of the present?" (Greenaway in http://bombsite.com/ issues/60/articles/2068 [accessed February 2, 2011]).
8.   See http://bombsite.com/issues/60/articles/2068 (accessed February 2, 2011).
9.   Some of the film's uses of phrases and sentences are not exactly similar to those in the version of *Pillowbook* translated and edited by I. Morris in *The Pillowbook of Sei Shōnagon* (1991).
10. There are thirteen books in all, and the significance of this number in Western circles is not lost on me, but I'm unsure of its meaning in Japanese culture. To get revenge, she sends thirteen people covered in writing, and the publisher then commits suicide.

References

Aytemiz, P. (2011) 'Play, Create and Untie: Cognitive Participation as Interaction in Films' in *Image, Time and Motion: New Media Critique from Turkey, Ankara (2003–2010)*, ed. A. Treske, U. Önen, B. Büyüm, and I. A. Degim (Amsterdam: Institute of Network Cultures), pp. 56–61.

Greenaway, P. (1996) *Pillowbook* (Paris: Dis Voir).

Pascoe, D. (1997) *Peter Greenaway: Museums and Images* (London: Reaktion Books).

Shōnagon, S. (1991) *The Pillowbook of Sei Shōnagon*. Trans. and ed. I. Morris (New York: Columbia University Press).

Willoquet Maricondi, P. (1999) 'Fleshing the Text: Greenaway's Pillow Book and the Erasure of the Body.' http://pmc.iath.virginia.edu/text-only/issue.199/9.2willoquet. txt (accessed June 1, 2011).

13 Doing the Translation Sums
Colonial Pasts and Digital Futures

Michael Cronin

Robert Young, in his *Postcolonialism: A Very Short Introduction*, is explicit about the centrality of translation to any conceptualization of the postcolonial. He claims, "Nothing comes closer to the central activity and political dynamics of postcolonialism than the concept of translation" (2003: 138). For Dipesh Chakrabarty, in *Provincializing Europe: Postcolonial Thought and Historical Difference*, it is the relationship of translation to the politics of incommensurability that makes translation and the translator indispensable figures for the understanding of difference:

> what translation produces out of seeming "incommensurabilities" is neither an absence of relationship between dominant and dominating forms of knowledge nor equivalents that successfully mediate between differences, but precisely the partly opaque relationship we call "difference." (2000: 17)

The figure of difference in translation can, of course, itself be understood in many different ways, but what I would like to focus on in this chapter is the differences that are likely to emerge in the relationship between translation and postcolonial writing in the context of a new digital ecology.

Extensive Universality

In an essay published posthumously on the 'geopolitics of translation theory,' the translation scholar Daniel Simeoni returned to his interest in the contingent origins of theory, situating the work of polysystem theorists and Bourdieusian sociology in a specifically European notion of the state and state development. He used the term 'cultural loyalty' to characterize "the researcher's internalized preferences for homogenous groupings representative of the culture under study, more often than not his or her own" (2008: 337), a remark that clearly echoes the concerns of postcolonial translation scholars from Spivak and Niranjana to Bassnett and Trivedi. He goes on to claim that:

This loyalty has often taken the guise of a theoretical agenda modeled after the cohesive strength entailed in European state building (but where is the alternative model, even today?). Few scholars are aware of this connection, so much so that much of the work that goes on in the discipline of the social sciences and the humanities follow traditions closely linked to the development of their institutions, even as they question them, may in fact be steeped in a geopolitical unconscious, *l'impensé géopolitique de la théorie*. (337)

In Simeoni's view, theories that claim to transcend borders are often inescapably defined by them. In particular, there are forms of the universal that seek to repress this geopolitical unconscious. What these are and how they might illuminate Simeoni's claim can be illustrated by attending to a distinction made by a theorist cited in Simeoni's essay, Jean-Claude Milner.

Milner, in a discussion of Jean-Jacques Rousseau's famous declaration at the beginning of his *Social Contract*, "L'homme est né libre et partout il est dans les fers" [Man is born free and everywhere he is in chains], claims that the opposition appears initially to be chronological. Man is born free at birth and then he becomes enslaved. Milner argues that a deeper opposition resides at a logical level:

> I hear the sound of the clash between the universal proposition in the singular, *Every man is free* and the proposition in the plural, *All men are free*. The first one is true, the second false. But, at the same time, we understand that the proposition in the singular is only true in an intensive sense. It is universal in the strict sense that it brings out the maximum intensity in the name *man*. It would still be universal even if men were nowhere to be found free. (2011: 36)[1]

The kind of 'intensive' universality evoked by Milner, where there is an exploration of the maximal meaning or meanings of what a word might signify (the use of 'l'homme' and the translation is itself immediately problematic), contrasts with an extensive universality primarily concerned with extension and plurality, as in mass consumer products, where what is most characteristic is their interchangeability and omnipresence (the Starbucks phenomenon). The translation of postcolonial literature in the digital age is arguably faced with the tension between forms of extensive universality that drive the translation industry worldwide and the claims of intensive universality that underline the maximally difficult and maximally complex nature of words and their use in different languages and different literatures. Although literature is not an explicit referent, the remarks of Brian McConnell from the software company Worldwide Lexicon point to the competing demands of intensive and extensive universalism in the contemporary, digital moment. McConnell's watchword for translation into future is, "Don't let perfect be the enemy of the good":

His example of a model platform for a world of ubiquitous translation functionality where simplicity is the watchword is Twitter. The focus should be exclusively on defining conventions for the most common tasks and interactions between the various [*sic*] involved, and then regularly improving them. (Joscelyne 2011: 1)

If the 'perfect' is the drive toward intensive universality, the 'good' as defined here is the move toward extensive universality where the prior definition of conventions will allow for the cheap, fast, and efficient circulation of messages in a 'world of ubiquitous translation.' The somewhat glib utopianism of the MD of Worldwide Lexicon might appear to be at an unimaginable remove from the specific pressures of rendering African, Caribbean, or South Asian literatures into different languages. However, the epistemic bias of digital connectivity toward extensivity captured in the very moniker of the 'World Wide Web' means that the question of the production and accessibility of postcolonial literatures in translation must address the nature of the digital contexts in which they are presented and disseminated. I want to examine, in particular, one kind of context that has come to the fore in the promotion of translated postcolonial literatures.

Brand-New

In its mission statement *Words without Borders*, the online magazine for international literature (www.wordswithoutborders.org), makes explicit its commitment to make particular kinds of literature visible:

> Words without Borders translates, publishes, and promotes the finest contemporary international literature. Our publications and programs open doors for readers of English around the world to the multiplicity of viewpoints, richness of experience, and literary perspective on world events offered by writers in other languages. We seek to connect international writers to the general public, to students and educators, and to print and other media and to serve as a primary online location for a global literary conversation. (Words without Borders 2012)

The avowed aim is to start a "global literary conversation," but that conversation is unlikely to happen if, firstly, the participants cannot access the conversation, and, secondly, if they cannot understand what the participants are saying even if they do. Although the technology potentially allows for the conversation between different kinds of literature (on the crucial politico-economic condition that one has Internet access), the conversation cannot take place in the absence of translation. Thus, what we might define as ostensible transparency points up the fiction of digital immediacy or pseudo-transparency, the notion that because a text can be technically accessed, it can be readily understood. Translation as a function of ostensible transparency is in a sense making ostensible or visible the necessity of translation in order to give effect to the global, transmissive possibilities of information technology. Of course, what it is that is being made ostensible is not simply the agency of translation but particular forms of content that address widely varying sociopolitical motivations in the postcolonial world.

In the case of *Words without Borders*, the project is predicated on the widely reported Anglophone indifference to literature in other languages and the markedly low percentage of translated titles published in English (Assouline 2011). The ostensible project is one of monolingual internationalism, by this we mean the translation of different literatures in different languages into one language, in this case English. In contrast, the online poetry platform Lyrikline (www.lyrikline.org) engages in what can be termed multilingual internationalism, where poems are translated into German, French, English, Slovene, and Arabic. In both cases, the inward direction of the translations is not subject to prior selection other than on the grounds of quality. The ostensible project is a making available of the literatures of the world in one or more languages. The online magazine and the online poetry platform want to give effect to a form of digital cosmopolitanism where the global promise of access promised in theory by the technology is matched by the cultural contents on offer via the technology. However, as has been remarked on by many commentators, any viable notion of the cosmopolitan must have a credible theory of the local (see Vertovec and Cohen 2002).

The project of ostensible transparency in the context of digital translation practice can be linked to a making manifest of the local to the global as opposed to presentation of the global to the local. The online website of *Mediterranean Poetry* (www.mediterranean.nu) is specifically devoted to making available, in English translation, poetry from writers from Mediterranean countries in addition to contributions by Anglophone poets on Mediterranean themes. *Transcript*, described as 'Europe's online review of international writing' (www.transcript-review.org), available in German, English, and French, has the specific aim of promoting "quality literature written in the 'smaller' languages [of Europe] and to give wider circulation to material from small-language literary publications through the medium of English, French and German." Thus, special issues of the review have covered writing from Malta, Macedonia, Latvia, Slovenia, Croatia, Brittany, and Northern Catalonia. The postcolonial paradigm is never invoked as a founding rationale for any of the sites mentioned, but it is clear that it is both internal and external colonialism that have led to the marginalization and occlusion of particular kinds of literature in the languages of present and former colonial powers. If *Mediterranean Poetry* and *Transcript* practice a form of diffuse localism, giving a platform to a variety of local literatures, the digital presence of other specifically national or quasi-national bodies has a more explicit vision of what constitutes the local, a local that is inextricably bound up with the economic-political power asymmetries of a postcolonial world.

The Center for Slovenian Literature, the Danish Literature Centre, the Dutch Foundation for Literature, the Finnish Literature Information Centre, the Ireland Literature Exchange, the Korean Literature Translation Institute (KLTI), the Polish Book Institute, to name but a few such bodies, are dedicated to the promotion through translation of particular national literatures. Joo-Youn Kim, the president of the KLTI (www.klti.or.kr), makes clear the connection between the promotion of particularism and the enablement of the digital:

> Korean literature has prospered and built up wonderful cultural assets on the soil of its long traditions, and commands a wide pool of works and writers being produced at this very moment. Indeed, literature got in full bloom at an earlier stage in Korean history, with the first-ever invention of metal movable type-based printing. Now a new chapter is being written with Korea's globally recognized IT power [. . .]. In the era of cultural convergence, we simultaneously endeavour to actively accommodate the ever-changing cultural environments within the paradigm of information technology and, thereby, to set forth a new role of literature, which has prospered around the traditional concept of printing. (Kim 2011)

What the institute is seeking to make transparent are the ostensible achievements of Korean literature, and information technology is seen as the primary medium for the globalization of Korean literature in translation. In Joo-Youn Kim's statement, it is noticeable that the foregrounding of the local is situated in a material history of translation transmission, which goes from the invention of "metal movable type-based printing" to the emergence of Korea as a "globally recognized IT power." This history is a tacit rebuke to the colonial hubris of the Japanese occupier who would seek to conceal or minimize the scale of Korean technical and literary achievement (see Hwang 2010). The history of tools is seen as inextricably bound up with the fortunes of Korean writing and what is possible through translation. In the postcolonial moment that dovetails with the advances of the developmental state, Korean preeminence in the field of IT is seen in a national narrative as a logical extension of the country's precocity in the area of printing.

The use of translation for the purpose of ostensible transparency in a digital context brings with it potential tensions that are intrinsic to the interaction between the medium and the message. For example, on the KLTI website under 'Vision' we find the statement, "Korea as Cultural leader in Global Community." The global reach of the medium is explicitly harnessed to the national interests contained in the message of the institute that sees the promotion of Korean literature in translation as a way of establishing leadership in the global community, an aspiration echoed in the presentation of Korea as a globally recognized IT power. What the KLTI is doing here is no different from what informs the many centers around the world that promote national literatures in translation, and a great many of these centers are from nations with a colonial history, namely, the development of a form of digital nationalism that sees the recognition value of a postcolonial, national identity as increasingly dependent on a prominent digital presence.

In a sense, what is implicit in this digital nationalism is the notion of 'soft power' enunciated by Joseph Nye (1991, 2004). Nye argued that attraction rather than coercion was much more effective in the medium to long term in terms of enduring influence in international relations. Although Nye's concept was first developed in the context of thinking about the limits to military and economic coercion ('hard power') as the preferred foreign policy instruments of the United States as a superpower, it was soon apparent that the distinction could be usefully employed by a whole range of actors on the world stage, from postcolonial states to major powers with previous or continuing colonial ambitions.

For smaller nations, the options of exercising 'hard power' are generally relatively restricted, either because of the lack of resources or, in certain cases, the unwillingness of populations with colonial or postcolonial histories to exercise such power. In this respect, the notion of 'soft power'—influence through attraction or co-option—appears both more feasible and more desirable or acceptable. Culture is frequently the arsenal that is drawn on for the weaponry of soft power, even for superpowers as demonstrated by the long association of Hollywood with the alleged superiority of the 'American Way of Life.' For countries lacking in significant economic or military resources, often in itself the legacy of colonial depredations, cultural promotion can be seen as a relatively inexpensive means of exercising soft power. The power, of course, is unlikely to exert any influence if it is not brought beyond the shores of the specific national or postcolonial culture. To this end, two types of translation are required: spatial (it must be moved from the point of origin to various points around the globe) and semantic (the content must be understood in various points of the globe). Soft power needs a medium (digital connectivity) and a message (translated content). Through the practice of ostensible transparency as engaged in by multiple government-sponsored translation bodies and institutes across the planet, it is possible to argue that translation has become a key component in the incorporation of postcolonial literatures into the operation of soft power in the digital age.

Soft power as a concept is increasingly linked to the notion of 'nation branding' or brand nationalism (Anholt 2007). This was described in the *Boston Globe* as "shorthand for coordinated government efforts to manage a country's image, whether to improve tourism, investment, or even foreign relations" (Risen 2005). The connection between nation branding and soft power was made explicit by Mikhail Margelov, chairman of the International Affairs Committee of Russia's Federation Council. The Russian government was concerned that the external image of the country was poor and that many public associations with the country included, 'cold weather,' 'vodka,' and 'authoritarianism.' Margelov argued that the nation's new branding campaign:

> needs to push *"the image of a 'good' rather than a 'strong' Russia"* as part of the "soft power" approach that is now so popular. And to do that it must have a co-ordinated plan, one that will be *"pro-active rather than defensive"* in order to ensure that Moscow gets in the first word in any dispute. (Volcic and Andrejevic 2011: 599; their emphasis)

The 'nation brand' is one that inescapably marries positive associations to the profit imperative. These are associations that help bring foreign investment and tourists into a country while also acting as a stimulus to the sales of nationally produced goods and boosting the international image of the country. The emphasis on image is seen to parallel the transition from modernist industrial production to postmodern consumption, "a move from the modern world of geopolitics and power to the postmodern world of images and influence" (van Ham 2001). Moreover, as Volcic and Andrejevic argue:

> The promoters of nation branding market it as a powerful equalizer—a way that countries without the economic or military clout of superpowers can compete in the global marketplace. They claim that nation branding can help such nations to achieve greater visibility, attract tourists and foreign investors, expand exports, and promote their profile among the member states of various international organizations (such as the EU), all the while cultivating patriotism at home. (2011: 604)

In the context of a research project, Volcic and Andrejevic interviewed a nation brand marketing specialist in New York, who argued:

> Branding is *the only* power available to small, unknown, peripheral nations [. . .] it can help them strengthen their economic position, attract investors, skilled labour, and travellers [. . .] Do you honestly believe that Kosovo has any other option than to brand itself? Kosovo *has* to market itself [. . .] this will also strengthen citizens' identity and increase their self-esteem [. . .] there is no other way for Kosovo to persuade the rest of the world that they are a young, peaceful, stable and dynamic country [. . .] even if they are not. (2011: 604–605; their emphasis)

It is perhaps inevitable that the "small, unknown, peripheral nations" are those places or peoples who found themselves at the mercy or on the edges of empire. In the contemporary, postcolonial moment, the concert of nations becomes the global trading floor, each nation clamoring for competitive advantage as the notion of political sovereignty becomes subservient to market position or positioning. Although nation branding is generally seen as an instance of the privatization of public functions (promotion of foreign trade, diplomacy), it is possible to see how publicly funded translation institutes and centers can be co-opted into a version of postcolonial brand nationalism, if only to justify their continued funding in an era increasingly dominated by what Cerny (1997: 272) calls the "competition state," the state that is almost exclusively focused on the economic fortunes of the polity.

For the competition state, the perceived added value of distinctiveness means the mobilization of the historical, cultural resources of the nation-state and this obviously includes literature to bring people, goods, and money into the national economy. A dimension to nation branding in the age of the interactive web is the role of a form of reciprocity in the construction of the 'brand.' This is, in part, because of the notion that it is only through the active participation of the citizens that the 'brand' will acquire any credibility. As the *Handbook of Brand Slovenia*, a nation with a long and checkered history of colonial occupation (see Carmichael and Gow 2010), expresses it, "The power of the brand lies in the consent and motivation of the Slovene citizens to live the brand" (cited in Volcic and Andrejevic 2011: 610). The use of lateral and participatory rather than top-down and one-way message transmission is at one level an expression of the commercial logic of Web 2.0. A version of the lateral and the participatory in the context of postcolonial literatures is the presence of organizations like Ireland Literature Exchange or Books from Lithuania on Facebook. The possibility for interaction that is allowed by social media is not only a way of spreading the message of translation organizations to broader, nontraditional constituencies, but it also implicitly co-opts Facebook respondents into the proselytizing project of the organizations. By expressing an interest in the organization (even through the simple gesture of a 'like'), Facebook users are mobilized to become a part of the community dedicated to spreading the good news in translation about Irish, Lithuanian, or whatever literature is being promoted by an organization.

Just as brands are primarily about associations, so social media carries its own associative potential in terms of organizations' own expressed 'likes.' Thus, Ireland Literature Exchange lists among its 'likes': Sweny's Pharmacy, Lincoln Place, Dublin, Digital Arts Marketing Training, the Festival of World Cultures, the New York Review of Books, National Concert Hall, Dublin, Ireland, Irish Arts Center, ABSOLUT Fringe, Dublin Theatre Festival, the National Campaign for the Arts, Theatre Forum Ireland, the *New Yorker*, *Irish Theatre Magazine*, Publishing Ireland, Gallery of Photography, Abbey Theatre (http://www.facebook.com/IrelandLiteratureExchange). The mixture of national cultural institutions, national representative organizations, national festivals, and a limited number of high-profile journals and magazines with a more idiosyncratic reference to a pharmacy mentioned in James Joyce's *Ulysses* positions the informal interactivity of 'likes' in a strategic economy of national, cultural promotion. If, at present, the engagement with the social media and the mobilization of interactivity is primarily at the level of marketing and publicity, it is possible to imagine how wiki-translation, fansubbing, and other forms of group translation might be incorporated into evolving forms of digital, postcolonial identity construction.

In a trenchant critique of nation branding, Jansen argues that "nation branding is a monologic, hierarchical, reductive form of communication" (2011: 141). Given that the associative power of brand lies in its simplicity (less is more), the dangers of the conflation of commercial self-interest with national representativity become uncomfortably obvious. Being 'on message' means leaving a lot out, and what must inevitably get left out is what is seen as sending out the 'wrong,' that is, negative message. This is where a mission of ostensible transparency in translation enters into explicit conflict with the willed opacity of brand logic. The translated literatures of Ireland, Poland, Lithuania, Korea, or whatever literature is supported in translation by a public body from a democratic, postcolonial state cannot be assimilated to 'a monologic, hierarchical, reductive form of communication.' Literature that practiced this form of communication would not be literature but propaganda, and it is precisely the dangers of the assimilation of postcolonial literatures to forms of nationalist, identitarian rhetoric that have troubled postcolonial translation scholars in the past (Niranjana 1992).

In other words, a project of ostensible transparency in the domain of postcolonial literary translation must contest simple identity narratives that any particular sectional interest might wish to foster for the purposes of narrowly defined economic gain or self-aggrandizement. What is at stake is all the more important in that it is precisely simplified identitarian narratives conveyed through translation that often functioned as the most powerful agents in justifying various forms of colonial subjection (Tymoczko 1999). In this respect, it is important that literary translation, even if predominantly published by private sector or commercial publishers, should be defined as a public good in postcolonial polities. It is only as a public good in a democratic state that literary translation can be promoted in a way that gives due expression to the multiple and conflicted identities of any body politic. The current potential for digital interactivity points to the possibility of a global cybercitizenship of a World Republic of Letters, where nations would be held accountable to citizen-readers for the nontranslation of important literary works in different national languages, but such accountability implies not only access to material infrastructures and knowledges of languages (to know what is missing); it also implies the integrity of inclusiveness that runs counter to the often reductive banalities of brand. There is another dimension to the fate of postcolonial literatures in translation in the contemporary digital context, and this relates to the convergence of the human and the technological.

The Company of Strangers

The convergence of the human and the material, the interaction between humans and technology that we have described in terms of a particular form of digital postcolonial translation practice of dissemination situates translation at one level in the emerging intellectual and cultural movement of transhumanism (Hansell and Grassie 2012; Blake, Molloy, and Shakespeare 2012). A core tenet of transhumanism is that evolving technologies will greatly enhance human intellectual, physical, and psychological capacities. Posthumanist thinkers, for their part, share the transhumanists' belief in the significance of technology in our lives but are deeply critical of the unreflective scientism they see at work in transhumanist philosophy and are more anxious to situate humans and human reason within an overarching ecological framework (Wolfe 2009). It is obvious that any future discussion of postcolonial translation paradigms in digital settings will become part of the dialogue around transhumanism and posthumanism if only because of the fundamental interplay between human language, technology, and sociohistorical pressures in past and present developments in translation practice.

One of the recurrent topics of debate in the area of the transhuman and the posthuman is of course the human body. Not only how the body itself mutates through interactions with the digital tools it manipulates, but also how human bodies do or do not come into contact with each other in digital worlds. This concern with contact or connectivity in a digital age has a direct bearing on the specific position of postcolonial literary translation within cultures of origin and reception and in the response of the academy to the translation paradigm. To see why this might be the case, we will begin by looking briefly at an episode from James Joyce's *Ulysses*.

In the Nestor section of the novel, Stephen Dedalus, in the guise of teacher, observes the slow progress of one of his less able students, Cyril Sargent. The pupil's first name is an ironic allusion to the saint who was both translator and inventor of an alphabet, Saint Cyril the Philosopher. Sargent has been punished by the headmaster, Garret Deasy, for his failure to solve mathematical problems and has been set to writing out algebraic solutions from the blackboard into his copybook entitled 'Sums':

> In long shaky strokes Sargent copied the data. Waiting always for a word of help his hand moved faithfully to the unsteady symbols, a faint hue of shame flickering behind his dull skin. *Amor matris*: subjective and objective genitive. (Joyce 1971: 163–164)

Stephen repeatedly reflects in this section of the novel on his own 'amor matris,' his own relationship with his mother and his biological family. As Barry McCrea notes, Stephen finds parallels between his own situation and that of the hapless Sargent:

> Stephen, who is generally given to seeing parallels and symbols, immediately identifies the slow, unrealized Sargent with his own situation. He associates Sargent's abjection with what he imagines to be his own imprisonment in his biological family and the paradigms associated with

it. Sargent's "Sums," his book of selves, is a *copy*book, and a copied, genealogical self is what Stephen feels gloomily condemned to. (McCrea 2011: 112; his emphasis)

Of course, one of the most common reasons for a failure to appreciate the complexity of translation is that it is viewed as the activity of the hack, a kind of slavish copying of the original that deserves all the scorn the romantic critic can muster for the curse of the derivative. Cyril Sargent may be an unworthy successor to the gifted Cyril who was one of the inventors of the first Slavic alphabet and translators of the Bible into Old Church Slavonic. His association, however, with the rote activity of copying suggests the reductive, almost dismissive approach to translation. The relationship between the original and 'an inferior copy' as analogous to the relationship between the colonial power and the colony is explored by Robert Young who claims:

> Languages, like classes and nations, exist in a hierarchy: as does translation itself [. . .]. Under colonialism, the colonial copy becomes more powerful than the indigenous original that is devalued. It will even be claimed that the copy corrects deficiencies in the native version. The colonial language becomes culturally more powerful, devaluing the native language as it is brought into its domain, domesticated and accommodated. (2003: 164)

Sargent's schooling, of course, takes place in the language of the colonial master, English, and one of Dedalus's dilemmas as the day of June 16, 1904, unfolds is the extent to which he masters or is mastered by the 'colonial copy.' Is his translation of the colonized self a successful transformation or merely the punitive repetition of the master's *pensum*? There is, however, another dimension to the episode that is of equal importance when examining potential futures for postcolonial literature in translation.

The social anthropologist Tim Ingold makes an important distinction in his writings between 'genealogy' and 'relation.' In the genealogical model, individuals are seen as entering the lifeworld with a set of ready-made attributes they have received from their predecessors. The essential parts that go to make up a person, his or her culture, are handed on, more or less fully formed. The popular image for this conception of personhood and community is that someone has something in their 'blood' or more recently, 'in their genes.' The relational model, on the other hand, relates to the concept of 'progeneration,' which Ingold defines as the "continual unfolding of an entire field of relationships within which different beings emerge with their particular forms, capacities and dispositions" (2000: 142). That is to say, whereas the genealogical model is concerned with past histories of relationship, with the unfolding development of a bundle of preset attributes in a given space, the progenerative model is primarily concerned with current sets and fields of relationships for persons in a given lifeworld.

The genealogical model has obvious affinities with the notion of 'family' or, indeed, 'diaspora' in both a narrow nuclear and wider kinship definition of the notion, and both notions feature prominently in discussions of the postcolonial literature of exile (see, for example, Jones and Jones 2000). It is the model that clearly informed the 2004 Citizenship Referendum in the Republic of Ireland that introduced the notion of bloodline into definitions of Irish citizenship. In the genealogical model the descent line is separate from the lifeline, and life and growth become the realization of potentials that are already in place. So being Irish is to be a member of a family that through immediate (domestic) or extended (diasporic) bloodline is endowed with a culture that is determined by essence rather than context.

One consequence of this model is that cultural difference is almost invariably construed as 'diversity.' That is to say, the notion of diversity, which is becoming something of a mantra of beatific official pronouncements on postcolonial literature and our multicultural world, supposes that different groups are possessed of different sets of ready-made attributes. These are juxtaposed in the shop windows of different contemporary postcolonial states, and each group acting out their predefined cultural script contributes to the effervescent display of cultural diversity. So the invocation of diversity that is often seen as a way of countering nativist genealogical exclusiveness in fact tends to partake of the same logic but simply multiplies the examples of genealogical inheritances rather than challenges the basic logic.

McCrea argues that what marks the emergence of the modernist narrative is the move away from the genealogical model toward alternative forms of kinship, whether it be Stephen Dedalus's relationship with Leopold Bloom or Marcel's leaving his much-loved family to enter into the transformative worlds of Swann and Charlus. It is arguable, however, that it is not simply the advent of modernism, but it is the inescapable presence of translation in colonial pasts and postcolonial presents that bring speakers of a language, whether willingly or unwillingly, into the 'company of strangers.' The translation imperative that is central to the experience of the colonized (Cheyfitz 1991) generates a pressure to move outside or beyond the genealogical model toward a mode of development that is progenerative. It is precisely the progenerative dimension to translation that must make it a recurrent object of suspicion for genealogical narratives of community and nation to be found in postcolonial contexts.

In 1905 when Douglas Hyde, the future president of Ireland, went on a fund-raising trip for the devalued 'Indigenous original,' the Irish language, to the United States, he paid a visit to then president of the United States Theodore 'Teddy' Roosevelt. Entertainment was not lavish, and after a simple main course they proceeded to a dessert of apples and green grapes washed down by a cup of tea and a glass of sherry. Roosevelt was in garrulous form and was no stranger to strongly held opinion. He revealed to his Irish guest his own vision of the multicultural:

> He was of the opinion that there was still too much "colonialism" in America, that it was a nation made up of a lot of other nations and because there were so many Irish in the country, Americans should take anything that was good or worthwhile or interesting in the Irish and make it into their own. (Hyde 1937: 15)[2]

Roosevelt's primary concern was to construct a national community, but a community that would make a virtue of appropriative diversity. In order for this post-'colonialism' society to emerge, he was, like Hyde, greatly preoccupied with the question of language; however, his concern was not to see minority languages triumph, but to see English, the dominant host language of the United States, prevail. It was English that would allow for "anything that was good or worthwhile" to be assimilated into the body politic. In a statement to the *Kansas City Star* in 1918 he offered a *précis* of his thinking on the issue, "Every immigrant who comes here should be required within five years to learn English or leave the country." A year later, in a letter he wrote to the president of the American Defense Society, he declared, "We have room for but one language here, and that is the English language [. . .] and we have room for but one sole loyalty and that is a loyalty to the American people" (Pearson 1920: 19). The object, in a sense, was to subordinate the progenerative energies of the translation contact with the foreign to a controlled project of genealogical continuity of one people speaking one language.

A more contemporary manifestation of this form of recuperation is the extraordinary lack of interest that continues to be shown by many English Literature departments throughout the English-speaking world in the phenomenon of translation despite the fact that translation has been central to the evolution of literature and language in English (Ellis 2008; Braden, Cummings, and Gillespie 2010). It is as if to teach English literature in a predominantly chronological fashion is to imply a sense of genealogical relation or continuity, a role that was, in a sense, allotted to English 'Polite Letters' in the nineteenth century in British universities as part of the project of fashioning national and imperial subjects (Readings 1997). It is in this context that both the fact of translation as central to the postcolonial literary experience in many different settings and the presence of translated postcolonial literatures from a host of different languages have the potential to subvert the genealogical paradigm and unleash the progenerative potential of the 'company of strangers.' The scale, extent, and spread of users of the Internet mean, of course, that the company of strangers is now global. One of the challenges for students and scholars of postcolonial literatures in translation is to understand how the global, digital community of writers and readers of translated literatures will enable or hinder the emergence of new forms of expression and engagement.

Notes

1. "J'entends résonner un entrechoc entre la proposition universelle au singulier *Tout homme est libre* et la proposition au pluriel *Tous les hommes sont libres*. La première est vraie, la seconde est fausse. Mais du même coup, on comprend que la proposition au singulier n'est vraie qu'en intensité. Elle est universelle dans la mesure exacte où elle porte le nom *homme* à son intensité maximale. Elle demeurerait universelle, quand bien même les hommes seraient libres nulle part."

2. "Badh é a bharamhail féin go raibh an iomarcaidh "coilíneachta" i nAmerice fós, go mbadh náisiún é a raibh móran náisiún fighte le chéile ann, agus ó bhí oiread sin Éireannach 'na measg gur cheart d'Americe gach rud maith nó fiúntach nó spéisamhail ar bith do bhí i mbeatha na nGaedhael do ghlacadh uatha, agus a gcuid féin a dhéanamh de."

References

Anholt, S. (2007) *Brand New Justice: The Upside of Global Branding* (Oxford: Butterworth-Heinemann).

Assouline, P. (2011) *La condition du traducteur* (Paris: Centre National du Livre).

Blake, C., Molloy, C., and Shakespeare, S. (eds) (2012) *Beyond Human: From Animality to Transhumanism* (London: Continuum).

Braden, G., Cummings, R., and Gillespie, S. (2010) *The Oxford History of Literary Translation in English*. Vol. 2 (Oxford: Oxford University Press).

Carmichael, C., and Gow, J. (2010) *Slovenia and the Slovenes: A Small State in the New Europe* (London: Hurst).

Cerny, P. (1997) 'Paradoxes of the Competition State: The Dynamics of Political Globalization' *Government and Opposition* 32: 2: 251–274.

Chakrabarty, D. (2000) *Provincializing Europe: Postcolonial Thought and Historical Difference* (Princeton, NJ: Princeton University Press).

Cheyfitz, E. (1991) *The Poetics of Imperialism: Translation and Colonization from* The Tempest *to* Tarzan (Philadelphia: University of Pennsylvania Press).

Ellis, R. (2008) *The Oxford History of Literary Translation in English*. Vol. 1 (Oxford: Oxford University Press).

Hansell, G. R., and Grassie, W. (eds) (2012) *H+/-: Transhummanism and Its Critics* (New York: Xlibris).

Hwang, K. M. (2010) *A History of Korea* (London: Palgrave).

Hyde, D. (1937) *Mo Thurus go Meiriceá nó i measg na nGaedheal ins an Oileán Úr* (Dublin: Oifig Díolta Foilseacháin Rialtais).

Ingold, T. (2000) *The Perception of the Environment: Essays in Livelihood, Dwelling and Skill* (London: Routledge).

Jansen, S. (2011) 'Redesigning a Nation: *Welcome to E-stonia, 2001–2018*' in *Branding Post-Communist Nations: Marketizing National Identities in the 'New' Europe*, ed. N. Kaneva (London: Routledge), pp. 120–144.

Jones, E. D., and Jones, M. (eds) (2000) *Exile and African Literature* (Trenton, NJ: Oxford University Press).

Joscelyne, A. (2011) 'Interoperability and Open Tools.' http://www.translationautomation.com/technology/interoperability-and-open-tools.html (accessed November 28, 2012).

Joyce, J. (1971) *Ulysses* (Harmondsworth: Penguin).

Kim, J.-Y. (2011) 'President's Message.' http://www.litkorea.net/ke_01_02_011.do (accessed December 20, 2012).

McCrea, B. (2011) *The Company of Strangers: Family and Narrative in Dickens, Conan Doyle, Joyce and Proust* (New York: Columbia University Press).

Milner, J.-C. (2011) *Clartés de tout: de Lacan à Marx, d'Aristote à Mao* (Lagrasse: Verdier).

Niranjana, T. (1992) *Siting Translation: History, Post-Structuralism and the Colonial Context* (Berkeley: University of California Press).

Nye, J. (1991) *Bound to Lead: The Changing Nature of American Power* (New York: Basic Books).

Nye, J. (2004) *Soft Power: The Means to Success in World Politics* (New York: Public Affairs).

Pearson, E. L. (1920) *Theodore Roosevelt* (New York: Macmillan).

Readings, B. (1997) *The University in Ruins* (Cambridge: Harvard University Press).

Risen, C. (2005) 'Re-Branding America. Marketing Gurus Think They Can Help "Re-Position" the United States—and Save American Foreign Policy,' *Boston Globe.* http://www.boston.com/news/globe/ideas/articles/2005/03/13/re_branding_america (accessed November 15, 2012).

Simeoni, D. (2008) 'Norms and the State: the Geopolitics of Translation Theory' in *Beyond Descriptive Translation Studies*, ed. A. Pym, M. Shlesinger, and D. Simeoni (Amsterdam: John Benjamins), pp. 329–341.

Tymoczko, M. (1999) *Translation in a Postcolonial Context* (Manchester: St. Jerome).

Van Ham, P. (2001) 'The Rise of the Brand State,' *Foreign Policy.* http://www.globalpolicy.org/component/content/article/162/27557.html (accessed December 24, 2012).

Vertovec, S. and Cohen, R. (eds) *Conceiving Cosmopolitanism: Theory, Context, Practice*, Oxford: Oxford University Press.

Volcic, Z., and Andrejevic, M. (2011) 'Nation Branding in the Era of Commercial Nationalism' *International Journal of Communications* 5: 598–618.

Wolfe, C. (2009) *What Is Posthumanism* (Minneapolis: University of Minnesota Press).

Words without Borders. (2012) 'About Words without Borders.' http://www.wordswithoutborders.org/about (accessed October 4, 2012).

Young, R. (2003) *Postcolonialism: A Very Short Introduction* (Oxford: Oxford University Press).

Contributors

Bill Ashcroft is Professor of English at the University of New South Wales, a founding exponent of postcolonial theory, and coauthor of *The Empire Writes Back* (Routledge, 1989), the first text to examine systematically the field of postcolonial studies. He is author and coauthor of sixteen books and more than 160 chapters and papers, translated into several languages. Among his most recent publications are: *Caliban's Voice: The Transformation of English in Post-Colonial Literatures* (Routledge, 2009) and *Post-Colonial Transformation* (Routledge, 2001).

Simona Bertacco is an Assistant Professor of Humanities at the University of Louisville, USA, and was previously a 'ricercatrice' at the University of Milan, Italy. Her research focuses on issues in postcolonialism, women's and gender studies, and translation studies. Her publications include: 'Skepticism and the Idea of an Other: Reflections on Cavell and Postcolonialism' in *Stanley Cavell and Literary Studies* (Continuum, 2011); *Death and Its Rites in Contemporary Art & Culture (Altre Modernità #4 2010)* coedited with N. Vallorani; 'Postcolonialism' in *The Oxford Companion of Philosophy and Literature* (2009).

Franca Cavagnoli's most recent book is *Il proprio e l'estraneo nella traduzione letteraria di lingua inglese* (Feltrinelli, 2010). She lectures in translation studies at ISIT, Università degli Studi di Milano and Università degli Studi di Pisa, and has translated into Italian works by Toni Morrison, Nadine Gordimer, Jamaica Kincaid, J. M. Coetzee, and V. S. Naipaul. She has written two novels: *Una pioggia bruciante* (Frassinelli, 2000) and *Non si è seri a 17 anni* (Frassinelli, 2007). She has edited two collections of Australian short stories for the Italian public: *Il cielo a rovescio* (Mondadori, 1998) and *Cieli australi* (Mondadori, 2000). Her articles have been published in newspapers and journals such as *Corriere della sera*, *Il manifesto*, *Diario*, and *Linea d'ombra*.

Evelyn Nien-Ming Ch'ien is currently a member of the Institute of Transcultural and Transtextual Studies at the Université Jean-Moulin 3

(Lyon, France) and a researcher affiliated with the Ronin Institute (New York,). In 2012, she spent a year in Guangzhou, China, as a Fulbright Senior Research Fellow at the Sun-Yat Sen University in the History and Anthropology Departments. She has published in both scholarly and popular domains. Her first book, *Weird English* (Harvard University Press, 2004), was considered a breakthrough in the field of vernacular literature and linguistics. *Weird English* received a Choice award; was reviewed in *Library Journal, Far Eastern Economic Review, Politics and Culture*, the *Globe and Mail*, the *New York Sun*, the *Chronicle of Higher Education, RMMLA*, the *Texas Observer*, NPR station *The Morning Show* at KPFA Radio in Berkeley, and Hyphen (top ten book in 2006), among others; and cited in many academic publications.

Roberta Cimarosti teaches English and Translation at the University of Venice *Ca' Foscari*. Her scholarly work is based on world literatures in English and her publications include a monograph on the poetics of Derek Walcott and several essays on Caribbean, African, and British poetry and fiction as well as on Shakespeare's theater.

Michael Cronin holds a Personal Chair in the Faculty of Humanities and Social Sciences at Dublin City University, Ireland. He is author of *Translating Ireland: Translation, Languages and Identity* (Cork University Press, 1996); *Across the Lines: Travel, Language, Translation* (Cork University Press, 2000); *Translation and Globalization* (Routledge, 2003); *Time Tracks: Scenes from the Irish Everyday* (New Island, 2003); *Irish in the New Century/An Ghaeilge san Aois Nua* (Cois Life, 2005); *Translation and Identity* (Routledge, 2006); *The Barrytown Trilogy* (Cork University Press: Ireland into Film Series, 2007); *Translation Goes to the Movies* (Routledge, 2009); *The Expanding World: Towards a Politics of Microspection* (Zero Books, 2012); and *Translation in the Digital Age* (Routledge, 2013). He is coeditor of *Tourism in Ireland: A Critical Analysis* (Cork University Press, 1993); *Anthologie de nouvelles irlandaises* (L'Instant même, 1997); *Unity in Diversity? Current Trends in Translation Studies* (St. Jerome Press, 1998); *Reinventing Ireland: Culture, Society and the Global Economy* (Pluto Press, 2002); *Irish Tourism: Image, Culture and Identity* (Channel View Publications, 2003); *The Languages of Ireland* (Four Courts Press, 2003); *Transforming Ireland*, coedited with Peadar Kirby and Debbie Ging (Manchester University Press, 2009). He is editor of the New Perspectives in Translation Studies series for Routledge and he is coeditor of the *Irish Review*.

Michelle Keown is Senior Lecturer in English Literature at the University of Edinburgh, Scotland. She has published widely on Maori and Pacific writing and is the author of *Postcolonial Pacific Writing: Representing the Body* (Routledge, 2005) and *Pacific Islands Writing: The Postcolonial*

Literatures of Aotearoa/New Zealand and Oceania (Oxford University Press, 2007). She has also produced various publications focusing on translation/ multilingual studies, including the edited volume *Comparing Postcolonial Diasporas* (Palgrave Macmillan, 2009), which investigates a range of Anglophone, Francophone, Hispanic, and Neerlandophone literary and cultural contexts.

Naseemah Mohamed is a 2013 Rhodes Scholar, a Rockefeller Fellow, and a 2012 honors graduate of Harvard College, where she completed a Joint A.B. in Social Studies and African Studies with a primary focus field on education in Africa. Her thesis, 'The Art of Literacy: A Post-Colonial Pedagogical Intervention,' received the 2012 Dorothy Lee Hicks Award for the most outstanding thesis concerning African/African-American Literature in Harvard College. In 2012 she cofounded the Center for African Cultural Excellence, a nonprofit organization that supports African writers and artists and advocates for African heritage preservation and the advancement of cultural expressive forms. She is currently completing a MSc in International Education Policy at Oxford University.

Susan Philip teaches in the English Department of the Arts Faculty, University of Malaya. Her main area of research is in the English-language theaters of Malaysia and Singapore, though nowadays her focus is more on Malaysia. She is particularly interested in ideas of identity and of belonging within the nation.

Biancamaria Rizzardi is the founder and the director of the MA in Postcolonial Translation at the University of Pisa, Italy. She is the editor of the Italian version of several British Victorian and Canadian poets, such as C. A. Swinburne's *Poems and Ballads* (*Poesie e Ballate*, 1995); Elizabeth Barrett Browning's *Sonnets from the Portuguese* (*Sonetti dal portoghese*, ETS, 2006); Margaret Atwood's *The Diaries of Susanna Moodie* (*I diari di Susanna Moodie*, Piovan Editore, 1985); and Sheila Watson's *Five Stories* (*Cinque racconti*, ETS, 2007).

Sherry Simon teaches in the French Department at Concordia University. Among her many publications are *Gender in Translation* (Routledge, 1996), *Le Trafic des langues, Translating Montreal: Episodes in the Life of a Divided City* (McGill-Queens University Press, 2006), and *Cities in Translation. Intersections of Language and Memory* (Routledge, 2011).

Doris Sommer is Ira Jewell Williams, Jr., Professor of Romance Languages and Literatures and of African and African American Studies, and Director of the Cultural Agents Initiative at Harvard University. She is the editor of *Cultural Agency in the Americas* (Duke University Press,

2006) and *Bilingual Games: Some Literary Investigations* (Palgrave, 2004), and she is the author of *Bilingual Aesthetics: A New Sentimental Education* (Duke University Press, 2004), and *Proceed with Caution When Engaging Minority Literature* (Harvard University Press, 1999).

Stephanos Stephanides is Professor of Comparative Literature at the University of Cyprus. As poet, critic, scholar, translator, and documentary filmmaker, he has a special interest in dislocation, memory, and forgetting. He has a special interest in India and the Caribbean as well as the Mediterranean. He is fluent in Greek, Spanish, and Portuguese, but his dominant and literary language is English. Selections of his poetry have been translated into more than twelve languages. He has served as a judge for literary prizes, including the Commonwealth Writers Prize (Europe and South Asia region) in 2000 and 2010.

Chantal Zabus holds the "Institut universitaire de France" (IUF) Chair of Comparative Postcolonial Literatures and Gender Studies at the University Paris 13 Sorbonne-Paris-Cité, France. She is the author of *Between Rites and Rights: Excision in Women's Experiential Texts and Human Contexts* (Stanford University Press, 2007); *The African Palimpsest* (Rodopi, 1991; rpt. 2007); and *Tempests after Shakespeare* (Palgrave, 2002). Her latest book, *Out in Africa: Same-Sex Desire in Sub-Saharan Literatures and Cultures*, is forthcoming with Boyden and Brewer (Oxford: James Currey Series) in December 2013. She has also edited, with Jacques Derrida, *Le Secret: Motif et moteur de la littérature* (Louvain, 1999); *Changements au féminin en Afrique noire: Littérature et Anthropologie* (L'Harmattan, 2000; Italian trans. 2003); *Fearful Symmetries: Essays and Testimonies on Excision and Circumcision* (Rodopi, 2009); with Silvia Nagy-Zekmi, *Colonization or Globalization? Postcolonial Explorations of Imperial Expansion* (Lexington Books, 2010); with Silvia Nagy-Zekmi, *Perennial Empires: Postcolonial, Transnational and Literary Perspectives* (Cambria Press, 2011). Two edited volumes, *Transgender Experience: Agency, Erotics, and Intimacy* (with David Coad) and *The Future of Postcolonial Literature* are forthcoming with Routledge in 2013 and in 2014, respectively. She is the editor-in-chief of *Postcolonial Text*.

Index

For Product Safety Concerns and Information please contact our EU
representative GPSR@taylorandfrancis.com
Taylor & Francis Verlag GmbH, Kaufingerstraße 24, 80331 München, Germany